Gerard

28th November 1979

Woman's Day
CELEBRATING CHRISTMAS

Woman's Day
CELEBRATING CHRISTMAS

A complete family reference book for Christmas this year and ever after

Edited by Nancy Schraffenberger

Robert J. Kasbar
Book Coordinator/Production Manager

Designed by Allan Mogel Studios

 Columbia House

ISBN 0-930748-11-5

Published by Columbia House, a Division of CBS Inc. 1211 Avenue
of the Americas, New York, New York 10036

Printed in the U.S.A.

PHOTOGRAPHY CREDITS

Ben Calvo—All photography except pages listed below.
Carmen Schiavone—Pages 75, 101, 103, 104, 105 (Pinafore),
108, 110, 111 (Scarf and Hat), 114 (Tie).

DESIGNER CREDITS

Martha Albert—Pages 24, 66 (Window Ornaments).
Linda Osborne Blood—Page 104.
Beattie Bodenstein—Page 111 (Scarf and Cap).
Casey Bradford—Pages 41, 43 (Crocheted Ruffle Tree).
Nan Brown—Page 103.
Linda Cross—Pages 40 (Nuts-and-Apples Wreath), 43 (Fragrant
    Centerpiece), 44 (Colonial Centerpiece), 52, 56, 60, 66
    (Banister Trim), 68, 116.
Susan Daly with Pamela Burns—Page 108.
Stan Dunaj—Page 55.
Mrs. C. Garigan—Page 59.
Isabel Garrett—Page 72.
Esther Ginsberg—Pages 16, 109.
Carol Inouye—Page 57 (Bells).
Veronica Kiem—Page 75.
Hilde Liu—Page 106.
Elizabeth D. Logan—Pages 31 (Cookie Creatures), 37 (Foam Bird
    and Star).
Diane Lowe—Page 113.
Margaret McNeely—Page 22.
Patricia C. Miller—Pages 35 (Crocheted Bells), 37 (Flowered
    Apples), 40 (Dainty Wreath), 65.
Barbara Muccio—Pages 35 (Crocheted Stocking), 101, 102, 117
    (Message Boards).
Dolores Olson—Pages 37 (Nut Santa), 48.
George C. Pfiffner—Page 23 (Cards).
Ruth Pollack—Page 57 (Fascinator).
Dale L. Rohmann—Page 42 (Popcorn Wreath).
Barbara Sestok—Page 76.
Marcia Shenton—Pages 34 (Play-dough Basket), 63.
Ellen Silver—Page 117 (Frames).
Shelly Skewis—Page 42 (Evergreen Wreath).
Josephine Springer—Page 111 (Mittens).
Mrs. E. O. Travis—Page 33 (Bargello Balls).
Diane Wagner—Pages 34 (Felt Ornaments), 110 (Necklaces).
Marilyn Wein—Pages 54, 114 (Eyeglass Case).
Noreen E. Wint—Page 38.
Woman's Day Staff—Pages 26, 31 (Wooden Bird), 33 (Patchwork
    Ball, Yo-Yo Chain), 35 (Popcorn Chain), 45, 47, 50 58, 61, 64,
    69, 70, 71, 73, 100, 105, 110 (Pouch), 114 (Tie), 115.
Timothee Wood, Page 67.

INTRODUCTION

Woman's Day Celebrating Christmas is a compendium of information that is intended to be useful to you and your family this Christmas as well as a dozen Christmases from now. In preparing it, we reviewed hundreds of pages of material published in *Woman's Day* over the past four decades, selecting the ideas for Christmas that are truly classic . . . of recognized and permanent value. The focus is on the home, the homemade and the human touch, with emphasis on accomplishing the work of Christmas as easily and enjoyably as possible. You might call the content "old-fashioned" in that it is entirely based on traditional aspects of the Christmas celebration, yet the ways and means we suggest—the time-saving methods and products—are thoroughly contemporary.

To the best of our knowledge, no other book puts so much of Christmas between two covers. Whether you're looking for an explanation of Advent, a fruitcake recipe, a party plan, a gift to make, an activity to amuse a child, a decorating idea, the second verse of "Silent Night" or a work schedule for all your Christmas preparations, you'll find it here. Our sincere hope is that our guide will be a friend—a helpful, cheerful Christmas companion through the years to come.

The Editors of *Woman's Day*

"I WILL HONOUR CHRISTMAS IN MY HEART..."

"I WILL HONOUR CHRISTMAS IN MY HEART . . ."

With this vow, a troubled old man makes a new beginning. He is Ebenezer Scrooge in the famous Dickens tale, *A Christmas Carol,* and his simple words provide an answer to a question asked more and more often as the holiday season becomes increasingly harried, hurried and complex: What is the best way to celebrate Christmas?

Scrooge honored Christmas with a newborn joy in the privacy of his heart, an inward celebration. The wonderful happiness he felt within led to many kind and generous acts in the outside world. But it all began with enjoyment of his own feelings—a gift to himself.

The aim of this book is to put you in the spirit and help you find the time to make that gift to yourself. For it can't be denied that the more we become involved—sometimes burdened—with the production of the great Christmas festival (and with responsibilities for making it all happen), the less likely we are to participate freely in the event.

What is *not* true, however, is the observation that "Christmas is for children." You've probably heard this remark as often as we have, and it's usually possible to detect a hint of resignation or wistfulness beneath the words. It's as if the speaker is also saying that after one's first decade or so of Christmases, the capacity—or even the right—to experience wholeheartedly the grace, joy and eye-widening excitement of the holiday is somehow lost.

The point is, Christmas doesn't belong exclusively to any age group. It is the festival of the Holy Family and of the family of man: of sons and daughters and *their* sons and daughters. We are never not children. And at no time of year are men and women more apt to be in touch with their own childhoods in thought and deed than at Christmas. Through memories of our early Christmases we create the celebrations of the present for ourselves, our families and our friends. Just as our parents used their recollections to keep Christmas for us, so we pass on the beloved old traditions to new generations who will cherish them in the future.

You needn't be a child to experience the magic of Christmas. Magic is realizing that Christmas is a birthday, one so miraculous that each of us becomes a celebrant; a birthday when everyone enjoys saying, "Thank you" and "I'm happy" and "I love you." Magic is the anticipation of grown-ups and children looking forward to a visit from a grandfatherly man known to all and seen by none, a man of secrets and surprises, all of them good. Magic is the giddy smell of pine boughs, roasting meat and bayberry candles all mixed together. Magic is shabby boxes that hold glittering treasures of Christmas ornaments and fancily wrapped packages whose contents are dark mysteries waiting to be solved. Magic is the soaring chords of the organ playing "Joy to the World" and the not-quite-clean stocking hung at the foot of the bed.

The magic of Christmas is its ancient and continuing presence in our lives. May you know it "by heart."

CHRISTMAS USA:
SIGNS, SYMBOLS,
CUSTOMS

Three hundred and twenty years ago, you could have been punished with a fine for celebrating Christmas in America. Two hundred and thirty years ago, December 25th fell on what is now January 6th on the calendar. A hundred and sixty years ago, Christmas was not a legal holiday in a single one of the states and territories, and Santa Claus was almost unheard of.

The development of Christmas as a national holiday in the United States has been just as innovative as you would expect, and the origins of present-day Christmas customs and folklore are both older and younger than you may think.

It was not until the middle of the fourth century, A.D., that church authorities established the birthdate of Christ as December 25th. In any case, the end of the year was associated with jubilant festivals long before Jesus was born. The same time period encompassed the Natalis Solis Invicti, the Mithraic cult's sun-god feast celebrating the "birth of the unconquerable sun"; the Roman Saturnalia, honoring the god of agriculture; Chanukah, the Jewish Festival of Lights; and the winter solstice in northern Europe, celebrated by the Celtic and Teutonic peoples.

These earlier festivals included various elements such as displays of lights, blazing fires, garlands of evergreens, singing, gift-giving, feasting and liberal merrymaking. Although the Christmas celebration is rooted in the scriptural account of the Nativity, the influence of pre-Christian rites is evident. In fact, one of the objections that Puritans in the American colonies had to the celebration of Christmas was the revelry connected with it, and in 1659 they enacted a law imposing a fine of five shillings on anyone "found observing by abstinence from labor, feasting, or in any other way, such days as Christmas day."

The Massachusetts court repealed the anti-Christmas law in 1681, but several religious groups in America continued to oppose festivities. In general, the character of your Christmas depended on what church you attended and what country you came from. For example, Catholics and Episcopalians celebrated; Baptists and Quakers didn't. The Dutch burghers welcomed St. Nicholas, German settlers decorated Christmas trees and the English (Church of England, not Puritans) caroled and wassailed. In 1752, an event occurred that contributed to the unsettled pattern of Christmas celebrating. The New Style Calendar was adopted in England—and subsequently in her colonies—and 11 days were lopped off the year. Thus December 25th became January 6th. Some

people began to celebrate the 6th as "Old Christmas" and in a few corners of rural America they still do.

Controversy over religious practice, at Christmastime or any other, began to diminish during the latter half of the 18th century with new waves of immigration, the War of Independence and the tolerance fostered by the separation of church and state established by the American Constitution in 1791. However, it took another century for a "united" Christmas to evolve. In 1890, Oklahoma became the last of the 48 states and territories to enact legislation declaring December 25th a legal holiday—and it is the only religious celebration that is, by law, a national holiday.

Christmas in America today reflects many cultures in a unique merging of religious ceremonies and folk customs.

The Church Christmas

Christmas is literally the mass of Christ or, more formally, the Feast of the Nativity of Our Lord. In the Christian church, the period preceding December 25th is the holy season of Advent—from the Latin *adventus*, "coming"—which is used to prepare for the coming of Christ. It begins on the Sunday nearest November 30th and ends at midnight on Christmas Eve. In many homes, an Advent wreath with a candle is hung on the first Sunday of Advent and another candle is added on each of the three succeeding Sundays. An Advent calendar is a popular gift for children. Typically, it depicts a Christmas scene on heavy

cardboard with small die-cut openings numbered 1-24. Each day during the Advent season a "door" is opened to disclose a tiny picture, a Bible verse or perhaps a phrase from a Christmas song. The last opening traditionally reveals a nativity scene.

The twelve days of Christmas end January 6th with Epiphany (a Greek word meaning "appearance"), which commemorates the arrival of the three wise men or Magi at the manger in Bethlehem. It is celebrated as the first appearance of Christ to the Gentiles. To people with Spanish backgrounds, January 6th is "Three Kings Day," which is the occasion for giving gifts rather than Christmas day.

Of all the signs and symbols of Christmas, those most closely related to the church are derived from the information about the Nativity given in the gospels of Matthew and Luke (see page 167) in the New Testament of the Bible. They are the Holy Family, the manger and guiding star, the angels, shepherds and wise men, worship services and joyous praising or singing.

Stars, candles and radiant angels—in fact, lights of any kind—symbolize the enlightenment the birth of Christ brought to the world. Bonfires and the blazing Yule log have become traditional over the centuries, but their origins are in early Scandinavian rites connected with the winter solstice. The word "Yule" has its roots in *giul* or *huil*—"wheel"—referring to the wheel of the year, the annual revolution of the sun. Particularly in Scandinavian countries and later in England, many ceremonies went along with finding the Yule log, bringing it into the house, lighting it, keeping it burning and saving part of it to kindle the next year's log.

To rejoice in Christmas with special songs of celebration is strongly connected to the church. However, not all Christmas songs are carols. The word "carol" originally referred to songs associated with round dances (carousel = carol) and linked with the seasons, especially Christmas. In the strictest sense, only songs with a repeated refrain are carols and the others are hymns or folksongs. The custom of going from house to house caroling apparently comes from the old English practice of wassailing. "Wassail" derives from the Anglo-Saxon *wes hál*, "be well," a toast. Originally, the wassail bowl held spiced ale and it was a part of every convivial occasion, including Christmas. Wassailing often took place outside with the bowl carried from door to door by merrymakers who drank the health of those who gave them a friendly welcome.

The custom of setting up scenes depicting the stable where Christ was born began with St. Francis of Assisi early in the thirteenth century in Italy. The founder of the Franciscan order wanted to make the Christmas story more real to his followers and he assembled a manger scene with live animals and real people to represent the Holy Family, shepherds and Magi. His effort was so successful that it was imitated throughout southern Europe; gradually, small figures made of materials ranging from carved wood to wax came into use. Today the manger tableau is seen throughout the world in churches, homes and community parks.

The Folk Christmas

Greenery has been a symbol of survival and eternal life since pagan times; the use of it in this country at Christmas is particularly associated with German and English settlers. The custom of decorating evergreen trees came from Germany, where the Reformation leader Martin Luther is said to have set up a tree with lighted candles for his children in the early 1500s. Holly, ivy and mistletoe were popular Christmas decorations in England as long ago as the 1400s, and their use here was introduced by English colonists. But that familiar Christmas plant, the poinsettia, was not known in this country until the 19th century. Its namesake, Dr. Joel Roberts Poinsett, an American diplomat who admired the starlike, green and red *flor de la Noche Bueno* during his ambassadorship in Mexico, brought it to the United States in the 1820s.

The tradition of card sending is another one that began in England, although it is almost new compared to decorating with greenery. The first card is thought to have been commissioned in the 1840s by an English lord who was "too busy to write Christmas letters." The practice of printing Christmas greetings spread and in America a Bostonian, Louis Prang, put high quality cards on the market in the 1870s. The popularity of printed cards was increased by an influx of cheaper imported cards. In about 1890, Mr. Prang went out of business rather than lower his design and printing standards to meet competitive prices, but his work had given the greeting-card business a solid footing. In the 1970s, Americans sent several billion Christmas cards annually.

eight reindeer (an earlier description of Santa Claus written in 1809 by Washington Irving is thought to have influenced Moore). The poem was published the following year and as it was in the process of becoming widely known during the middle years of the century, various artists were also providing illustrations of St. Nicholas and/or Santa Claus. Among the many who portrayed the jolly old elf, it was Thomas Nast, whose Christmas cartoon sketches were printed annually in *Harper's Weekly* from 1863 into the 1880s, who contributed most to our present conception of a big, hearty Santa Claus wearing a red suit trimmed with fur.

Nowadays most Americans, despite differences in cultural or religious heritage (and time zones and temperatures) enjoy the same kind of Christmas—with school vacations, days off from work, church services, exchanges of cards and gifts, decorated trees, festive dinners and parties, and visits from that thoroughly Americanized fellow, Santa Claus.

The name "Santa Claus" suggests a Spanish origin, but it is actually an American modification of the Dutch *Sinterklaus,* for St. Nicholas, who was a bishop of Myra in Asia Minor during the first half of the fourth century. This generous, charitable and beloved man made many anonymous gifts during his lifetime and became known as the protector of children, travelers, bakers, mariners, virgins, scholars and merchants—as well as the patron saint of many cities in Europe. Dutch settlers brought to America the custom of celebrating St. Nicholas' feast day, December 6th. On the eve of the 6th, Sinterklaus—who wore the red robe of a bishop and traveled on a white horse—visited Dutch homes and left small presents for good children. In the homes of German settlers in Pennsylvania, the gift-bringer was the *Christkindl*—Christ Child, later Americanized to Kris Kringle—who left presents on the eve of the 25th.

However, the name "Santa Claus," the date of his arrival and other attributes of his visit were not really "standardized" until late in the nineteenth century. The general recognition of Santa Claus was largely due to two Americans, a clergyman and a cartoonist, respectively. Dr. Clement Clarke Moore wrote *A Visit From St. Nicholas* (see page 168) in 1822, adding new details about the magical gift-bearer—his looks, his clothing, his transportation via a sleigh and a team of

EVERYTHING DONE BY DECEMBER 25

If you've ever said you'd be glad when Christmas was over (and who hasn't?), the practical program in this chapter will help you manage your planning, work and strength so you won't be making that sad statement.

The trick is to take the initiative and plan the kind of Christmas you want early enough so that everything flows smoothly and enjoyably for everyone, especially you! These are the priorities for gearing up for action, followed by tips and guidelines:

1. Establish a social calendar.
2. Set deadlines.
3. List, plan and organize.
4. Assign work.

1. Establish a Social Calendar

Where are you going to spend Christmas this year? Which meals where? What parties? House guests? Early in November is not too soon to get out a good-size calendar (with enough space for notations) and to start thinking.

· Certain relatives and friends usually have to be considered. Discuss with your parents, sisters, brothers, grandparents and in-laws plans that involve entertaining them or going to their homes. Write them down and put a star by the absolute musts.

· Cross off any things you know in your heart will simply be too much to squeeze in—gatherings that seem to have become more work than fun, parties in far-off places that require tiresome traveling time, often in miserable weather. Make fewer involved plans, but include the most important ones.

· Extend invitations early in the season so that you can plan your own entertaining for the time and date that is best for you. Avoid conflicting dates by finding out if and when the So-and-Sos are giving their usual party. Telephone all your invitations so you'll know right away who will be coming.

· Consider doing the same party twice with the same menu, decorations and preparations. Or team up with a friend or two to entertain mutual friends and share the work.

· Note the date, time and location of important community, church, club or school events that you and your family will want to have time and energy to help with and/or attend. For other plans that involve

the whole family, take a vote on what activities mean the most—cut out the rest. *Some things have to be skipped.*

· Include all details of the comings and goings of family and guests on the calendar—chauffeuring, meetings of trains, planes, buses, etcetera.

2. Set Deadlines

Your work schedule will depend on where dates fall on your social calendar and on the "size" of your Christmas—the number of people in your family, the number of guests, gifts, cards, parties and events. Adjust these deadline suggestions accordingly:

November 1.	Plans completed and supplies purchased for cards, decorations or gifts you will make (see Chapters 4, 5 and 6).
	Shopping for "bought" and mail-order gifts underway.
	Post office consulted on final dates on mailing overseas, military, any long-distance cards or packages (adjust your schedule, if necessary).
November 30.	Final entertaining schedule established.
December 4.	All cards and gifts made or purchased. Wrapping and mailing supplies purchased. Food planning complete.
	Basic food staples and household supplies purchased.
December 10.	Out-of-town gifts wrapped and mailed. Cards mailed.
	Fruitcakes, candies and cookies made. Special cleaning and party preparation finished.
	Tree purchased (see "Tree Tips" on page 20); lights and ornaments checked.
	Outdoor decorations set up.
December 17.	Tree and interior decorations in place. Special Christmas-dinner food ordered. Special food gifts in the works.
December 24.	Hand-delivered gifts wrapped. Last-minute foods prepared.

3. List, Plan and Organize

To make your schedule serve you well, you'll need plenty of lists. Keep them in a loose-leaf "master plan" notebook so you can remove pages to carry with you for reference.

Gifts Making a gift list early in the season is important because buying, making, wrapping and mailing gifts can be the most time-consuming part of Christmas. Be as detailed as possible, noting sizes, colors, ages, any pertinent specifications. Include any materials needed for gifts you'll make. Some hints to save your time, feet, energy and nerves:

• Order gifts by mail or phone. Shop the newspaper ads and mail-order catalogs for standard items on your gift list. For unusual gifts, scout the specialty-house catalogs. Keep a record of what you order, from whom and when.

• Don't forget such send-for items as theater and concert tickets or magazine subscriptions.

• Shop in the morning. Crowds are thinner, lines shorter, clerks more available and gift boxes more plentiful.

• Choose easy-to-find gifts. Often the obvious gift is the one most likely to hit the mark. Any woman loves to get more nightgowns, panty hose or a refill of her favorite perfume. What man can't use another shirt? Teen-agers can always use socks, sports equipment, "message" tee shirts, a gift certificate from the local record store. And who wouldn't like one of the books everyone is talking about this year?

• Buy family gifts—one big item that both children and parents can use, such as a croquet set, a charcoal grill, a complete set of gorgeous towels for the bathroom or beach, a globe or map, a bushel basket of special fruit.

• Shop in the stores that don't collect crowds. Here are some gifts you can get at hardware stores, drugstores, stationery shops and art-supply houses or on one of your regular trips to the supermarket.

—A collection of unusual herbs and spices.
—All kinds of exotic eye makeup and a pair of false eyelashes.
—Cooking utensils (packaged with a favorite recipe and the ingredients to make it).
—An ice-cream scoop and assortment of nuts and syrups.
—Three or four adult carpentry tools.

—Sketching, painting or calligraphy supplies.
—A selection of paperback books.
—Party candles, paper hand towels, matches, coasters, paper napkins in coordinated colors.
—Film and flash-attachment gear.

Cards If you don't keep a list from year to year, make up one now that you can save—many people like to do this on index cards which have space for address changes and notations such as birthdays and anniversaries. If your list is last year's, review it for new entries, possible deletions and address corrections. Check your stamp supply so you can replenish it, if necessary, before post-office traffic builds up.

Christmas cards that you get in the mail can be used to decorate a wall or can be placed in an attractive bowl. Put envelopes with new addresses with your card list.

Cleaning, House Organization List any general cleaning you *must* do—only what's unavoidable. Defer the rest to less-busy January or February.

• Take a sturdy basket or box and tour the house. Collect bric-a-brac and doodads that require care and actually will be in the way when the holiday decorations get put out. They will also be safely out of reach of small visitors.

• For the daily pick-up of toys and whatnots that litter the house, just toss whatever is lying about into a plastic clothesbasket. Let everyone sort through it to retrieve his or her own things so that you don't waste time sorting out and putting away.

• Clean and polish silver and brass way ahead (or get it done by others). Tie it in plastic bags or wrap it in plastic wrap or foil and label so you will know the contents.

• Wash glassware, punch bowls, large platters and china pieces that are stored away. Plastic-wrap them until they're needed.

• Every pair of scissors and utility knife in the house should be sharpened well ahead of their heavy-use time.

• When you plan table decorations, reserve your heirloom linens for Christmas dinner. For other festive meals, bright permanent-press cloths and colorful holiday paper napkins are convenient and decorative—matching paper cups and plates may be suitable, too. Buy candles early so you'll be sure of getting the right colors and sizes. Order special plants or flowers from the florist well in advance.

• For on-going jobs such as gift wrapping, card

writing and decorations making, a desk, card table or workbench can be used as a work station. You'll save time and effort if you have a place where materials and tools can be left out for easy accessibility.

· Holiday tapes or records can be stashed in a brightly colored straw basket on the floor next to the hi-fi; put the carol books on the piano or in a magazine rack where they'll be handy.

· To make room for holiday foods, clear the refrigerator of everything that needn't be kept cold. Many items don't belong there anyway. You can make space safely by removing jellies, jams, oils, peanut butter, catsup, chili sauce, Worcestershire sauce, dry grated cheese, and unopened canned foods. (The latter can be chilled when needed—in a rush, by a short stay in the freezer.)

· Stock the bathroom just once. Put extra rolls of toilet paper, boxes of tissues, paper cups, clean towels where they can be found easily—scouring powder and sponges, too.

· Don't forget family clothing. Make a list of any special dry-cleaning or laundry requirements, shoe repairs, replenishment of lingerie-hosiery supplies and dress-up accessories. Book appointments at the beauty salon early.

Food Planning, Preparation Before you make any lists, take an inventory of your freezer, refrigerator and pantry, noting existing supplies that you can work into pre-holiday family meals. Knowing what you have on hand will cut down on unnecessary spending, and as you use up supplies you will create space for the holiday specialties you will be making or buying.

· Make menus for all family meals (see "Two-week Busy-day Meal Plan," page 158) as well as those times you plan to have parties or guests.

· List all the cookies, cakes, candies and other goodies you will be making to have on hand or give as gifts (see Chapter 7).

· Find your recipes so you don't have to be searching at the last minute for ones that may be loaned or even lost. Note the book and page number on the menu; put loose recipes in an envelope and tape it in your master-plan notebook.

· Make an early-bird shopping list for food staples you'll need for preparing make-ahead items. They take a lot of toting and putting away properly and you'll be using far more than usual: flour, various sugars, extracts, candied fruits, nuts, shortening, oils, herbs, spices, crackers, nonperishable dairy products, mixes of all sorts. Get all the canisters filled and have

refills on hand.

· Make dated shopping lists for picking up perishable items you'll need for specific occasions throughout the month.

· Be sure you have enough paper and plastic goods, foil, sponges, cleaning and maintenance products. Check on toothpaste, mouthwash, shampoo, adhesive bandages, etcetera.

· Plan to stock up gradually on carbonated and alcoholic beverages and other staples that are too heavy to carry all at once. Some liquor stores also sell drink mixers and will deliver.

· Save time and clean-up by cutting, grinding, chopping and measuring amounts required for recipes ahead of time; label, wrap and store appropriately in the refrigerator, freezer or cupboard. For example, make crumbs, prepare chestnuts or fresh coconut, chop onions. Cut up candied fruits and nuts. Measure dry ingredients for cakes, cookies, breads or waffles.

· Cook ahead. Cookies, candies and fruitcake aren't the only things you can prepare in advance. You can make and freeze meat dishes, bread, dough for rolls and desserts.

· Rely on every conceivable shortcut by taking advantage of convenience goods, mixes and disposables. Roast in plastic bags; line pans with foil to make scouring and oven cleaning unnecessary.

4. Assign Work

Making decorations, trimming the tree, cooking special treats and so on are all part of the holiday fun—activities that children and parents traditionally do together. But the more routine, monotonous and peripheral works can also be shared. Let adults and teen-agers know what has to be done and let them pick the chores that are most suitable for their schedules.

Ideas For Younger Children

· Household chores. Children can have fun making a work chart and pasting a fancy sticker after each job done (bed making, dish washing, room cleaning, garbage emptying).

· Kitchen assistance. Kids are great hands at cutting up fruitcake fruit with scissors, shelling nuts, making bread crumbs, grating cheese, decorating cookies, popping corn. Put a piece of plastic down and let them work on the floor or at a small table somewhere out from underfoot.

· Christmas card display. Children have wonderful imaginations. If you let them think up a way to display incoming cards, they'll take the whole job off your hands.

· Party prep. For their own parties, kids are perfectly capable of deciding on the menu, making the favors, fixing the table and planning the program. For adult parties, they're often surprisingly willing to help just to be in on the excitement.

· Managing the music. Your youthful music director can get out all the Christmas records and carol books; recommend new selections; see to it that the house is filled with music all season.

Houseguests

· Tasks that make them feel useful while keeping them out of your path are making beds, setting the table, keeping the living room tidy, doing a daily sweep with the vacuum cleaner.

Party Guests

· Emptying ashtrays. Provide a large metal container with a little water in the bottom for dumping, a clutch of dampened paper towels for wiping clean and an out-of-the-way location to do the work.

· Clearing away drink glasses and hors d'oeuvres plates before you sit down to dinner. Provide a tray and a signal for when to start. That way the living room won't still be littered when you get up from the table.

· Keeping an eye on the self-service bar or punch table to replenish the beverages.

· Picking up the ice on the way to your party. Have payment ready in an envelope for the favor-doer. (A picnic cooler is a good storage place for cubes.)

Tree Tips

Before you go tree shopping, know where your tree will be located in the house so you will buy one that's the right height. Trying to alter it later on by cutting large portions off either end is likely to spoil the natural taper. Also, if the tree will be placed in a corner or near a wall, it needn't be perfect on all four sides.

Freshness is the key when you consider an individual tree. Bounce it on the ground lightly. If the branches are springy and only a few needles drop off, signs are that the tree has a good indoor life expec-

tancy. Run your fingers down a branch, too. The needles should be resilient, not brittle. Look for a full, symmetrical shape with limbs strong enough to hold strings of electrical lights and ornaments. The tree should have a healthy color, strong fragrance and clean appearance.

Care, Feeding, Safety Plan to leave the tree outside, if you've bought it well ahead of time. Saw the butt at a diagonal about one inch above the original cut to open the pores and let it absorb more moisture; then stand the tree in a container of water. Just before you bring it in the house, saw the butt again, squaring off the diagonal.

· Keep the butt of the tree in water as long as it's inside and refill the container daily—trees are very thirsty. Sprinkling water on the branches and needles before you decorate will help retain freshness.

· Be sure the tree is firmly supported by the stand and placed away from exits, fireplaces, radiators, electric heaters, televisions or any source of heat.

· Don't have lighted candles—or any combustible material—on or near the tree. Be sure electric cords and light sockets are not worn and that you don't overload circuits. Never leave your home or go to bed with the tree lights still on.

· Double-check that your decorations are flame-proof; don't put electric trains or toys under the tree.

The longer a tree stays indoors, of course, the drier it becomes. But with these protective measures, it should remain in safe, attractive condition for at least ten days.

CARD-MAKING AND GIFT-WRAPPING GUIDE

The Christmas season, more than any other, is a time to communicate love and goodwill to people we care about—as the millions of Christmas cards mailed each year testify. While these greetings do enrich our friendships, a card made by hand brings a uniquely personal message from the sender and evokes a one-to-one feeling that conveys the essence of Christmas.

Have you ever felt the urge to make your own cards and resisted it on grounds that you "lack the knack"? Humbug! All you need for the designs in this chapter is the ability to cut out, stick on and follow easy directions. Besides the knowledge that you've really put something of yourself into your holiday greetings, another satisfaction of custom card-making is that you can avoid feeling rushed and anxious because you can do it well in advance of the other seasonal preparations. In fact, it's a good end-of-summer project to do with children who have the "nothing-to-do blues."

Cards Made with Stick-ons

Easiest of all—just inexpensive notepaper with surprisingly elegant designs made from notary seals, signal dots, stars, labels and photo-mounting corners. If you like, add smaller matching motifs to the envelopes.

MATERIALS: Box of plain white notepaper with matching envelopes; ¼″-diameter and ¾″- diameter red and green gummed signal dots, ½″- diameter gold and blue gummed notary seals, ¼″ and 4″ silver gummed stars, silver gummed photo-mounting corners, 1¾″ x 3¾″ gold-edge gummed labels, all available at most variety or stationery stores; scrap ribbon.

Following photograph, attach various stick-ons to notepaper in desired designs. Make related designs on back flap of envelope. Write greeting inside.

Tissue, Ribbon and Typed Greetings

You don't even need glue to put these cheerful cards together. All six designs are produced from one setup of materials shown in the separate how-to photograph—ribbon, tissue paper, tape, clear vinyl and rows of typed greetings. For color photograph of cards, turn to page 92.

Note: For all cards we used blank note cards with matching envelopes, available at most stationery and variety stores.

RIBBON CARDS

MATERIALS: ¼″-wide green and ⅜″-wide red curling ribbon; ¾″-wide red and green and ½″-wide red satin ribbon; ½″-wide double-faced tape; typing paper.

TREE: Mark a 3¾″-wide band on typing paper and cover with double-faced tape. Referring to how-to

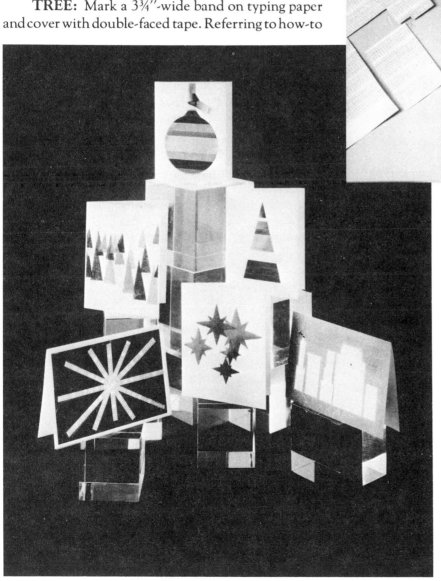

photograph, arrange bands of red and green ribbon over tape, leaving some white. Turn sheet over and draw lines along edges of ribbon band. Beginning at one end, divide one line into 2″ intervals. Beginning at same end, mark second guideline 1″ in from end, then at 2″ intervals. Connect marks zigzag fashion to outline triangular trees. Cut out trees, center on note cards and press in place on cards with tabs of double-faced tape.

ORNAMENT BALL: Cut typing paper to 6″ x 9″ and cover sheet with double-faced tape and ribbon. Turn sheet over and, using compass, draw 6 evenly spaced 3″-diameter circles. Carefully cut out circles; use excess for ornament neck. Cut out and tape neck pieces to backs of balls, as in photograph. Center and press balls on note cards with tabs of double-faced tape. To finish card, tie an overhand knot near end of a piece of ⅜″-wide ribbon. Tape knot in place and cut excess ribbon at edge of card.

TISSUE-PAPER CARDS

MATERIALS: One package assorted colors tissue paper; 18″-wide clear self-adhesive vinyl; masking tape.

TREES: Cut vinyl strip as wide as height of note cards. On protective backing draw 3 undulating guidelines, simulating rolling hills, across length of strip (guidelines should not cross or touch). Peel off backing and tape it to work surface so that guidelines are visible. Line up and tape vinyl on top, sticky side up.

Using bright blue and 4 shades of green tissue paper, stack sheets and cut a 1¾″-, a 1¼″- and a 1″-wide strip. With colors still stacked cut out triangular trees, beginning with 1¾″ strip (see how-to photograph). Separate trees and place on vinyl along bottom guideline one at a time, overlapping and spacing at random and mixing colors. Position 1¼″ trees on middle guideline and 1″ trees on top guideline. When trees are in place, cut vinyl strip into segments the size of note cards. Press segments on cards.

STARS: Cut vinyl strip as wide as height of note cards. On protective backing draw lines dividing strip into card segments. Peel off backing and tape to work surface with vinyl on top, as described for trees.

For each card, cut 5 tissue-paper squares, varying from 1″ to 2½″, of different colors. Fold each square in half twice to form smaller square, then a third time to form a triangle with one edge unfolded. Cut out a V from one corner to the other of unfolded edge. Unfold stars and press 5 on each vinyl segment as shown. Cut vinyl along guidelines and press on note card.

TYPED CARDS

MATERIALS: Typing paper; typewriter with red ribbon; blue tissue paper; green and red metallic gift wrap; 18″-wide clear self-adhesive vinyl; masking tape; double-faced tape.

Using red typewriter ribbon, type out on paper rows of letters so that holiday greeting reads vertically (see how-to photograph). Space letters by turning roller by hand a click at a time; double-space between words. (**Note:** Test-type to check spacing. We used all capital letters with a minimum overlap between rows. If yours overlap too much, use small letters.)

STAR: Cut and mark vinyl as described for Tissue-Paper Stars. With masking tape secure vinyl to work surface. Type a page of "MERRY CHRISTMAS TO YOU." Cut page into vertical strips 2 letters wide so that message is readable. Cut 5″, 3½″ and 3″ strips for 3½″ x 5″ note card. (Adjust strip lengths for other note-card sizes.) Arrange strips, message face down, on vinyl. Center 3″ strip vertically, then a 5″ strip horizontally. Continue with two 5″ and 3½″ strips between vertical and horizontal to form star. Cut red gift wrap for background ½″ smaller all around than note card. Center red background, red side down, within card guidelines; press in place. Remove masking tape and press note cards to vinyl borders; cut away vinyl segment and smooth in place. Repeat for remaining cards.

CITYSCAPE: Cut and mark vinyl as described for Tissue-Paper Stars. Also mark a horizontal guideline ½″ from bottom edge. Tape paper and vinyl to work surface. Type page of "HAPPY HOLIDAYS." Cut vertical strips 5, 6, 7 and 15 letters wide. Cut to varying lengths, notching them to give the appearance of tiered skyscrapers. Following photograph, arrange 5 buildings on each vinyl card segment (2 buildings are 7 letters wide). Center group of buildings along bottom guideline. Cut blue tissue paper for background to cover entire strip. Press in place and cut to card width. Attach skyscraper scenes to note cards with tabs of double-faced tape. Cut a small piece of green and red gift wrap; press on double-faced tape; cut out holly berries and leaves and position one each on top of one building on each card, as in photograph.

Pop-up Cards

These take more time to make, but they're easy and fun to do—with cutouts of favorite motifs, colored and gold papers, dots, seals and stars.

MATERIALS: For cards: heavy-duty construction paper, pastel paper, lightweight Bristol board or other suitable paper; knitting needle or other blunt-pointed object; scissors; mat knife; ruler; pencil; white glue. **For pop-ups and decorations:** white construction paper, colored construction paper, gift wrap, foil paper or other papers on hand; floret sequins; gummed foil stars; gold doilies; gummed dots (or make dots with paper punch and glue in place); colored markers.

TO MAKE CARDS: Mark size desired with ruler and pencil; cut with scissors. (If you have access to a paper cutter, use it for easier and neater cutting.) Score centerfold with knitting needle; fold card at scoring.

To make pop-ups, enlarge pattern (see To Enlarge Patterns, page 30) for desired shape. Decorate, following specific instructions below. Fold outward at center. Follow diagram to fold hinges in or out.

To assemble, unfold card and pop-up. Following photograph for placement, glue hinges to card. Let glue dry before folding card.

Santa: Cut card 6½″ h x 9″ w. Cut out Santa in white (see pattern). Cut out suit and hat; glue on. Draw features on face with markers. Glue on dot buttons. Glue Santa to card; add stars and sequins.

Angel: Cut card 6″ h x 6¾″ w. Cut out angel in white (see pattern). Cut out hair and foil gown; glue on. Draw features on face with markers. Decorate with doily and sequins as shown. Glue to card; add sequins.

Wreath: Cut card 5½″ h x 10″ w. Cut out wreath and separate bow (see pattern). Glue bow and dots on wreath; glue to card.

Bells: Cut card 5½″ h x 7¼″ w. Cut 1 large and

2 small bells (see pattern). Score decorative lines on small bells with knitting needle; cut out round doily pieces and glue to bells as shown. Following photograph, glue small bells to card. Decorate large bell with glued-on doily pieces and glue bell to card.

Tree: Cut card 7½" h x 11" w. Cut out tree (see pattern). Make inside cuts with craft or mat knife. Cut out hinges in white and glue to back of tree. Glue on tree's dots and top star. Glue tree to card; add stars.

Snowflakes: Cut card 5¼" h x 9½" w. Cut out large snowflake and 2 small snowflakes (see patterns); make inner cuts first, outline cuts last. Following photograph, glue small flakes to card, then glue hinges of large one to card.

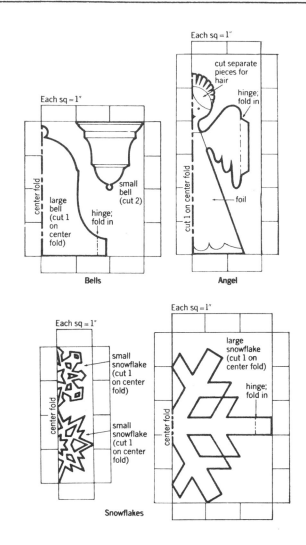

Bells

Angel

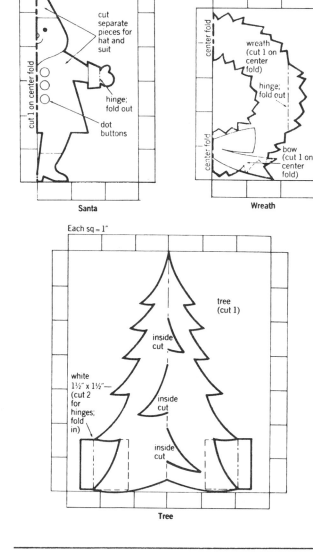

Santa

Wreath

Snowflakes

Each sq = 1"

tree
(cut 1)

inside cut

white
1½" x 1½" —
(cut 2
for
hinges;
fold
in)

inside cut

inside cut

Tree

Ready for the Big Wrap-up

Whether you love to be painstakingly elaborate in making packages look pretty or whether you can't wait to get them decently covered and done with, wrapping gifts always seems to take longer than you expect. But you *can* beat the clock without huffing and puffing. Like card-making, planning and lining up your Christmas gift-wrapping materials is an undertaking that you can get started as early as September, before fall holidays and school activities encroach on your time. Keep an eye out for sturdy cartons suitable for packing and mailing out-of-town gifts and put them aside. Begin to save plastic and aluminum containers, coffee cans and the like to use for food gifts (see page 120 for specific tips on packaging gifts from your kitchen).

Check through wrapping materials you have on hand—any leftover from last Christmas?—and make a list of what you'll need. Typical outer-wrapping supplies for parcel-post mailing include plain brown paper, strong cord, strapping or other heavy-duty tape, address labels, sharp scissors. As for decorative wrapping, the usual equipment is paper, ribbon, tags, seals, special trims, colored and clear adhesive-backed tape, plus your pen and scissors. Have enough of everything so you won't get caught short in the middle of a wrapping session. Keep all your gift-wrap paraphernalia in one big shopping bag or, ideally, plan to establish a holding area and wrapping station where you can assemble all your gifts and work materials and leave them out.

Peacock feathers, doilies, multicolor snippets of ribbon and yarn are the trims for these travelproof packages.

Now, before you actually shop for your gift wrap and tie, ask yourself these questions:

• One style for all? Using the same-theme paper, ribbon and tags for all your gifts is swift and efficient, reduces decision-making, makes shopping for wrap easier and you save money by buying big rolls.

• Will the gifts travel? No point in buying or fussing with fat bows and fragile decorations on gifts that will be mailed or stacked. Flat trimming can be highly effective—see "Noncrush Wrappings."

• Any problem shapes or sizes? You may need a few special materials and methods to deal with gifts that are big, bumpy or bulky. See "Wrapping the Unwieldy."

• Must you buy it? With economy and ecology in mind, you want to consider the alternatives suggested in "Recycled Wrappings" at the end of this chapter.

Noncrush Wrappings

The trick is to use trims that conform to the surface of your package. Directions for eight styles are given here, and they'll probably inspire other ideas. For example, you might also choose wide rickrack, eyelet, lace or double layers of ribbon in different widths and colors fastened down with a big gold notary seal. Or decorate the package with snips of origami paper, splashes of gold spray paint or designs of colored tape that take the place of bows.

GENERAL DIRECTIONS

MATERIALS: Glossy gift wrap in assorted colors; double-faced and standard clear tape; assorted gift-wrap ribbons plus decorations listed under specific directions. (**Note:** All references to tape are for double-faced; standard is called plain tape.)

Wrap boxes neatly with paper, sealing with plain tape. All ribbons are cut separately to fit around box, and each end is secured on bottom with plain tape. All details and decorations are placed with double-faced tape.

Feather Box: Wrap box with 2 crossing ¾"-wide ribbons. Cut off head and ½" of bare quill of 2 peacock feathers. Tape quills to ribbons at crossing. Following photograph, cut short piece of ribbon to cover quill ends and tape on.

Doily Star: Cut 6 wedge shapes from an 8"-diameter doily and tape in place in star arrangement, following photograph for placement.

Doily Corner: Fold one 10″-diameter doily in quarters. Unfold and cut along 1 fold to center. Following photograph, tape doily at corner with folds at box edges. Cut away excess doily ½″ from side edge of box. Bring rest of doily up to that corner; tape over ½″ wrap so that last end overlaps it.

Graph-Paper Box: Wrap box with 10-per-inch graph paper (large sheet, 19″ x 24″). Use ¾″-wide turquoise ribbon and matching rattail cord. Following photograph, split ribbon as required to narrow widths. Place on box and weave in pattern shown. Cut rattail 1″ longer than required and weave in place as shown, attaching it at bottom of box by wrapping ends together in one piece of plain tape.

Ribbon Tree: Cut triangular snippets of ¾″-wide ribbon and place in tree shape on box, following photograph for shape. Cut a piece of clear self-adhesive plastic just a bit larger than box top. Cover tree, placing plastic carefully in one motion to avoid puckering; trim at edges.

Diagonal Ribbon: Works best on long, narrow boxes. We used 1½″-wide checked rayon, 2 colors of ¾″-wide ribbon (single ribbon strip is split to narrower width) and ⅜″-wide curling ribbon. Cut lengths slightly longer than necessary to fit around box. Starting at center of box, establish desired angle and tape ribbons in place on bottom, following photograph for pattern.

Yarn Wrap: Cut ½″ to ¾″ snippets of yarn (use scraps on hand). Slightly unspin ends of yarn and place on tape as shown. Wrap 3 times above snippets with lengths of yarn, separating wraps neatly on top of box. Wrap 1 length below; secure on bottom as for ribbons.

Christmas Balls: From contrasting gift wrap cut 2½″-diameter circles with tops like ornaments, as shown. Decorate with ribbon on tape. Wrap ¾″-wide ribbon around box for top band; tape on ⅜″-wide ribbon, looping as shown. Tape balls to ends of ribbons.

Wrapping the Unwieldy

It's not impossible to Christmas-wrap a gift that's extra large or an odd shape. A huge carton can be quickly spray-painted or use spray glue to simplify the job of covering it with paper. An unboxed gift with bumpy parts—say a tricycle or ride-it truck—could go in a plastic trash bag that you've plaided or striped with colored self-adhesive tape and gathered at the top with a big ribbon bow. Or use corrugated paper to make a neat cylinder shape around an ungainly gift and roll it up snapper-style in a paper Christmas tablecloth. Finally, you can disguise an unwieldy gift in a second gift: stitch a burlap bag to size, embroider the recipient's name on it and pull it snug with a felt drawstring.

Burlap-bag Wrap Cut burlap to size, allowing 6″ at top edges for fold-over heading and casing for drawstring tie and 3″ at width for seams. (Plan to cut burlap so that bag will not have a bottom seam.) Stitch ½″ edges at either end for top. With wrong sides together, stitch ½″ side seams; trim. Turn bag wrong side out and stitch 1″ side seams. Fold over and stitch 5½″ heading along top; stitch 2½″ casing for drawstring along bottom edge of heading.

Turn bag right side out. Use 1½″ x 1½″ stencil from a variety store to mark letters for name. Mark letters with pencil. Chain-stitch name, using 6 strands of embroidery floss (see Stitch Diagrams, page 30).

For drawstring, piece 6′ x 2½″ felt. Use 1″-diameter welting cord or twist 6′ of Dacron batting into welting; make drawstring. Trim seam. Cut opening in casing; stitch raw edges; work drawstring through casing.

Recycled Wrappings

Everyone in your family can help collect and prepare these—and have fun doing it.

Road maps that are out of date. They're colorful, and a good size and weight for wrapping.

Newspaper comics, both black and white and in color. Great for children's presents.

Wallpaper remnants you may have kept, or wallpaper sample books. In fact, many wallpaper stores give these away and the books include dozens of sheets with grains, patterns and textures that are appropriate for Christmas.

Leftover white shelf paper or specially bought rolls of it. It's inexpensive and motifs that your children draw or cut out and paste on will make the present festive.

Supermarket bags and other store bags and wraps (if they're crisp and wrinkle-free). Like shelf paper, they're fun to decorate.

Scrap yarn and fabric in bright colors make ties and trims. Cut fabric in strips and simple shapes with pinking shears and "appliqué" it to paper with double-faced tape.

CHRISTMAS EVERYWHERE: DECORATIONS TO MAKE

Home is where Christmas happens, and the centuries-old custom of bringing signs of the celebration into the house is one of the most beloved. In the vigor and spicy tang of evergreen boughs we can sense—almost breathe—the Christmas spirit of renewal. With the blooming of lights in myriad colors, sizes and shapes, we know the presence of Christmas hope. The garlands and the glow are like a blessing on our homes and our families—and certainly they are a graceful way to extend our greetings to those who come to visit or who merely pass by. Most families consider Christmas trimming one of the most enjoyable activities of the holiday season because everyone of every age can take part. Even your toddler can share in making most of the decorations in this collection. You'll find ornaments for the tree, wreaths, centerpieces, "anywhere" pieces and imaginative outdoor trims. Many are keepsakes you can bring out year after year. And don't forget that decorations make thoughtful, thrifty Christmas gifts.

GENERAL DIRECTIONS

TO ENLARGE PATTERNS: You will need brown wrapping paper (pieced if necessary to make a large enough sheet for a pattern), a felt-tipped marker, pencil and ruler. (**Note:** If pattern you are enlarging has a grid around it, first connect grid lines across pattern with a colored pencil to form a grid over the picture.) Mark paper with grid as follows: First cut your paper into a true square or rectangle. Then mark dots ¼″, ½″, 1″ or 2″ apart or whatever is indicated on pattern around edges, making same number of spaces as there are squares around the edges of pattern diagram. Form a grid by joining the dots across opposite sides of paper. Check to make sure you have the same number of squares as shown in diagram. With marker draw in each square the same pattern lines you see in the corresponding square on the diagram.

If you want to avoid the trouble of drawing a grid to enlarge your pattern, you can order a package of four 22″ x 34″ sheets of 1″ graph paper for $1.50 postpaid from Sewmakers, Inc., 1619 Grand Avenue, Baldwin, New York 11510.

ABBREVIATIONS AND TERMS USED FOR KNITTING AND CROCHETING: Beg—beginning; ch—chain; cl—cluster; dc—double crochet; dec—decrease; dp—double pointed; h dc—half double crochet; inc—increase; k—knit; lp—loop; p—purl; psso—pass slipped stitch over; rnd—round; sc—single crochet; sl—slip; sl st—slip stitch; sp—space; st—stitch; tog—together; tr—treble crochet; y o—yarn over. *—**Asterisk**—means repeat instructions following asterisk as many times as specified, in addition to the first time. [ ]—**Brackets**—indicate changes in size. ( )—**Parentheses**—mean repeat instructions in parentheses as many times as specified. **Stockinette stitch**—K 1 row, p 1 row or k each round if using circular or double-pointed needle. **Garter stitch**—K each row.

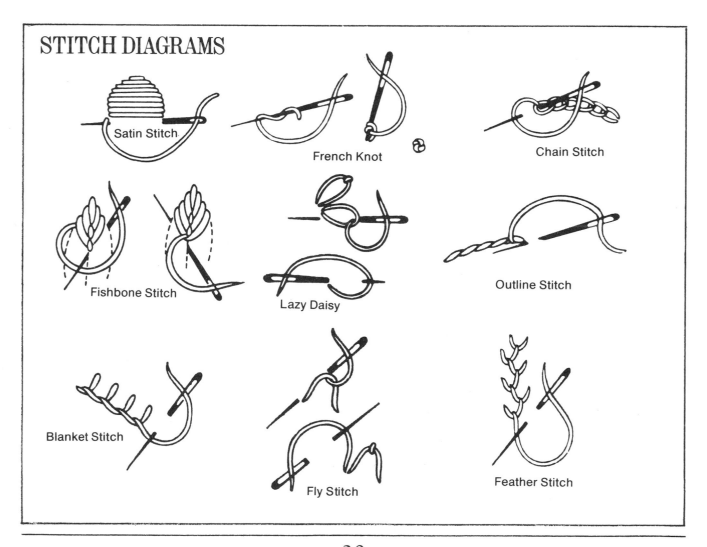

STITCH DIAGRAMS

Satin Stitch

French Knot

Chain Stitch

Fishbone Stitch

Lazy Daisy

Outline Stitch

Blanket Stitch

Fly Stitch

Feather Stitch

Old-fashioned Christmas Tree with Hand-crafted Ornaments

All the traditional festoons are here, crowned by a ten-point star: bells and balls, fruit and flowers, birds and angels, stockings and Santas, popcorn chains and candy canes.

Cookie Creatures

Bright with vegetable dyes and cake decorations.

MATERIALS: See recipe below for special dough; food coloring; small candies, red hots, cake decorations such as silver balls, confetti and florets; florist's wire; paring knife; cardboard; small artist's brushes; clear polyurethane or shellac (optional).

Enlarge patterns for elephant and bird on cardboard (see To Enlarge Patterns, page 30); cut out.

Follow recipe below to make dough for cookies, which are inedible. Recipe cannot be halved or doubled. Cookies measure about 5″, and recipe will make about 24.

Recipe: Preheat oven to 300°. Mix 4 cups flour

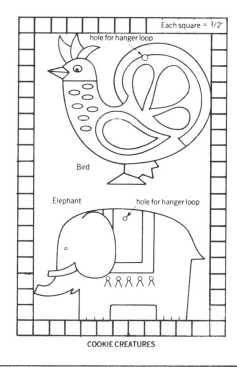

COOKIE CREATURES

with 1 cup salt. Dissolve ¼ cup instant coffee in 1½ cups warm water. Make a hole in center of flour-salt mixture and pour in 1 cup coffee. Mix thoroughly with hands or fork, adding additional coffee-water if necessary (dough should be smooth and satiny and neither crumbly nor sticky). Form into balls and store in plastic bags to prevent drying out. Using one ball at a time, roll out on cookie sheet to ¼″ thickness. Use cardboard patterns to cut cookie shapes with wet paring knife. Pull away excess dough, knead into ball and roll out again. To incise details on cookies follow pattern and use tip of ice pick. Work a hole centered at top of each ornament and insert and twist a piece of wire for hanger. Following photograph, paint cookies with undiluted food coloring and artist's brushes. Press small candies and cake decorations into dough as shown.

Bake ornaments in 350° oven ¾ to 1½ hours or until pin inserted in dough comes out clean. Remove from oven and cool on cake rack. Coat with polyurethane or shellac if desired.

Wooden Bird

Smoothly shaped of natural pine.

SIZE: 4″ long.

MATERIALS: 6½″ of 1 x 4 clear pine stock for two birds; white wood glue; decorative cord.

Enlarge pattern for body and wings (see To Enlarge Patterns, page 30) on cardboard; cut out. Rip 1 x 4 into two lengths 1½″ and 2″ wide. For bodies transfer pattern to 2″ piece in reversed position. Using coping, jig or band saw, cut out. Round and shape soft curves of each bird's body with sandpaper; taper into beak. For wings set table saw and rip 1½″ pine to ½″ thickness. Through long edge cut ½″ piece approximately in half at a 10° angle. Transfer pattern for wings to one half, keeping straight edge of wing on the long, thicker edge of wood. Cut out and sand, rounding all edges except those to be joined. Following photograph, glue wings to body, making certain they are aligned; let dry.

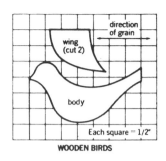

WOODEN BIRDS

To hang bird bore a hole large enough for decorative cord centered and straight through body. Place a single wrapping of transparent tape around end of cord as tip to push cord through hole to bottom of bird. Knot end of cord, dab with glue and pull up so that it is caught in hole. Loop top end for hanging.

Yo-Yo Chain

Could also garland a banister or mantelpiece.

MATERIALS: ½ yard 45″-wide cotton in 6 or 7 different small prints (each ½ yard makes 27 yo-yos); ¾″-diameter red wooden beads, one for every 2 yo-yos; absorbent cotton or Dacron polyester stuffing; needle and thread; heavy-duty nylon fishing line; scrap cardboard.

Draw 5″-diameter circle on cardboard; cut out for pattern. Using pattern, cut out fabric circles. To make a yo-yo sew tiny gathering stitches all around circumference of fabric circle. Draw up stitches, leaving opening for stuffing; stuff; knot ends. To string chain use needle and long length of fishing line and string two yo-yos and a bead; repeat until all yo-yos and beads are strung; knot ends to hold.

Bargello Balls

Worked in six sections with gold thread across center.

SIZE: Each ball measures about 3¼″ in diameter.

MATERIALS: One 6″ x 16″ piece mono (single-mesh) needlepoint canvas with 18 meshes per inch; D.M.C. 6-strand embroidery floss: **For Red Ball:** 1 (8.7-yard) skein each No. 818 (A), No 893 (B), No. 891 (C), No. 666 (D) and No. 816 (E); **For Green Ball:** 1 skein each No. 3348 (A), No. 704 (B), No. 702 (C), No. 700 (D) and No. 319 (E); 4 yards gold metallic thread (M); 1 yard ¼″-wide gold metallic braid; about 3¼″-diameter plastic-foam ball; tapestry needle; white glue.

Fold masking tape over canvas edges to prevent raveling. Use full 6-ply strand of floss and 1 strand of metallic thread, each cut into 18″ lengths. Following chart, work 6 hexagonal motifs. Brush glue over last stitches around motif edges to secure. When dry, trim canvas, leaving ⅛″ all around.

Draw a line completely around ball, then anywhere on line mark a small crossline to indicate top of ball. Apply glue to back of one motif. Using pins to hold in place, line up left edge of motif to the right of line ball, placing one pointed end at top crossline. Glue remaining motifs around ball, overlapping edges slightly where necessary. Press pinned motifs with damp sponge. When dry, remove pins.

Cut a 6″ length of metallic thread and tie ends to form hanging loop. Glue knotted portion of loop to top of ball.

Cut three 10½″ lengths of metallic braid. Slide one halfway through loop and glue over joining of 2 motifs; overlap ends slightly at bottom of ball. Glue remaining strips to other joinings in same manner.

Patchwork Ball

Stitched with festive cotton prints.

MATERIALS: 4″-diameter plastic-foam ball; scraps of colorful calico print fabrics and a related solid color in cotton or rough hopsacking; white glue; yarn scrap; stout needle.

To begin covering ball, cut two 1¼″-wide strips of solid-color fabric to go around circumference of ball

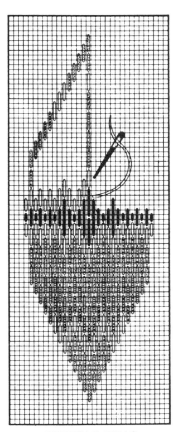

BARGELLO BALLS
Color Key

— M
— E
— D
— C
— B
— A

and overlap ends slightly. Brush glue on fabric strip and wrap around ball, dividing ball in half; glue overlapped ends. Smooth fabric strip in place. Brush glue on second strip and wrap around ball so it is divided into four equal sections. From print fabrics cut eight 1¼"-diameter circles for each section. Beginning at a narrow end of section, glue fabric circles in place. Overlap circles so that section is covered. Repeat for remaining sections.

For hanger, thread yarn through needle, then at center of one solid strip run needle under fabric and out again. Pull up yarn, remove needle and knot loose ends of yarn for loop.

Felt Tree, Bell and Angel

Stuffed and trimmed with embroidery.

MATERIALS: For Angel: Scraps white felt; light-blue, pink, yellow, bright-pink and green 6-strand embroidery floss; white thread; gold metallic thread; absorbent cotton. **For Christmas Tree:** Scraps green felt; red 6-strand embroidery floss; gold metallic thread; absorbent cotton. **For Bell:** Scraps red felt; green and white 6-strand embroidery floss; gold metallic thread; absorbent cotton.

Note: See To Enlarge Patterns, page 30, and Stitch Diagrams, page 30.

ANGEL: Enlarge pattern on brown wrapping paper; cut out. Cut two angels from white felt, using pinking shears. Lightly pencil outline for dress, candle and facial features on one felt angel. Following photograph as color guide and using 2 strands of floss throughout, embroider hair, eyes, cheeks, candle and hands in satin stitch. Use an outline stitch to frame face, make mouth and frame dress, sleeves and collar. Use chain stitch to trim bottom edge of dress. Make a halo with metallic thread as in photograph. Matching edges, sew angel together as in photograph, outlining wings in blue, then continuing with white thread. Leave opening to stuff loosely with cotton; stuff, then close. For hanger loop use needle to thread length of gold thread through top edge; knot ends.

CHRISTMAS TREE: Enlarge pattern on brown wrapping paper; cut out. Cut two trees from green felt, using pinking shears. Lightly pencil guidelines for garland and ornament balls on one felt tree. Following photograph, use a single strand of metallic thread to embroider garland in chain stitch

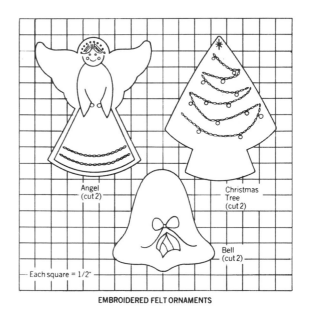

Angel
(cut 2)

Christmas
Tree
(cut 2)

Bell
(cut 2)

— Each square = 1/2″

EMBROIDERED FELT ORNAMENTS

and 2 strands of red floss to embroider balls in satin stitch. Make star at top as shown. Matching edges, sew tree together with red floss as in photograph, leaving opening to stuff. Stuff lightly and close opening. Attach loop as described for angel.

BELL: Enlarge pattern on brown wrapping paper; cut out. Cut two bells from red felt, using pinking shears. Lightly pencil outline for bow and leaves on one felt bell. Following photograph as color guide, use satin stitch for bow and outline stitch for leaves. Matching edges, sew bell together with green floss as shown, leaving opening. Stuff lightly and close opening. Attach gold hanger loop as described for angel.

Play-dough Basket

Enameled and filled with dried flowers.

SIZE: 3″ wide.

MATERIALS: 24 ounces play dough, available in most variety stores; empty 1-pound coffee can; 1″-diameter bottle cap; high-gloss enamel; clear cement; assorted dried flowers; ¼″-diameter wooden beads; 6-strand embroidery floss.

Note: Play dough will make 10 baskets.

Knead dough and roll out to ⅛″ thickness. Using 1-pound coffee can, cut out 10 circles for baskets. Pull away excess dough, knead into ball and roll out again. Using 1″-diameter cap, cut out 10 circles for bases. Find center and mark it on each basket circle. Use center point to divide circumference into 3 or 4 equal parts, then punch a hole at each point with ice pick for hanger. To flute edges of basket as shown in photograph press a blunt pencil point or nailhead into dough all around edge. To shape basket carefully lift and position dough circle onto top of an empty soda bottle. Using center mark, center dough over bottle mouth. Drape basket evenly, shaping each third or quarter as a unit. When complete, basket looks like a lampshade. Allow baskets and bases to dry overnight near a radiator; turn baskets right side up when outsides are dry and allow to dry an additional 12 hours. Keep turning flat base pieces every few hours to prevent warping. (**Note:** If weather is humid or damp, play dough will not air-dry. Place baskets on bottles and bases on cookie sheet in 170° oven 12 hours; turn over and dry another 12 hours.) Store dried baskets in an airtight container until ready to paint.

To decorate baskets brush 2 coats of enamel on all surfaces; let dry. Cement base in place. Puddle cement in basket; cut little bunches of dried flowers and place in cement in basket; let dry. Fill in any open area with individual flowers. To hang, cut short lengths of 6-strand floss for each hole. Thread floss through each hole, knot end and pull up. Join and knot ends at top, slip on bead and loop floss back through bead; knot ends. Clip excess floss and dab bead with cement to hold.

Crocheted Stocking

The right size for small candy canes.

SIZE: Each stocking measures about 6″.

MATERIALS: Coats & Clark's Speed-Cro-Sheen, 1 (100-yard) ball each white No. 1, Spanish red

No. 126 and hunter green No. 48 (1 ball will make 3 solid stockings or more striped stockings); steel crochet hook No. 1 **or the size that will give you the correct gauge.**

GAUGE: 6 dc = 1″; 5 rnds dc = 2″.

BASIC STOCKING: Starting at toe, ch 4. **1st rnd (right side):** Work 6 dc in 4th ch from hook. Join with sl st to top of ch 3 (7 dc, counting ch 3 as 1 dc). **2nd rnd:** Ch 3, work 2 dc in next dc and in each remaining dc (13 dc); join. **3rd rnd:** Ch 3, * dc in next dc, 2 dc in next dc. Repeat from * around (19 dc); join. **4th through 6th rnds:** Work dc in each dc around (19 dc); join.

To Shape Heel: 7th rnd: Ch 1, work sc in same sp as sl st and in each of next 2 dc, h dc in each of next 2 dc, dc in each of next 2 dc, 2 dc in each of next 2 dc, 2 tr in next dc (center back), 2 dc in each of next 2 dc, dc in each of next 2 dc, h dc in each of next 2 dc, sc in each of last 3 dc (24 sts); join to 1st sc. **8th rnd:** Ch 1, sc in same sp as sl st and in each of next 2 sc, h dc in each of next 2 h dc, dc in each of next 2 dc; work joined dc in next 2 dc as follows: (y o hook, insert hook in next st and pull up lp, y o and draw through 2 lps on hook) twice; y o and draw through all 3 lps on hook (joined dc made); work another joined dc in next 2 dc; work joined tr at center back as follows: * (y o hook) twice, insert hook in next st and pull up lp (y o hook and pull through 2 lps on hook) twice. Repeat from * once more, then y o and draw through all 3 lps on hook (joined tr made). Work 2 joined dc, dc in each of next 2 dc, h dc in each of next 2 h dc, sc in each of last 3 sc (19 sts); join.

9th rnd: Ch 3, work dc in each st around (19 sts); join. **10th through 15th rnds:** Repeat 4th rnd. **16th rnd:** Ch 2, work h dc in next dc and in each remaining dc; join. **17th rnd:** Ch 1, sc in same sp as sl st and in next 8 h dc; in next h dc work sc, ch 12 and sc (hanging lp made); sc in each remaining 9 h dc; join. Break off.

STRIPED VARIATIONS: Work in one color through 15th rnd or change colors after every 1 or 2 rnds.

Popcorn Chain

Snowy kernels strung on nylon thread.

MATERIALS: Corn for popping; large saucepan; cooking oil; nylon thread; needle.

Follow package directions to pop corn. When popped, pour out into large bowl. Thread needle with nylon thread and string long chains of popped corn.

Crocheted Bells

Each has a small ornament clapper.

SIZE: Each bell measures about 2½″ long.
MATERIALS: Coats & Clark's Speed-Cro-Sheen, 1 (100-yard) ball each white No. 1, Spanish red No. 126 and Killarney green No. 49-A (1 ball will make about 6 bells); steel crochet hook No. 1 **or the size that will give you the correct gauge;** 1¼″-diameter plastic drapery rings; 1″-diameter ornament balls.

GAUGE: 5 sc = 1″.
BELL: Starting at top, ch 4. Join with sl st to form ring. **1st rnd (right side):** Work 14 sc in ring; join with sl st to 1st sc. **2nd rnd:** Ch 1, sc in same sp as sl st, * 2 sc in next sc, sc in next sc. Repeat from * around, ending 2 sc in last sc (21 sc); join. **3rd through 12th rnds:** Ch 1, sc in same sp as sl st and in each sc around; join. **13th rnd:** Repeat 2nd rnd, ending with sc in last sc (31 sc); join. **14th rnd:** Repeat 3rd rnd. **15th rnd:** Work sl st in each sc around; join. Break off.

Stripes: Using contrasting color and with right side of bell facing you, work rnds of sl st around bell where desired as follows: Hold yarn on wrong side of bell, insert hook in bell and draw lp through, insert hook in bell about ⅛″ away from last insertion, draw a lp through bell and through lp on hook to make chain st. Continue around in this manner.

Clapper: Cut 10″ length of thread and tie one end to matching ball ornament. Pull other end through top of bell and tie overhand knot to secure clapper at proper length.

FOR EACH BELL GROUP: Make 3 bells, using different colors. To cover drapery ring, with green work 36 sc over ring; sl st in 1st sc to join. Break off. **To Assemble:** Tie bells to ring at various lengths, using free end of clapper thread. Cut one 10″ strand of each color and, holding them together, tie in bow over clapper threads at ring.

Plastic-foam Bird and Treetop Star

Both are cut from plastic trays.

MATERIALS: Smooth white plastic-foam meat trays; lightweight nylon thread; mat knife; white glue.

Enlarge patterns for bird and double star (see To Enlarge Patterns, page 30) on brown wrapping paper. Wash trays thoroughly. When dry, trace orna-

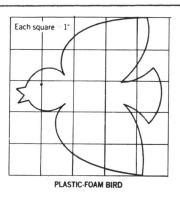

Each square = 1"

PLASTIC-FOAM BIRD

Each square = 1"

Cut 1
of each size

PLASTIC-FOAM DOUBLE STAR

ment shape lightly in pencil; use mat knife to cut out. Cut two stars for each ornament and use white glue to attach them with points positioned as shown in pattern. Cut one bird for each ornament. To hang ornaments punch a tiny hole centered near top edge of bird and centered on a point of double star and thread length of nylon thread through; knot ends for hanger loop.

Nut Santa

Felt hat and nose; movable eyes.

MATERIALS: Assortment of unshelled nuts, such as almonds, walnuts or Brazil nuts; scraps of bright pink, white and gold felt; ¼"-diameter movable eyes for toys; white glue; ¼"-diameter white bead; nylon thread.

To preserve nuts punch or drill a small hole in each one and quickly dip in boiling water. Remove and let dry. Cut a small triangle of pink felt and shape around one end of nut to form peaked hat; cut to fit. Wrap and glue hat around nut. Trim with narrow band of white felt as in photograph. Cut triangular nose from gold felt and glue two movable eyes and nose on nut for face. Thread needle with nylon thread and run it through peak of hat. Slip bead on; dab with glue to hold. Remove needle and knot loose ends of thread to form hanger loop.

Flowered Apples

Plastic fruit is painted, then lacquered.

MATERIALS: Small plastic apples, available at most variety stores; bright green, red, white and yellow acrylic paints; small pointed artist's brush; clear high-gloss polyurethane; gold gift-wrap cord; nylon thread.

Paint apples red or green with 2 or 3 coats of acrylic; let dry. Referring to photograph, use pointed brush to paint tiny 4-petaled flowers in contrasting color acrylic. Add leaves and connecting dots of paint between flowers to form rows. Let dry. Apply 2 coats of polyurethane to finish; let dry. Tie bow of gold cord at stem; loop and tie piece of nylon thread around base of stem for hanger loop.

One-of-a-Kind Wreaths

Unusual ingredients are featured in these charmingly different wreaths—the design elements range from citrus peel to pompons. They're well worth the bit of extra time and care it takes to make them because all but one of the six can be preserved for use in years to come. The exception is a whimsical ring of succulent plants that can be re-potted after the holidays.

Spice Wreath

An infinity of fragrances; lovely, subtle colors.

SIZE: About 17″ in diameter.

MATERIALS: 14″-diameter purchased straw wreath; the following dried flowers: 4 to 6 bunches of German statice, 12 miniature straw-flowers on 2″ wire stems and a few rosebuds or sprays of ammobium; 6 sweet-gum balls; 12 acorn caps; ¼ yd. 72″-wide ivory nylon net; small rubber bands; floral picks; thin flexible wire; 2 yds. ½″-wide pale-green velvet ribbon; glue gun and cartridge; white glue; various spices, herbs and dried flower petals (see Note below).

Note: Our wreath, though not difficult to assemble, requires patience and care. Listed below are a few of the spices, herbs and dried flower petals we used. You can substitute whatever is available in your area.

Use seed and spices such as star anise, caraway, cardamom, coriander, cumin, fennel, rosemary, mustard, poppy, sesame, whole or coarsely ground allspice, cloves, cinnamon bark or stick, nutmeg, gingerroot and whole bay leaves. From pharmacies you can obtain orrisroot, frankincense and myrrh; also dried flower petals such as lavender, potpourri, sassafras, bark, oakmoss, herbal and mint teas, lemon verbena, tansy and yarrow.

SACHETS

Cut nylon net into 5″ squares. Prepare various potpourris of dried petals and herbs. Add a pinch of orrisroot to each mixture to preserve the fragrance. Place 2 teaspoons potpourri mixture in center of each net square. Pull up edges to form a 1″-diameter ball. Bind sachet tightly with rubber band; cut away excess net. Also make sachets of sesame seed, rosemary, whole cardamom and caraway.

ACORN CAPS

Pour a few drops of glue in acorn cap and rub to coat inside of cap thoroughly. Sprinkle cap with seed

SPICE WREATH
Assembly Detail

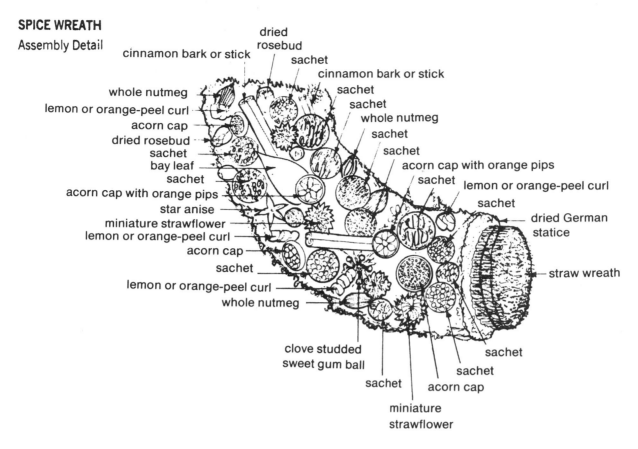

spices such as mustard, whole allspice and whole cardamom. Also arrange orange pips in flower or star shape. Shake out excess seed and set caps aside to dry.

SWEET-GUM BALLS

Dip tips of whole cloves in glue and insert 1 in each hole in sweet-gum ball until ball is half filled.

LEMON- AND ORANGE-PEEL CURLS

Remove peel from fruit in 4 lengthwise sections; scrape any pulp and soft white membrane away. Cut in thin strips. Allow strips to dry 1 to 2 hours, then twist pliable strips into spirals and secure with a toothpick. Allow to dry.

WREATH ASSEMBLY

Using flexible wire, make a strong double hanger loop around straw wreath; bind wire firmly. Push loop to back of wreath and tuck any sharp ends into straw.

Cut statice into sprays of 3″ to 5″ including stems. Wire a pick to each spray. Cover front and all edges of wreath with statice, making sure that sprays all go in the same direction. Overlap sprays so that front and sides of wreath are completely covered. Do not cover back.

Following manufacturer's directions for using glue gun, touch the underside of prepared sachets, acorn caps, sweet-gum balls, peel curls and all the individual dried flowers, bay leaves, cinnamon bark, star anise, etc. with gun and arrange on wreath as in photograph and assembly detail.

To finish, make a loopy bow with streamers from velvet ribbon as in photograph; wire bow to wreath.

Note: Store wreath in large plastic bag.

Dainty Wreath

Calico-covered bottle caps, eyelet edging.

SIZE: 13″ diameter.
MATERIALS: 60 pry-off-type metal bottle caps; scraps of 6 or 7 colorful cotton prints, ginghams or polka-dot fabrics in predominantly red and green; 2½ yards 2″-wide white eyelet trim; 2 yards 1″-wide bright-green grosgrain ribbon; matching thread.

Wash and dry bottle caps. On fabric scraps use a compass to draw sixty 2¼″-diameter circles; cut out. Fold over and press a ¼″ hem on all fabric circles. To cover bottle cap, center cap on wrong side of fabric circle. With needle and thread take tiny stitches around circle on hemmed edge. Pull thread tight so

Nuts-and-Apples Wreath

Pinecones and cinnamon sticks are tucked in, too.

SIZE: 18″ diameter.

MATERIALS: One large corrugated-cardboard carton; white glue; utility knife; 3 tubes clear cement; hanger plate; 16 small artificial apples, available from variety stores; 2 dozen small pinecones; assorted dried seed pods, acorns, thistles, etc.; assorted unshelled Brazil nuts, walnuts, almonds and filberts; 2 jars whole cinnamon sticks; 3 yards 3″-wide red-and-white-gingham taffeta ribbon; 1 skein red 6-strand embroidery floss.

Cut carton open and flatten. Laminate three layers of corrugated carton pieces (each at least 19″ square), using white glue and alternating direction of corrugation. Weight laminated pieces and allow to dry overnight, then draw 18″-diameter circle with a centered 6″-diameter inner circle. Carefully cut out for wreath background, using utility knife.

To preserve nuts, first punch or drill a small hole in each nut, then dip quickly into boiling water; put aside to dry. Also quickly rinse pinecones and pods

that fabric pulls around cap; knot thread to hold. Cover all caps.

To assemble wreath, tack 14 covered caps together to form ring; make a second ring of 20 and a third of 26, alternating fabrics for a colorful effect. Center smallest ring inside second one and tack edges together; repeat to join third ring. For ruffled edge, fold over and press raw edge of eyelet trim. With needle and thread gather with tiny stitches to fit circumference of third ring; tack to hold. Sew ends of eyelet trim together to form ring, then sew to third ring as in photograph.

Make a double-loop flat bow with 10″ streamers from grosgrain ribbon. Sew to top edge of wreath as in photograph. Hang wreath on wall or use as centerpiece.

gathered outdoors to remove any oozing resin or dirt. Spread out on a towel and let dry several days.

Following photograph, use clear cement to glue artificial apples and pinecones around wreath, spacing evenly. Glue nuts, dried pods and other dried items around inner and outer edges, extending slightly beyond cardboard edge to conceal it. Also fill any open areas with smaller nuts and seeds. Make bundles of 2 or 3 cinnamon sticks and tie around center with 6 or 7 wrappings of embroidery floss; knot to hold. Clip excess floss, leaving ¼" ends. Glue bundles at equal intervals around wreath. Let dry.

To finish, tie ribbon around bottom of wreath, then tie a big bow; pink loose ribbon ends. Cement hanger plate to back.

Crocheted Loop-stitch Wreath

Trios of pompons are the "berries."

SIZE: 16" diameter.

MATERIALS: Bernat Quickspun (bulky acrylic yarn), 8 (35-yd.) skeins emerald No. 2788; Bernat Berella "4" (acrylic knitting-worsted-weight yarn), 1 (4-oz.) ball scarlet No. 8933; aluminum crochet hook size K (or international hook size 7.00 mm); ¼ yd. red felt; cardboard; red sewing thread.

POMPON (make 15): Cut 2 cardboard circles 1½" in diameter. Cut ½"-diameter hole in center of each to make ring. Hold rings together and make cut from outer edge to hole. Wind scarlet yarn around and around rings, bringing it through cut with each wind. When cardboard is covered and hole filled, cut yarn. Snip yarn around outside edge of ring; separate cardboard rings slightly and tie yarn together tightly in center between rings. Remove cardboard and pompon will fluff out. Trim slightly if necessary.

WREATH FRAME: From cardboard, cut circle 14" in diameter. Cut 9"-diameter hole in center to form ring. (**Note:** If cardboard is thin, cut 2 rings and tape together.)

CROCHET: With crochet hook and emerald yarn, crochet chain to fit around outside of ring plus 1". **1st row:** Sc in 2nd ch from hook and in each ch across; ch 1, turn. **2nd row (wrong side):** Work lp sc in next sc as follows: * Make 2"-long lp over index finger of left hand; insert hook in next sc and draw a bit of both strands of lp through st; remove finger from lp, y o and draw through all lps on hook (lp sc made). Repeat from * across (lps appear on

right side of work). **Break off. Do not turn. Always work with wrong side facing you. 3rd row:** Make lp on hook; work lp sc in each lp sc across. Repeat from ** until piece is large enough to cover both sides of ring. Break off.

FINISHING: With lps outward, fold crocheted piece over cardboard frame and sew edges together. (You will have to pull in the crochet around inner edge to fit cardboard frame.) From felt, cut 3" x 20" piece for bow and 2" x 30" piece for ties. Fold wider piece to form bow shape, lapping ends at center back. Fold narrower piece in half crosswise, wrap fold around bow and tack at back. Cut ends on a diagonal. Following photograph, tack pompons and bow to wreath.

Evergreen Wreath

Pine sprays with replantable hens-and-chickens.

MATERIALS: Unadorned evergreen wreath; 10 hens-and-chickens succulents; thin flexible wire.

Use entire cluster of succulent with root intact. Twist wire near top of root. Following photograph, arrange succulents around wreath and twist wires around branches to hold in place. **Note:** After Christmas remove succulents from wreath and transplant in soil mix for cacti and succulents.

Popcorn Wreath

Sprinkled with peppermint candies and satin bows.

SIZE: Approximately 18″ diameter.
MATERIALS: 15½″-diameter x 2″-wide plastic-foam ring; 6 to 8 quarts unbuttered popcorn; 4 dozen round, flat peppermint candies; white glue; 6 yards ⅝″-wide red satin ribbon; thin flexible wire; 3 yards 1½″-wide red-and-white polka-dot cotton ribbon; round wooden cocktail picks; pipe cleaner; colorless nail polish.

Cover work surface with waxed paper. Unwrap candies and brush colorless nail polish on all surfaces; put aside to dry. Place plastic-foam wreath on waxed paper and pour container of undiluted white glue into bowl; allow glue to thicken slightly. Dip picks halfway into glue and stud plastic-foam wreath liberally but not densely with picks so that about 1″ projects out of ring; let dry.

Dilute ½ cup white glue with ½ cup water; mix well. Working with small amount (1½ quarts) at a time, pour diluted glue over popcorn and mix well to coat thoroughly. Working quickly, begin spreading popcorn on wreath, covering face and sides. Prepare more popcorn as you work and build up wreath as shown in photograph. Set wreath aside to dry a day or two.

Cut red satin ribbon into twenty-four 9″ pieces and make small bows. Wire a pick to each bow. Also make loopy bow from polka-dot ribbon as in photograph; wire a pick to it.

When wreath is dry, use undiluted glue to attach coated candies over wreath. Dip bow picks in glue and push in place over wreath as in photograph; add polka-dot bow at top, slightly off center. Allow wreath to dry.

To hang, bend pipe cleaner in *U* shape and work tips into back of plastic foam at top. Pull out and dip tips of pipe cleaner in glue; reinsert in holes; let dry.

Centerpieces, Sidepieces, Mantelpieces

In this group are "sit-down" ornaments (as opposed to hanging ones) that you can place on dining tables, cocktail tables, shelves—any flat surface. Some are sophisticated, some are amusing, some are edible, and one has finger-puppet favors for children.

Fragrant Centerpiece

Lemons, limes, a pineapple top.

SIZE: 21" high.
MATERIALS: 21" plastic-foam cone 5" in diameter; 8 each jumbo lemons and limes; top of fresh pineapple; sprays of evergreen and laurel leaves; 5½' of ¼"-diameter dowel.

Note: Our centerpiece of fresh lemons, limes and pineapple top will be fresh 4 to 5 days. If you wish, plastic lemons, limes and a pineapple top can be substituted.

Cut dowel into 5" lengths for each lemon and 3" lengths for each lime. Cut off stem end of lemons and limes and insert proper dowel length into each one. Following photograph, position lemons and limes equally over plastic-foam cone by inserting dowel into cone at 45° angle. Set cone in large plate or tray. Cut top off pineapple; let juices drain if necessary. Cut off tip of cone and secure pineapple top on cone with toothpicks or pins. Fill in open areas of cone with evergreen sprays and laurel leaves, sticking stems of greens directly into plastic foam.

Crocheted Ruffle Tree

Trimmed with pompons and candy canes.

SIZE: 16" high x 7" diameter at base.
MATERIALS: For tree: Bucilla Multicraft (acrylic bulky yarn), 6 (2-oz.) skeins emerald No. 33; aluminum crochet hook size J (or international hook size 6.00 mm); 15"-high x 4"-diameter plastic-foam cone; green acrylic or poster paint; paintbrush; straight pins. **For ornaments:** Bear Brand Winsom (acrylic sport-weight yarn), 1 (2-oz.) skein each scarlet No. 409 and white No. 101; aluminum crochet hook size F (or international hook size 4.00 mm); pipe cleaners.

TREE: Lightly cover plastic-foam cone with

green paint. Allow to dry thoroughly. **Crocheted Ruffle:** With green yarn and size J hook, crochet 16-ft. chain. Mark chain at 4-ft. intervals. Work 2 sc in 2nd ch from hook, 2 dc in each of next 2 ch, 3 dc in each ch to 1st marker, 3 tr in each ch to 2nd marker, 3 d tr (yarn around hook twice) in each ch to 3rd marker, 3 tr tr (yarn around hook 3 times) in each ch to end. Break off. Starting at top of cone, secure st at beg of ruffle with straight pin. Wind ruffle around cone (see photograph), securing other end with pin at base.

ORNAMENTS: Candy Cane (make 6): Spiral: With red and size F crochet hook, ch 32. Work 3 sc in 2nd ch from hook and in each ch across. Break off. With white, make another spiral. Intertwine spirals, wrap around 3″ pipe cleaner and bend to form cane. Cut off excess pipe cleaner.

Large Pompon: Cut two 3″-diameter cardboard circles. Cut 1″-diameter hole in center of each to make ring. Hold rings together and make cut from outer edge to hole. Wind red around and around rings, bringing it through cut with each wind. When cardboard is covered and hole filled, cut yarn. Snip yarn around outside edge of ring, separate cardboard slightly and tie yarn together tightly in center. Remove cardboard and pompon will fluff out. Trim slightly if necessary. Pin to top of tree.

Small Pompon (make 6): Cut two 1″-diameter cardboard circles. Cut ½″-diameter hole in center of each to make ring. With red, complete as for large pompon. Make 2 more red and 3 white pompons. With pins attach small pompons and candy canes to tree.

leaves or bunches to fill in bare spots. Top centerpiece with pineapple.

Colonial Centerpiece

Takes inspiration from Williamsburg.

SIZE: Approximately 18″ tall.

MATERIALS: 3′ of ½ x 6 clear pine; white glue; 1½″ finishing nails; flat green paint; 12 large red Delicious apples; 9′ of plastic holly garland; one well-shaped pineapple with leafy top.

For base, cut 4 sides from ½ x 6 pine as shown in construction detail. Sand cut ends and assemble base with glue and nails. Position and install nails for holding apples as indicated. Paint base; let dry.

Following photograph, impale apples on nails and wrap holly around base and between apples. Secure garland with tacks or staples. Use single holly

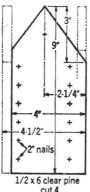

1/2 x 6 clear pine
cut 4

COLONIAL CENTERPIECE

Guardian Angel

Silver doilies and studs add sparkle.

SIZE: 16″ tall.

MATERIALS: 15″ plastic-foam cone 4¾″ in diameter; 3¾″-diameter plastic-foam ball; two 10″ x 12″ pieces ¼″-thick plastic foam; metallic silver doilies; three ¼″-diameter chrome-plated studs; blue, pink and red felt-tipped markers; special glue for plastic foam or Elmer's Glue; straight pins.

Cut 5″ tip off cone, using knife with serrated cutting edge; put tip aside and use for arms. Enlarge pattern for wings (see To Enlarge Patterns, page 30)

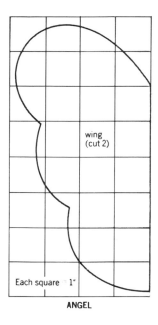

wing
(cut 2)

Each square = 1″

ANGEL

on brown wrapping paper; cut out. Trace wing shapes on ¼″-thick plastic foam and cut out with knife.

Referring to photograph, mark placement for eyes, nose, mouth and rosy cheeks. Color in cheeks with pink felt-tipped marker. Cut out tiny circles from scrap foam for eyes, nose and mouth. Color eyes blue, nose pink and mouth red with felt-tipped markers. Glue facial features in place with special glue. Cut out edges of doilies and cut in 2″ pieces. Following photograph, glue 3 overlapping rows of doily to head. Make a slight depression at top of cut-off cone; glue head to body. Cut tip of cone in half lengthwise for arms. Position arms ¾″ down from neck edge; pin securely in place. Cut decorative motif from doily for collar; glue around shoulders as in photograph. Center 3 studs on front for buttons. Trim lower edge

of angel's robe with doily motifs; glue in place. For halo, cut out and position 5¾″ foam disk as in photograph; work slight depression in halo where it touches back of head; glue in place. Glue wings to back as in photograph, adding pin through each to hold securely.

Ruffled Tannenbaum

Folds flat to store for next year.

MATERIALS: 2½ yards 45"-wide small-print green cotton fabric; 1 yard 18"-wide press-on bonding mesh; 7 yards ½"-wide red rickrack; matching thread; 16" piece two-part Velcro fastener; absorbent cotton; scrap yellow print fabric for star; T-pin; tissue paper for stiffening cone; brown wrapping paper.

Enlarge diagram for cone on brown wrapping paper as described under To Enlarge Patterns, page

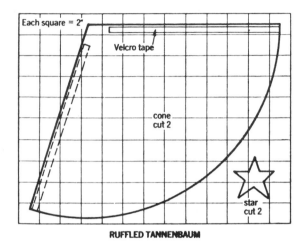

30. Using pattern, cut out two fabric cone shapes. Following manufacturer's directions, cut bonding mesh to shape of cone. Assemble two fabric pieces, right sides out, with mesh. Using warm iron, press pieces together; allow to cool. Following manufacturer's directions, stitch Velcro fastener along edges of cone indicated on pattern. Shape cone, overlapping edges, and stuff with tissue paper to stiffen into freestanding tree.

For ruffled layers, cut strips 3½" wide and 48", 42", 34", 31", 26", 23", 17" and 14" long. Turn up ½" hem along one long side of each strip; topstitch rickrack along hemmed edge as in photograph. Run machine basting stitches along opposite long side. Pin and stitch ends of each strip together to form ring. Slip largest ring over cone and fit around base by pulling up basting stitches. Repeat for remaining rings in sequence. Stitch gathers to hold. Finish top edge of smallest ruffle with rickrack. From remaining fabric make a small cone to fit peak of tree. Enlarge star pattern, transfer to yellow print fabric and cut out. With right sides together, stitch star pieces around edges, leaving opening. Turn star, press and stuff with absorbent cotton; close opening. With T-pin inserted at peak of tiny fabric cone, attach star and slip over tree. Assemble ruffled layers on tree as in photograph.

Grandpa Elf, Ho-Ho Santa

Simple foam balls, painted and trimmed.

Referring to photograph, mark placement for eyes, nose, mouth and rosy cheeks. Color in cheeks with marking pen. Make a slight depression in foam head for eyes and nose; glue eyes and nose in place. Cut out red felt mouth and glue in place. Glue small cotton moustache under nose.

From felt scraps cut white collar, two red buttons, red belt and yellow buckle as in photograph. Glue buckle centered on belt strip and wrap around green body, pinning ends to hold in back. Glue buttons and collar in place. With sharp-pointed knife cut vertical slots in sides of body for hands. Check fit and glue hands in place. Stick two long pins in flattened end of head, dip pins in glue and join head to body. Glue cotton beard and hair fringe in place and shape with fingers. Open paper clip full length or use wire to shape spectacles. Stick loose ends (ear pieces) into plastic foam to hold.

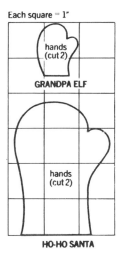

Each square = 1"
hands (cut 2)
GRANDPA ELF
hands (cut 2)
HO-HO SANTA

GRANDPA ELF

SIZE: 6″ tall.

MATERIALS: One each 4″-diameter and 2½″-diameter plastic-foam balls; scraps red, green, white and yellow felt; dark-green spray paint; spray Accent transparent paint; two green and one red ⅜″-diameter wooden beads; absorbent cotton; white glue; scrap Bristol board; straight pins; bright-pink felt-tipped marker; copper paper clip or flexible wire.

Very lightly sand a flat surface on one side of each ball. Spray-paint small ball light pink with transparent paint; set aside to dry. Lightly haze larger ball green, gradually building up color to dark green; let dry.

Enlarge pattern for hands (see To Enlarge Patterns, page 30) on brown wrapping paper; cut out and transfer to a 1¾″ square of Bristol board that has been covered on both sides with green felt. Cut out hands with sharp scissors.

HO-HO SANTA

SIZE: 12″ tall.

MATERIALS: One each 6″-diameter and 4″-diameter plastic-foam balls; scraps red, turquoise and yellow felt; red spray paint; spray Accent transparent paint; two ⅝″-diameter blue and one ¾″-diameter red wooden beads; absorbent cotton; scrap cardboard; bright-pink felt-tipped marker; white glue; straight pins.

Very lightly sand a flat surface on one side of each ball. Spray-paint smaller ball light pink with transparent paint; put aside. lightly haze larger ball red, gradually building up color; let dry.

Enlarge pattern for hands (see To Enlarge Patterns, page 30) on brown wrapping paper; cut out and transfer to a 4″ square of cardboard that has been covered on both sides with red felt. Cut out hands with sharp scissors. Trim each hand with band of cotton as in photograph. Glue in place.

Referring to photograph, mark placement for eyes, nose, mouth and rosy cheeks. Color in cheeks with felt-tipped marker. Make a slight depression in foam head for eyes and nose. (**Note:** You may wish to paint beads if you are unable to find the right colors and sizes. Thin acrylic paint with water; paint; let dry.) Glue nose and eyes in place. Cut out red felt mouth and glue in place. Glue cotton moustache under nose. From red felt cut a 6½"-high triangular shape to go around head for stocking cap. Wrap around head to form cone. Pin and stitch seam down back; trim away excess. Glue band of cotton around bottom edge of cap and cotton ball on top.

From turquoise felt cut wide strip for belt; cut buckle from yellow felt. Glue buckle centered on belt and glue belt around center of body as in photograph. With sharp-pointed knife cut vertical slots in sides of body for hands. Check fit and glue hands in place. Stick two long pins into flattened end of head, dip pins in glue and join head to body at an angle. Glue cotton beard, hair and furry collar in place and shape with fingers. Pin stocking cap on head.

Angel Pyramid

A choir of glorified clothespins.

SIZE: Overall pyramid, about 22" high; individual angels, about 7" high.

MATERIALS: One 4"-diameter x 13"-high plastic-foam cone; 1½"-thick x 8"-diameter plastic-foam disk; chunks of plastic foam; 2"-, 3"-, 4"-, and 5"-diameter metallic silver, gold, royal blue, magenta and kelly green doilies, available from most party-supply stores; 12 wooden clothespins; red, blue and green construction paper; gold tinsel stems; stemmed velvet holly and berries; pipe cleaners; 1/16"-diameter dowel, available from craft stores, or bamboo skewers; wooden toothpicks; acrylic paints; small brush; white glue; compass; scrap heavyweight cardboard; bank pins; spray silver metallic paint.

Study diagrams A through D to make basic angel. To make body (see diagram A), use compass to draw 5"-diameter circle on construction paper; cut out for dress. Wrap and glue circle around clothespin as shown. Add 5"-diameter silver or gold doily overskirt and 3"-diameter blue, green or magenta doily tunic. The tunic should match the color of construction-

paper dress. As in photograph, the tunic can be wrapped with edges of doily to the back or front.

If the angel is to stand, cut a piece of plastic foam to fit inside bottom edge of angel's dress as shown in diagram A. Also draw and cut a 2½″-diameter circle from cardboard. Assemble stand with glue and bank pins as shown. Make two standing angels. For pyramid angels paint a length of 1/16″ dowel or bamboo skewer with silver spray paint; let dry. Glue dowel or skewer to leg of clothespin. Make 10 pyramid angels.

Referring to diagram B, make wings. Draw and cut a 3″-diameter circle from construction paper to match the dress. Divide circle in half and cut out semicircles for wing liners. Assemble wings with glue, using 4″- and 3″-diameter gold or silver doilies and colored liner as shown.

Referring to diagram C, make arms. Fold and cut one 2″-diameter silver and one 2″-diameter blue, green or magenta doily in half. The colors should match overskirt and tunic. Cut two 3″ lengths of pipe cleaner for each angel's arms. Bend back one end of each to make small rounded hand as in diagram. Fold and glue silver or gold and colored doilies so that silver or gold edge shows at wrist edge.

For halo cut two small circular motifs from either silver or gold doilies. With wrong sides facing, glue pairs of motifs together.

To assemble angel, follow the step-by-step procedure indicated on diagram D. Bend tinsel stem around head for hair and glue in place. Bend velvet holly on top of hair; arrange and glue as in photograph. Paint eyes, brows, nose, mouth and rosy cheeks, using acrylic paints and small brush. Allow angel to dry.

To assemble pyramid, cover one flat surface of plastic-foam disk and entire plastic-foam cone with overlapped silver doilies; glue in place. Fold 3″-diameter silver doilies in half; arrange, rounded edge up, around edge of disk as in photograph; glue. Center and glue cone shape on disk, pushing two or three bank pins through bottom of disk into cone to reinforce bond. Following photograph for placement, insert skewered angels into plastic-foam cone, arranging in pyramid. Cut pairs of silver doily motifs as described for halo. Spray-paint several toothpicks silver. Glue doilies together in pairs with toothpicks sandwiched between. When dry, insert these motifs in cone between angels. Place standing angel at base pyramid.

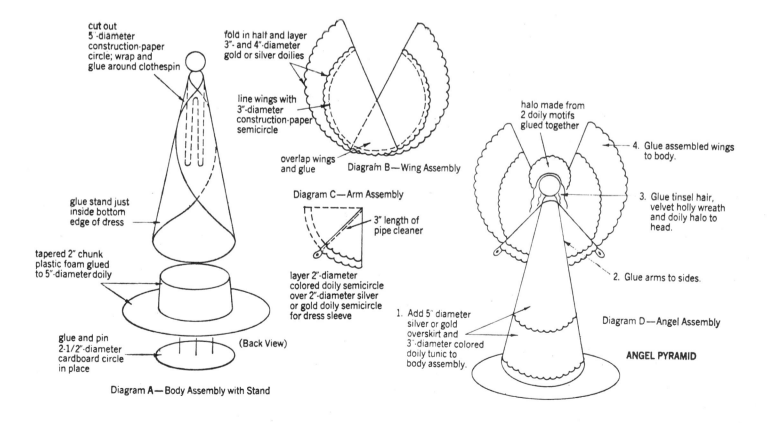

cut out 5″-diameter construction-paper circle; wrap and glue around clothespin

line wings with 3″-diameter construction-paper semicircle

glue stand just inside bottom edge of dress

tapered 2″ chunk plastic foam glued to 5″-diameter doily

glue and pin 2-1/2″-diameter cardboard circle in place

(Back View)

Diagram A—Body Assembly with Stand

fold in half and layer 3″- and 4″-diameter gold or silver doilies

overlap wings and glue

Diagram B—Wing Assembly

Diagram C—Arm Assembly

3″ length of pipe cleaner

layer 2″-diameter colored doily semicircle over 2″-diameter silver or gold doily semicircle for dress sleeve

halo made from 2 doily motifs glued together

4. Glue assembled wings to body.

3. Glue tinsel hair, velvet holly wreath and doily halo to head.

2. Glue arms to sides.

1. Add 5″-diameter silver or gold overskirt and 3″-diameter colored doily tunic to body assembly.

Diagram D—Angel Assembly

ANGEL PYRAMID

Marshmallow Tree

Perfect project for a child.

Children's Favors

Ice-cream-cone trees, felt finger puppets.

FINISHED SIZE: 13″ high.

MATERIALS: 12″ cone of plastic foam; scrap of foam rubber, plastic foam or stale loaf of bread for drying stand; 6 or 7 dozen marshmallows with firm surface; round wood toothpicks; food coloring set.

Mix colors as in set directions. Hold marshmallow with toothpick and follow photograph to paint design with a cotton swab or small brush. Insert in stand; let dry 24 hours in cool place.

ICE-CREAM-CONE TREES

SIZE: Approximately 8″ tall.

MATERIALS: Icing (below); cup-shaped and cone-shaped ice cream cones; table knife; assorted small hard candies; 1½″-diameter lollipops.

ICING: In large bowl of electric mixer combine ½ teaspoon lemon juice and 1 egg white. Gradually beat in 1½ cups confectioners' sugar until stiff peaks form, adding a little more sugar if necessary. **Note:**

Icing hardens quickly, so keep bowl covered with a damp towel.

Snip tip off cone-shaped cone, then cut away top edge of cup-shaped cone so that first cone, inverted, fits snugly into it to form tree shape. Use knife to spread icing around inside edge to seal joint. Spread icing to top of tree. Imbed candies in rows or desired patterns; allow to dry. Stick lollipop in hole at treetop.

Note: These trees are completely edible and will keep for the holiday season. Do **not** refrigerate.

FELT FINGER PUPPETS

MATERIALS: Assorted colors felt scraps; 1/4"-diameter movable eyes; pink, rose and red felt-tipped markers; absorbent cotton; scraps lace, yarn and ribbon; white glue; silver glitter; stout needle; 1/2"-diameter dowel; chunk of plastic foam; small wooden bucket; individually wrapped peppermint candies or other hard candies; cardboard scrap.

Note: See To Enlarge Patterns, page 30.

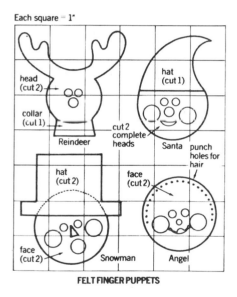

Each square = 1"

FELT FINGER PUPPETS

REINDEER: Enlarge pattern for reindeer on cardboard; cut out. For each reindeer cut two heads from dark-gold or brown felt. Following line on pattern, cut collar and nose from red felt. Glue felt heads together, matching edges. Glue collar in place. Following photograph, squeeze 3 small blobs of glue across collar; sprinkle silver glitter on glue. When dry, shake off excess glitter. Glue eyes and nose in place. For finger ring cut a felt strip 3/4" x 1 1/4"; shape into ring, center and glue on back of head.

SANTA: Enlarge pattern for head including hat on cardboard; cut out. For each Santa cut two com-plete heads from white or pale-pink felt; cut one hat, nose and mouth from red felt. Glue heads together, then add hat. Use felt-tipped marker to color cheeks. (**Note:** If head is cut from white felt, color face area on one felt piece pale pink; let dry and add rosy cheeks.) Glue nose, mouth and eyes in place. Glue cotton pompon and cuff on hat. Add cotton beard and moustache as in photograph. Make finger ring as described for reindeer.

SNOWMAN: Enlarge pattern for face and hat on cardboard; cut out. For each snowman cut two faces from white felt and two hats from turquoise felt. Cut nose and mouth from red felt. Glue face pieces together. Use felt-tipped marker to color cheeks. Glue eyes, nose and mouth in place. With face sandwiched between, glue hat pieces together. Make finger ring as described for reindeer.

ANGEL: Enlarge pattern for face on cardboard; cut out. For each angel cut two face pieces from either white or pale-pink felt. Use felt-tipped markers to color rosy cheeks, pink nose and red mouth. (**Note:** If angel face is white felt, color it pale pink on one side with felt-tipped marker; let dry and add facial features.) Glue on eyes. Using a tiny-hole punch, make holes around top of head as indicated on pattern. Using stout needle and yarn scraps, make double loops of yarn through each hole for hair; knot loose ends. Cut piece of lace for collar and glue face pieces together with lace sandwiched between as in photograph. Make small ribbon bow and glue under chin to lace collar. Make finger ring as described for reindeer.

ARRANGEMENT: Cut 10" or 12" pieces of dowel for each puppet. Apply primer and enamel to each dowel to finish; let dry. Push plastic-foam chunk in bucket and stick dowels into foam as in photograph. Slip a puppet on each dowel. Cover foam with candies.

Toy-Shop Mantel Decor

Rocking horses, trumpets, drums and carts nestle throughout the greenery.

MATERIALS: **For Rocking Horse:** 1- or 2-ply Bristol board; paper-towel tube; scrap 1″-wide white fringe; scrap of thin white yarn; black felt-tipped marker; ¼″ green satin ribbon; red enamel; white glue; spring-type clothespin. **For Drum:** 2 lids about 3½″ in diameter from 8-ounce yogurt or cottage-cheese containers; scrap thin cardboard; gold tinsel cord; red and green enamel; white glue. **For Gift Box:** 1 empty regular-size gelatin-dessert box; gold foil gift-wrap paper; ¼″ red satin ribbon; transparent tape. **For Cart:** 1 empty box of kitchen matches; 1 plastic straw; red enamel; masking tape; 1- or 2-ply Bristol board;

black felt-tipped marker. **For Trumpet:** Flexible plastic straws; metallic gold enamel; masking tape. **Accessories:** Garland of live greens; gold ornament-bead garland; oblong woven basket; potted greens; red plastic apples; holly sprigs; green string.

ROCKING HORSE: Enlarge patterns for head and rockers (see To Enlarge Patterns, page 30) on brown wrapping paper. Cut out two heads and two rockers from Bristol board. Cut paper tube to 4½″ and cut two disks from Bristol board to close ends. Glue horse's heads together at nose; clip with clothespin until dry. Following photograph, glue rockers on sides of tube body; close ends of tube with disks. Glue 3″ strip of fringe in place for mane; let dry. Glue head to body. Carefully paint horse red; let dry. Make tail from short strands of yarn knotted together at one end; glue knotted end to back disk. Add round black eyes with

TOY-SHOP MANTEL DECOR

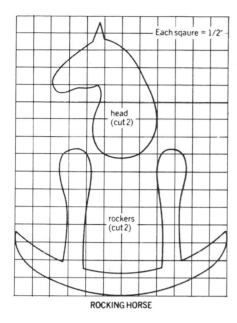

ROCKING HORSE

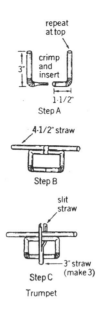

Trumpet

felt-tipped marker. Tie green ribbon around body.

DRUM: Clean lids in soap and water; let dry. Paint red and put aside. Form a 3″-high cylinder from thin cardboard to fit circumference of lids; tape abutted ends. Work holes around top and bottom edges of cylinder and 2½″ apart. Paint cylinder green; let dry. Lace gold cord through holes from top to bottom to form zigzag trim; glue ends. Assemble drum by gluing lid to each end and adding gold cord handle at one end as in photograph.

GIFT BOX: Wrap gelatin box as though for gift, using foil paper and satin ribbon.

CART: Use bottom tray of matchbox for body and paint red; let dry. Cut 4″ piece from plastic straw for handle. Slit straw at both ends. Open one slit end flat and tape to one end of cart. Open, then abut ends of other end of straw to form handle grip; tape to hold. Paint handle and touch up cart. Cut 1½″-diameter wheels from Bristol board. Paint black rings for tires; glue wheels to body as in photograph.

TRUMPET: From flexible straw cut two 4½″ pieces to form valve frame, another 4½″ piece for body mouthpiece and three 3″ pieces for valves. Following Step A in diagram, bend two 4½″ pieces at right angles, crimping one end to fit into opposite piece; repeat at top to form frame for valves. Tape remaining 4½″ piece along top as shown in Step B. To make valves, see

Step C and slit 3″ piece at one end so that slit ends extend ½″ beyond top of frame; tape tips of slit to form neat end. Bend and flatten other end of valve and tape to frame. Make two more valves.

From Bristol board cut 4½″-diameter circle. Cut slit from circumference to center. Shape circle into cone and tape to hold. Snip peak of cone and work one end of extended straw into it; tape to hold. Paint trumpet gold; let dry.

TO ARRANGE: Wind gold ornament beads around live garland; attach to mantel by most feasible means. Make hanger loops for toys from green string and hang toys along garland as in photograph.

For basket arrangement nestle toys in potted live or artificial greens in basket. Add apples and holly.

Hall, Walls and Everywhere

Hang these signs of Christmas cheer almost anyplace in the house—on doors, windows, wall areas, lighting fixtures, mirrors. Fresh greenery is incorporated in the kissing bough and banister trim, but otherwise all are "keepers."

Airy Angels

Craft straws, bound with thread.

SIZE: Approximately 15" tall.

MATERIALS: For each angel: forty-two 17"-long white craft straws, available from hobby- and craft-supply stores; white buttonhole or carpet thread; long needle or T pin; white glue.

BODY: Cut 25 straws to 14" and bind together 2" from one end with several wrappings of thread. Trim 2" ends to points. Turn bundle so 2" ends are down, then bend long ends over, covering 2" ends as shown in diagram, Step A. Bind again with thread 2" from fold-over to form head as shown.

ARMS: Cut 5 straws to 10" and bind together at center. To form wrists, tie straws together ¾" from one end as in Step B. For elbows, tie again 1½" from wrist ties. Trim straw ends for fingers.

WINGS: Cut 12 straws to 14" and bind together at center. Insert long needle or T pin through center of straws 3" from one end so it holds straws together in a row. Wind thread in and out between straws as well as around straws. After winding in one direction, turn and wind in opposite direction as in Step C. Pull thread up, forcing straws to flare out;

knot thread. Remove needle. Trim wing ends to point.

ASSEMBLY: Following Step D, insert arms below head; tie so that 13 straws are forward for skirt front and 12 are in back. Leaving 2 straws between arms, insert wings. Pinch body straws to close opening. Tie waist tight.

For halo, use scrap straw pieces. Flatten one piece to form ring and use a second for halo support. Glue halo pieces together as in photograph. Insert halo support in head as shown.

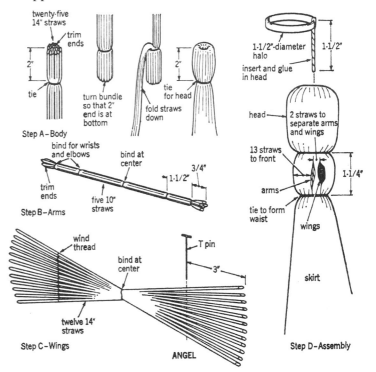

Window-shade Tree

Ornament balls are attached through pinholes.

SIZE: Approximately 20" x 40".

MATERIALS: Inexpensive light-color window shade or a clean 40"-long portion of used shade; bright-green and olive-green wide-tip waterproof markers; thirteen 2½"-diameter ornament balls; ornament hooks; 20"-long dowel or shade roller; two 1"-diameter hollow-brass or plastic-foam finials; white glue; masking tape; double-faced tape.

If using an old shade, remove roller and cut a 20" x 40" piece from best section. Cut roller and bottom pull slat to 20" length. Fold one end of shade to form pocket and secure with masking tape. Slip shortened slat in pocket.

Enlarge pattern, (see To Enlarge Patterns, page 30) on brown wrapping paper, then transfer to shade.

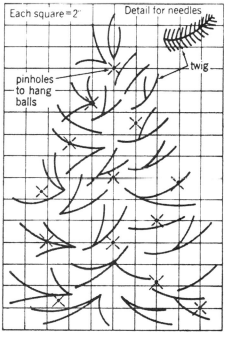

WINDOW-SHADE TREE

Use bright-green marker to draw twigs and small branches and olive and bright-green markers to draw needles. (**Note:** Our shade was slightly textured, which gave lines a fuzzy effect. If shade material is untextured, keep marker strokes light for a softer look.)

Use a length of double-faced tape or staples to attach shade to roller and a second strip of tape to stop unrolling. Add finials to ends. Hang shade on wall. To attach ornament balls push 13 pins into tree branches. Remove each pin in turn and insert an ornament hook. Hang one ball per hook.

Birds-of-a-Feather Tree

Accented with wheat fronds, checked bow.

SIZE: 30″ tall.

MATERIALS: 9′ of ¼″ x 1¼″ pine lattice; 18″ x 24″ piece ¼″ hardboard; 3 bunches natural dried wheat; 2 skeins 6-strand red embroidery floss; 1 yard 2″-wide red and white gingham ribbon; white glue; fine flexible wire; pigmented-shellac primer; high-gloss red enamel.

For tree, cut following pieces from lattice: 25″ vertical strip and 22″, 18″, 14″, 10″ and 6″ crosspieces. Following photograph, center and glue longest crosspiece across one end of vertical strip, then glue remaining crosspieces to strip in descending order 3″ apart. Drill hole through top of vertical strip for hanging. Put aside.

Enlarge pattern for bird (see To Enlarge Patterns, page 30) on brown wrapping paper; cut out. Using pattern and jigsaw, cut 10 birds from hardboard. Sand cut edges. Apply primer to all birds; let dry. Spray-paint birds red; let dry. Glue birds on ends of crosspieces as shown.

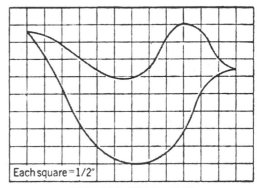

Each square = 1/2″

BIRDS-OF-A-FEATHER TREE

Cut 6 to 8 pieces of wheat to make double sheaves as in photograph. Bind each sheaf in middle with embroidery floss; knot ends. Center and glue sheaves on crosspieces.

To finish, bind wheat sheaf for treetop with wire. Make flat 10″-wide bow as shown. Glue wheat and bow to treetop.

Calico and Gingham Bells

Softly stuffed and beribboned.

SIZE: About 35″ long.

MATERIALS: ½ yd. red calico fabric for large bell; two 7″ squares each of 6 different calico or gingham prints for small bells; 9″ square green gingham for band on large bell; red plaid taffeta ribbon, 3 yds. 1″-wide and 1 yd. 1½″-wide; 3 yds. ¼″-wide gold metallic trim; Dacron polyester for stuffing.

CUTTING: Enlarge patterns (see To Enlarge Patterns, page 30) and cut out, adding ½″ to all edges for seam allowance. Cutting on straight of fabric, cut 2 bell shapes from red fabric and 2 bell shapes from each 7″ square green fabric. Cutting on the diagonal, cut 1 band for large bell from 9″ square green fabric.

LARGE BELL: Turn under and press seam allowance on long edges of band. Blindstitch to a red bell piece. Blindstitch a strip of gold trim above and below band. Cut four 8½″ strips and two 2½″ strips of gold trim. With ends of strips matching raw edge of bell, pin 1 end of each long strip to right side of a red

bell piece at an X dot and 1 end of each short strip at a Y dot. With right sides facing and gold strips sandwiched between, stitch red bell pieces together, leaving opening at top for turning. Turn and stuff. (Gold strips will hang from lower edge.) For hanging loop, cut 4″ gold strip; fold in half and insert ends in top opening of bell. Sew opening closed, catching ends of strip. Tie 1½″-wide ribbon in bow; notch ends. Tack bow to bell as in photograph.

SMALL BELLS: 3 top bells: Choose the 3 bells you wish to place at top. Cut six 7″ strips of gold trim. Working in same manner as for red bell, pin an end of each strip to a dot on 1 piece of each of the 3 bells. With right sides facing and strips sandwiched between, stitch front and back of each bell together, leaving opening at top. Turn and stuff. (Strips will hang from lower edges.) Insert ends of strips from red bell into top openings in 3 small bells and sew openings closed.

3 lower bells: For each bell, with right sides facing, stitch bell pieces together, leaving opening at top. Turn and stuff. Insert ends from a top bell in opening and sew opening closed.

Cut 1″-wide ribbon in 6 equal lengths. Tie each piece in a bow and notch ends. Tack a bow to each small bell.

Egg-carton Fascinator

The cups frame glittering ornament balls.

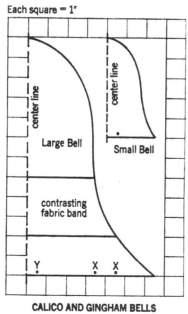

Each square = 1″

center line

center line

Large Bell

Small Bell

contrasting
fabric band

Y · X · X ·

CALICO AND GINGHAM BELLS

MATERIALS: Seven cardboard egg cartons; white glue; white acrylic paint; ten 1″-diameter red and thirteen ¾″-diameter green stemmed ornament balls; one ¾″-diameter and twenty-five ⅝″-diameter gold ornament balls; gold glitter.

Cut 78 individual cups from bottoms of egg cartons. Make a pattern for a 3″-wide 5-pointed star; cut out. Trace pattern and cut star from flat top of any egg carton. Discard excess carton pieces. Cut 10 cups 1″ high for side trim as in photograph. Thinning acrylic paint with slight amount of water, paint all cups, trims and star on all surfaces; let dry.

To attach red and green ornament balls insert one end of stem through center of cup base and dab with glue to secure. Beginning at lower edge of tree and working on a flat surface, follow photograph for a guide to the arrangement of cups. Glue cups together to form diamond-shaped openings between cups and triangular and diamond-shaped openings between rows; let dry. Brush glue on each side of star in turn; dust with glitter. When dry, shake off excess. Glue star to top cup as shown. Add side trims as shown. Glue all gold ornament balls as shown with largest at top.

Trapunto Tree

Calico ornaments, rickrack outline.

SIZE: 18″ x 23″.

MATERIALS: Large corrugated-cardboard carton; white glue; ⅔ yard 36″-wide green-and-white gingham; 1 yard 36″-wide solid-green cotton fabric; scraps of tiny-print fabrics for ornaments and solid brown fabric for tree trunk; 2⅓ yards ½″-wide green rickrack; 2 yards ¼″-wide red rickrack; matching thread; thin cardboard; absorbent cotton or Dacron polyester for stuffing; stapler and staples.

Cut carton and flatten. Laminate three layers of corrugated carton pieces (each at least 24″ square), using white glue and alternating direction of corrugation. Weight laminated pieces and allow to dry overnight. Trim square to 18″ x 23″ with utility knife for backing.

Enlarge pattern for tree sections, ornaments and trunk (see To Enlarge Patterns, page 30) on brown wrapping paper. Cut tree sections from green fabric, ornaments from assorted prints and trunk from brown fabric. Cut gingham to 24″ x 30″ for background. Following photograph for placement, arrange

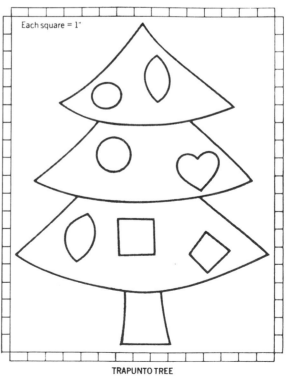

Each square = 1″

TRAPUNTO TREE

tree ornaments on each tree section; tucking raw edges under, topstitch in place. Make a tiny slit through back of tree where each ornament is placed and stuff ornaments lightly. Arrange tree sections and tree trunk centered on gingham background; baste in place. Finish raw edges of tree with green rickrack topstitched in place. Tuck raw edges of trunk under; topstitch. Remove basting. Turn gingham to wrong side and cut a centered slit on each tree section and trunk; stuff each lightly. Center corrugated-cardboard backing on wrong side of gingham and wrap excess gingham around edges to back. Fold raw edges under neatly and miter corners; staple edges in place. Turn tree over; make tiny bows of red rickrack to trim top of each ornament; tack in place.

Cut 1″-wide strips of cardboard to frame tree as in photograph. Cut strips of green fabric to cover each strip. Wrap each in turn. Glue covered strips around frame as shown. For bowed hanger, cut three 2½″-wide strips of green fabric for 10″-wide flat bow and two 7″ connecting streamers. Fold strips in half lengthwise; stitch and turn, leaving ends open. Slip paper or very thin cardboard into strips to stiffen; close ends. Make flat bow and two streamers as in photograph. Staple streamers to back of bow and top edge of backing.

Dancing Santas

A chain of six jolly men swinging.

MATERIALS: 10″ x 36″ piece 2-ply Bristol board; 10″ x 36″ piece green construction or Color-Aid paper; 13″ x 36″ piece red construction or Color-Aid paper; rubber cement; lightweight cardboard; absorbent cotton; black felt-tipped marking pen; ¼″-diameter paper punch; transparent fishing line; mat knife or scissors.

Brush rubber cement on one side of Bristol board and one side of red construction or Color-Aid paper. When surfaces are dry, carefully place paper on board and press smooth. Turn board over to cover with green paper in same manner. Save remaining red paper for Santas' tunics and hats.

Enlarge diagram, as described under To Enlarge Patterns, page 30, and transfer to lightweight cardboard; cut out. Trace pattern for six Santas on colored Bristol board, flopping pattern for every doll and matching fold lines. Cut out Santas with mat knife or scissors. Referring to diagram, enlarge and cut patterns for tunics and hats. Using patterns, cut out six red tunics and hats. Cement tunics and hats to green side of Santas. Also shape bits of cotton for beards and fur trim on hats; cement in place. Make faces, using

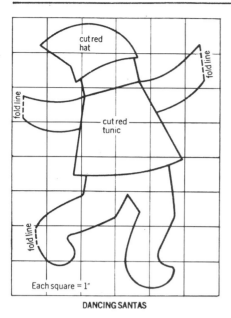

cut red
hat

fold line

fold line

cut red
tunic

fold line

Each square = 1"

DANCING SANTAS

felt-tip marker for eyes and paper punch to punch out red noses from scraps of red paper; attach noses. Join strip of Santas in ring by overlapping arms. To hang as mobile, punch tiny holes in each abutted arm as in photograph. Cut six long lengths of fishing line and knot one end of one length in each hole as shown. Bring all lengths together and knot. Tie another piece of line in loop at the top knot.

Boxwood Kissing Bough

Mistletoe, papier-mâché birds.

SIZE: About 17" in diameter.
MATERIALS: For birds: Six 2½" x 3" plastic-foam eggs; six 2"-diameter plastic-foam balls; six ½"-diameter screw eyes; lightweight cardboard; toothpicks; red poster or tempera paint; black felt-tipped pen; 8 yds. ¼"-wide red satin ribbon; white glue; all-purpose flour; newspaper. **For wreath:** 16"-diameter green plastic-foam ring; fresh boxwood greens; artificial holly berries; fresh mistletoe; 4 yds. 1"-wide red satin ribbon; floral picks; masking tape; thin flexible wire; nylon monofilament.
BIRDS: Enlarge patterns for beak and tail (see To Enlarge Patterns, page 30) on cardboard; cut out 6 tails and 6 beaks. Following assembly diagram, with serrated knife make a slot in narrow end of the plastic-foam egg for tail and in the plastic-foam ball for beak. Insert cardboard tail and beak in slots and tape securely. Join ball-head to egg-body with a toothpick dipped in glue. Repeat to assemble 5 more birds.

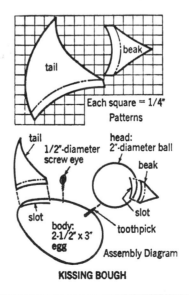

tail

beak

Each square = 1/4"
Patterns

tail

1/2"-diameter
screw eye

head:
2"-diameter ball

beak

slot

body:
2-1/2" x 3"
egg

slot

toothpick

Assembly Diagram

KISSING BOUGH

In bowl mix thoroughly 1 cup flour, ½ cup water and 1 teaspoon glue. Tear newspaper into ½" x 2" strips. Cover work surface with several thicknesses of newspaper or waxed paper. Dip newspaper strips into flour paste and begin wrapping them around bird in overlapping layers. Continue adding strips, tearing them into smaller pieces when necessary to make a smooth surface. Work layers over head and beak, body and tail as in photograph. Place completed bird on wire rack to dry 1 to 2 days. Apply papier-mâché to remaining birds. When dry, turn a screw eye centered in top of bird's body so it will balance when suspended from wreath. Paint birds red and set aside to dry. Add round eye with black felt-tipped pen.

WREATH: To assemble hanging wreath, cut four 26" lengths nylon monofilament. Tie 1 end of each length around plastic-foam ring so that it hangs from 4 equidistant points. Join loose ends of monofilament and tie around key ring at equidistant points. Leave these knots loose so that length can be adjusted. Add a separate piece of monofilament to key ring for hanger loop. Hang ring to check balance—the plastic-foam ring should hang about 10" below hanger loop. Tape monofilament line in place on plastic-foam ring.

Cut boxwood greens into 6" sprigs and wire each sprig to a floral pick. Dip pick end in glue and insert in plastic-foam ring. Overlap sprigs until ring is completely covered. Wire holly berries to picks and insert among boxwood sprigs.

ASSEMBLY: Cut six 24" and six 12" pieces ¼"-wide red ribbon. Tie and knot a 24" length through screw eye on each bird. Thread 12" length through eye and tie into bow to conceal eye and knot. Tie loose end of 24" lengths around wreath, arranging birds so they hang evenly spaced about 8" below wreath. Hide ribbon loop and knot in boxwood.

Cut length of ¼" ribbon to suspend small bunch of mistletoe as in photograph. Tie 1 end of ribbon around bunch and the opposite end to key ring. From remaining ¼" ribbon make small bow and tie around mistletoe bunch.

Cover lines of monofilament with 1" ribbon. Cut ribbon to length, pin 1 end to wreath, run ribbon along line and tie loose end at key ring. Repeat to cover all lines. Make loopy ball at top of ring with remaining 1" ribbon.

Santa Claus Mobile

Strung on thread, his features twist and turn.

MATERIALS: 72"-wide felt, 1 yard of white, ⅜ yard red and scrap of pink; scrap black vinyl; shirt cardboard; white glue; diamond dust; spray adhesive; brown wrapping paper; strong thread.

Note: Santas in 3 sizes are shown in photograph. To simplify the mobile, we give pattern for largest size only. You can make 3 identical Santas if you want to simplify the project. To graduate sizes as we did, allow each square on the pattern to measure ¾″ for the middle Santa and ½″ for the smallest Santa.

Enlarge pattern (see To Enlarge Patterns, page 30) and transfer each shape to brown paper; cut out. Trace shapes on thin cardboard and cut pieces for

S. CLAUS MOBILE

the three Santa heads. Referring to photograph, use cardboard pieces as templates to cut out felt to cover both sides of cardboard.

Dilute white glue with slight amount of water, brush on cardboard and cover with felt. Repeat until all pieces are covered. To make eyes, first insert black vinyl eyelashes between layers of pink felt and cardboard, then glue.

Arrange each Santa face, run needle through and string pieces together, using doubled thread. Make loop at top to hang. Spray Santas lightly with adhesive and apply diamond dust.

Gleaming Window Ornaments

Plastic beads melted in the oven.

SIZE: Approximately 7″ to 9″.

MATERIALS: Transparent plastic beads in assorted sizes, shapes and colors, available in most hobby and craft stores; cookie sheet; clear cement; thin flexible wire or nylon thread.

Note: Each design consists of both melted and unmelted beads. In the finished design melted beads appear glassy and light in color. The unmelted beads give texture and are darker.

From each package of beads melt about 15 beads of each color. Preheat oven and cookie sheet to 375°. Remove sheet and place beads ½″ apart on sheet, making certain that only beads of the same size are melted at one time. Colors can be mixed on the same sheet. Return sheet to oven and allow beads to melt 7 to 9 minutes or until they form into drops. Remove sheet and submerge it in cold water. As beads cool they slide off pan. Repeat until you have enough melted beads to start design.

To make ornament, copy designs in photograph or create your own on brown wrapping paper to provide a basic pattern shape for you to fill in as desired. For practice, assemble beads directly on patterns, then transfer to cookie sheet in same order of assembly. Combine colors, shapes and sizes of beads, using both melted and unmelted beads and making sure they touch each other. At top make a loop or ring of small beads for a hanger loop.

Bake ornament in 375° to 400° oven 10 to 17 minutes. Watch carefully that beads melt together, forming design. Remove cookie sheet and submerge in cold water. As ornament cools it will slip off sheet. Colors fade slightly during baking. If you wish to intensify color or add texture to some areas, position a second layer of beads on ornament, place on cookie sheet and bake another 7 minutes. Remove and cool in water.

To hang ornament, thread a strand of wire or nylon thread through ring; knot ends for hanger loop.

Note: If some layered beads fall off, secure them with a dab of clear cement.

Tissue-paper Cutouts

Children's art preserved in clear vinyl.

SIZE: 5″ to 6″ tall.
MATERIALS: White tissue paper; clear self-adhesive vinyl; several colors waterproof felt-tipped markers; metallic gold thread.

Have a child draw Christmas symbols with felt markers on tissue paper. (**Note:** Put newspaper under tissue, because markers will bleed through.)

Cut out rough shapes, leaving excess tissue paper around each design. Cut out a large but manageable piece of clear vinyl. Following manufacturer's directions for using vinyl, peel back protective-paper corners and tape vinyl to work surface, adhesive side (with protective backing) up. Remove backing. Place edge of tissue shape on adhesive and hold the rest up; with other hand gradually smooth shape against vinyl.

Cut around shape and repeat procedure to cover second side with vinyl. Cut shape, following design contours. To hang, thread needle with metallic thread and pierce drawing near top with needle. Pull thread through and make loop.

Lacy Nylon-net Ornaments

Aglow with gold stick-on trims and gems.

SIZES: Angel: 7¾″ high; **dove:** 7¾″ wide; **snowflake:** 5″ diameter.

MATERIALS: for 3 ornaments: 18″ x 24″ piece white nylon net; 2′ of 18″-wide iron-on bonding mesh; ⅜″-diameter, ½″-diameter and ¾″-long (teardrop) glue-on gems; gold doily trims, available from most hobby, craft or party-supply stores; white glue; white acrylic paint; art tip, available in art-supply stores; nylon monofilament.

Enlarge patterns (see To Enlarge Patterns, page 30) on brown wrapping paper. From nylon net cut two pieces each 5″ x 8″ for angel, 5″ x 8″ for dove and 5″ x 5″ for snowflake. Cut a piece of iron-on bonding mesh for each pair of nylon-net pieces. Following manufacturer's directions, fuse pairs of nylon net with bonding mesh; allow to cool.

Tape paper pattern to a work surface covered with waxed paper and position doubled nylon net on top, taping it to hold. (The design on pattern can be seen through the net.) Using art tip screwed onto acrylic-paint tube, pipe the design and outline ornament shape in white as in photograph. Allow raised design to dry thoroughly. Referring to photograph, glue on gold trims and gems with white glue.

To hang ornaments cut a length of monofilament, insert through hole in netting near top edge and tie ends in knot to form loop.

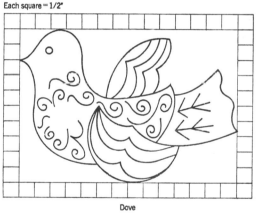

Each square = 1/2″

Dove

Each square = 1/2″

center line

Snowflake

Each square = 1/2″

Angel
NYLON-NET ORNAMENTS

"Stained-glass" Window Ornaments

The "glass" is tissue-paper strips.

SIZE: About 6″ in diameter.
MATERIALS: Lime-green, turquoise and hot-pink tissue paper; black construction paper; sharp mat knife; metal ruler; white glue.

Enlarge patterns (see To Enlarge Patterns, page 30) on brown wrapping paper; cut out. Trace pat-

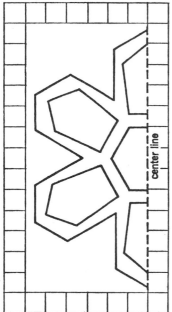

Each square = 1/2″

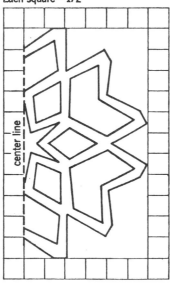

Each square = 1/2″

terns onto black construction paper and cut out two shapes for each ornament, using mat knife and metal ruler.

Mark and cut 1¼″-wide strips about 7″ long from various colors tissue paper. On work surface covered with waxed paper, dab black filigree cutout with glue, then place strips of tissue paper across cutout, overlapping strips irregularly. Dab a second filigree piece with glue, align on top of tissue-paper strips and press in place. Cut away excess tissue paper around edges.

These ornaments look best when hung against a window or light.

Banister Trim

Greenery with wreaths of calico yo-yos.

MATERIALS: **For 6 calico yo-yo wreaths:** ¼ yard each 36″-wide fabrics, 2 red and 2 green prints; six 24″-long No. 12-gauge covered green wires for stems; matching thread. **For gingham bows:** 18 yards 2″-wide red and white plaid taffeta ribbon; thin flexible wire; live evergreen boughs or garland.

To make wreaths, use a compass to draw a 4½″-diameter circle on brown wrapping paper for yo-yo pattern. For each wreath cut 5 each red and green fabric circles. Fold over and press a ¼″ hem all around each circle. With needle and thread make tiny running stitches around edge to gather circle into puffed yo-yo as in photograph. Pull thread tight and tie off.

Following photograph, join 10 yo-yos in a ring, alternating colors; tack edges together. Bend a wire stem into a 6½″-diameter ring, twisting ends together. Center wire ring on yo-yo ring so that gathered edges face out; whipstitch yo-yo ring to wire.

To decorate banister, entwine garland or attach boughs with flexible wire as in photograph. Make 6 double-loop ribbon bows with streamers, leaving about a yard of ribbon between bows for draping swag. Arrange bows with swags on evergreen, holding in place with wire as in photograph. Suspend a yo-yo wreath between bows with wire as in photograph.

Snowman Stocking

All crocheted, even the angora snowman appliqué.

SIZE: About 13″ long.

MATERIALS: Knitting-worsted-weight yarn, 4 ounces red (color R), 1 ounce white (W) and small amount green (G); small amount white angora yarn; aluminum crochet hook size F (or Canadian hook No. 9) **or the size that will give you the correct gauge;** tapestry needle.

GAUGE: 4 dc = 1″; 5 rnds = 2″.

STOCKING: Granny-square Top: the first square: starting at center with W, ch 6; sl st in 6th ch from hook to form ring. **1st rnd (right side):** Ch 4, (work dc in ring, ch 1) 7 times; sl st in 3rd ch of ch-4 (8 dc, counting ch-3 as 1 dc). **2nd rnd:** Sl st in first ch-1 sp, ch 3, in same sp work dc, ch 1 and 2 dc (first corner made); ch 1, 2 dc in next ch-1 sp (shell made), *ch 1, in next sp work 2 dc, ch 1 and 2 dc (another corner made); ch 1, shell in next sp. Repeat from * twice more; ch 1, sl st in top of ch-3. Break off W; attach R. **3rd rnd:** Sl st in first ch-1·sp, work a first corner in the same sp, * (ch 1, shell in next sp) twice; ch 1, work corner in next corner sp. Repeat from * twice more; (ch 1, shell in next sp) twice, ch 1; join. Break off. Square should measure about 2¾″.

Make 3 more squares.

To Join Squares: Holding 2 squares with right sides facing, whipstitch together along 1 edge with tapestry needle and R. Join 3rd square to 2nd and 4th to 3rd to form strip. Whipstitch 4th square to first square to form ring; break off.

Leg: With wrong side of ring facing you, using R, sl st in joining between any 2 squares. **1st rnd:** Ch 3, work 44 dc evenly spaced around edge of ring (45 dc, counting ch-3 as 1 dc); join with sl st to top of ch-3. Drop R; attach W. **2nd rnd:** With W ch 3, dc in each dc around; join. Drop W; pick up R. **3rd and 4th rnds:** With R repeat 2nd rnd. Drop R; pick up W. **5th rnd:** Repeat 2nd rnd. Break off W.

With R work even until piece measures about 9″ from beg. Drop R; attach W. Work stripes as follows: 1 rnd W, 2 rnds R, 1 rnd W. Break off W.

Foot: 1st rnd (inc rnd): With R sl st in center dc of last rnd, ch 10 for instep, 2 dc in 4th ch from hook, dc in each of next 6 ch, dc in each dc around leg; working along opposite edge of ch-10, dc in each of next 6 sts (60 dc); sl st in top of ch-3. **2nd rnd (inc rnd):** Ch 3, 3 dc in next dc, dc in each remaining dc around (62 dc); join. **3rd rnd (inc rnd):** Ch 3, dc in next dc, 3 dc in next dc, dc in each dc around (64 dc); join. **4th rnd (inc rnd):** Ch 3, dc in each of next 2 dc,

3 dc in next dc, dc in each dc around (66 dc); join. **5th and 6th rnds:** Ch 3, dc in each dc around; join. Do not break off. Fold stocking flat and working through both thicknesses, sc in each dc across to close bottom edge of foot. Break off.

SNOWMAN: **Head:** Starting at center with angora, ch 4. Sl st in 4th ch from hook to form ring. **1st rnd (right side):** Ch 1, work 6 sc in ring. Do not join but mark beg of each rnd. **2nd rnd:** Work 2 sc in each sc around (12 sc). **3rd rnd:** Repeat 2nd rnd (24 sc). Break off.

Body: Work as for head through 3rd rnd. **4th and 5th rnds:** Work sc in each sc around. Break off.

Hat: Starting at lower edge of brim with G, ch 13 to measure about 3″. **1st row:** Sc in 2nd ch from hook and in each ch across. **2nd row:** Sc in each sc across. Break off. **3rd row:** Skip first 3 sc, make lp on hook, sc in each of next 6 sc for crown; ch 1, turn. **4th row:** Sc in each sc across; ch 1, turn. **5th row:** Repeat 2nd row. Break off.

String Tie: With G crochet 7″ chain. Break off. Tie in bow.

FINISHING: Following photograph for placement, using tapestry needle and yarn, sew head and body of snowman to stocking. Add hat and string tie.

With G embroider 2 French-knot buttons (see Stitch Diagrams, page 30) on body of snowman.

Christmas Outdoors

Weather-wary decorations for your doorway and yard are created from plastic, newspaper cores, aluminum foil, moldings, dowels and plywood. Although the makings are as plain and practical as can be, the finished displays are utterly captivating.

Twin Door Trees

Plastic boxwood and fruit; finger-weave chains.

SIZE: Approximately 24″ wide x 42″ high.

MATERIALS: For two trees: Three 9′ garlands of plastic boxwood; 42 plastic red apples, approximately 2½″ in diameter; two 6″-tall plastic pineapples; 18′ of 1 x 2 pine; 3′ of 1 x 10 pine; 2′ of 36″ -wide chicken wire (any gauge); 3″ finishing nails; pigmented-shellac primer; dark-green paint; flexible wire; staples and staple gun; 35 yards 2-ply sisal package cord.

Following diagram, cut 1 x 2 and 1 x 10 pine for uprights and base of tree frame. Assemble two frames with nails as shown. Apply primer to frames; when dry, paint dark green. With staple gun attach chicken wire along one side edge of upright, as shown. Wrap chicken wire over wooden frame and attach along base and remaining side edge. Cut excess wire

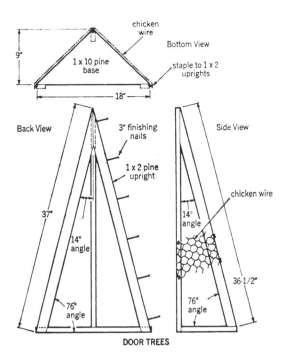

DOOR TREES

Fruit-bearing Lawn Tree

Bird and fruit shapes wrapped in colored metallic foil.

away and cover second frame in same way. Add 7 finishing nails equally spaced along each upright. Cover frames with plastic garland, beginning by stapling lengths down each upright, then filling in between uprights by wiring lengths to chicken wire. Fill in open spaces with small pieces of boxwood cut from garland. Cut a slit in base of each apple and pineapple. Impale fruit on finishing nails as indicated in photograph.

For finger-crocheted garland, cut sisal into two 17-yard lengths. Form loop at one end of length, pinching ends together; with fingers and thumb bring loose sisal through loop from underside to form second chain loop. Continue forming chains in this manner until entire length is worked. Try to maintain an even tension so that chain loops are the same size. To keep end loops from slipping, knot each end through its end loop. Following photograph, wrap garland, crisscrossing, around tree.

To make fruit, crush and shape newspaper into desired shapes, keeping them large for greater effectiveness. Wrap snugly in plain aluminum foil and rubber-cement edges to hold in place. Cover outside of each with crinkled colored foil and cement edges. Punch hole and insert medium-weight flexible wire for hanger and stem. Partially wrap with foil to simulate stem.

To make birds, crush and shape newspaper into plump body shapes; cover with plain foil. Fold newspaper into long strips for wings and wrap with plain foil. Tape wings to breast and sides of each body. Make tail in same way and attach. Wrap in colored foil and cement foil features and trimmings. Add wire for attaching. Wire a cluster of foil grapes to back of bird on treetop.

Star-spangled Lawn Tree

Foil chains; stars cut from aluminum casserole dishes.

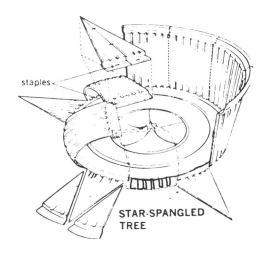

STAR-SPANGLED TREE
staples

aluminum foil. Tear off 4" sections; cut each section to 9" lengths. Fold each piece to 2" width, then to a 1" x 9" strip. Staple through middle of strip for strength. Form ring, staple end; connect next ring. One roll of 18"-wide foil makes a 35-foot chain.

Wooden-fantasy Lawn Tree

Gaily painted toylike ornaments cut from moldings and dowels.

Use cut pieces of 1" quarter-round, 11/16"x 2¼" cove molding, 1" and ¾" dowel. Following photograph, spray-paint parts before assembly; let dry thoroughly. Sand edges and sides to be glued. Use thermal glue gun to join parts, holding them together for 30 seconds until glue cools. Add screw eyes and wire for hanging. See sketches for individual decorations.

A. Cut four 3⅜" lengths of quarter-round and cut one end of each at a 45° angle. Glue square ends as in end view.

B. Cut two 4" and two 4¾" lengths of molding; cut ¾" dowel 1⅝" long. Following end view, glue 4¾" molding together and dowel at end. Following side view, glue on 4" molding lengths.

C. Cut four 3" lengths of molding. Glue flat edges together, making square center opening.

D. Cut four 3½" lengths of molding and 1" dowel 6" long. Glue molding to dowel as in end view.

E. Cut four 4" lengths of molding; saw one end of each at a 45° angle. Glue molding together with points coming together at the center and add 1" dowel 1¼" long. Attach screw eye to dowel.

F. Cut four 6⅜" lengths of molding; saw all ends to 45° angle. Glue into an X shape with points on the outside; add screw eye at center.

To make star, use a 3" x 10"-diameter aluminum casserole. Reverse dish; mark ten equidistant points around base. (Our dish had 60 flutes so we marked every sixth one.) Push a heavy pin through markings to indicate cutting lines; cut ten rectangular flaps with scissors. Cut a 5-pointed center opening as in diagram; curl back points. Flatten five alternate flaps and cut into points; retain cut pieces. Bend rectangular flaps in, overlapping and stapling corners to form pentagonal frame. Join pairs of cutoff points and staple together, then staple to pentagon. Punch a hole in an outer star point for an 8" wire hanger.

To make chain, use 18"-wide heavy-duty

WOODEN FANTASY

B. End View

A.

C.

D.

E.

F.

B. Side View

Tissue-trimmed Lawn Tree

The "confections" are wrapped with colored tissue, then clear plastic.

Work on a large surface. To make balls, cut # 18 nylon cord three feet longer than garland length; wad a sheet of newspaper into a compact ball, about 3″ in diameter, and insert section of cord about 18″ from one end. Cover newspaper completely with a sheet of colored tissue paper. Working with two wide rolls of plastic wrap, unroll enough of each to cover tissue ball; tie off each side of ball with paper-covered wire ties. Leave 1½″ to 2″ of wrap and cord between balls; begin next ball.

To make bells, use 2½″-diameter conical paper cups. Snip off peaked end of cup. Double-knot one end of a 10″ length of nylon cord and insert through snipped end with knot inside. Cut a sheet of tissue paper in half, then fold the cut sheet in half. Place cup peak on folded corner edge of paper; wrap and tuck loose ends inside cup. Cut a square of plastic wrap; stand cup in center and pull corners of plastic up and around. Keeping cord outside, twist paper-covered wire tie around peak; trim away excess. Loop cord for hanger.

Red-nosed Reindeer

The antlers on Rudolph's hinged head are twined with frosted lights.

MATERIALS: 4′ square piece ¾″ exterior plywood; two 1½″ x 2″ flat hinges; 1½″ alphabetical stencil set; glossy white exterior paint; glossy red exterior paint; two sets of multicolored frosted-bead outdoor lights (12 lights in each set); 3′ of 1 x 2 cedar or redwood strips; brown wrapping paper; lath nails; 1½″ x #8 wood screws. **Note:** Before constructing and setting up Rudolph, make certain that you have an outdoor outlet close by.

Enlarge pattern for Rudolph's body and head on

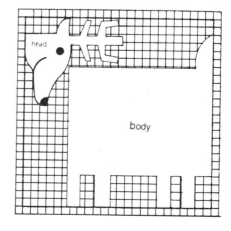

brown wrapping paper (see To Enlarge Patterns, page 30); then transfer to plywood and cut out, using a saber saw. Sand all cut edges. Mark and pre-drill screw holes for hinging head to body. Prime and paint both sides of Rudolph's head and body, sanding lightly between coats. Attach head to body with hinges. Referring to photograph, paint features and use stencil to paint "Merry Christmas" across body with red paint. Let dry. Arrange lights around antlers, concealing wires behind head; fasten bulbs to edges of antlers with lath nails.

To prop up Rudolph, drive two 18″ stakes cut from 1 x 2 redwood or cedar into ground, leaving 8″ above the ground. Position and screw Rudolph against stakes, making certain that the legs conceal stakes.

NEEDLEWORK AND CRAFTS GIFTS TO MAKE

When the three wise men came to the manger in Bethlehem, "they saw the young child with Mary, his mother, and fell down and worshipped him: and when they had opened their treasures, they presented unto him gifts; gold, frankincense and myrrh."

In the gospel according to St. Matthew, we learn of the first Christmas gifts. Nearly two thousand years later, Christmas and gift-giving are inseparably associated: the holiday inspires us to reach out, to touch; the gift is our tangible expression of gratitude, respect, affection. Nothing seems to convey these special feelings better than a gift you've had a hand in making.

Every year much is said and written about the commercialization of Christmas. But even though the annual "push" to get out, shop and buy shows little sign of diminishing, you may have noticed that more and more people are using their own human resources to make their giving more meaningful.

The gift of a personal service or skill—your thought, time and effort—is a priceless offering of your very self, and an affirmation of the original meaning of Christmas. In the following pages are many of our best ideas for gifts that you can make with ordinary materials—and extraordinary love.

Openwork Shawl

Crocheted in shells and chain loops, thickly fringed.

SIZE: Shawl measures about 70" across top edge and 28" from top edge to lower point at back, not including fringe.

MATERIALS: Bear Brand Winsom Orlon-acrylic yarn, 6 (2-ounce) skeins lapis blue No. 310 (color W); Bucilla nylon/wool fingering yarn, 3 (1-ounce) skeins rust No. 33 (color F); aluminum crochet hook size H (or international size 5.00 mm) **or the size that will give you the correct gauge.**

GAUGE: 3 shells = 4".

Starting at top edge with W, ch 270. **1st row:** Sc in 10th ch from hook (1st lp made), * ch 6, skip 4 ch, sc in next ch. Repeat from * across (53 lps); turn. **2nd row:** Sl st in each st to center of 1st ch-6 lp, sc in center of lp * ch 6, sc in center of next lp. Repeat from * across (52 lps). Break off; turn. **3rd row (shell row):** Make lp on hook with one strand each F and W and sc in 1st lp, * work shell of 3 dc in next sc between lps, sc in center of next lp. Repeat from * across (51 shells); turn. **4th row (shell row):** Sl st in sc and 1st dc, sc in next (center) dc on 1st shell, * shell in next sc (between shells of last row), sc in center dc of next shell. Repeat from * across (50 shells). Break off; turn. **5th row:** With W, sc in center dc of 1st shell, * ch 6, sc in center dc of next shell. Repeat from * across (49 lps); turn. **6th row:** Repeat 2nd row (48 lps).

Repeat 3rd through 6th rows 11 times more, decreasing 1 shell or lp on each row; then repeat 3rd through 5th rows (1 W lp on last row). Break off. With W work sc evenly around all edges.

Fringe: To make tassel cut five 16"-long pieces W; fold in half and insert fold through sc at edge; draw ends through fold and pull to tighten. Make 105 tassels, evenly spaced, around diagonal edges.

Little Crocheted Pets

Not for babies only—children of all ages will love them.

GENERAL DIRECTIONS

MATERIALS: All animals shown were made with either Coats & Clark's Red Heart Wintuk or American Thread Dawn Sayelle (both are knitting-worsted-weight yarns). All yarns are machine-washable. For stuffing, you can use Dacron polyester stuffing or use any of your leftover yarns that are machine-washable.

Both of the above yarns are sold in 1-oz., 3-oz. and 4-oz. skeins. We have listed some of the colors needed by ounces and those that are less than 1 ounce by yardage.

Important: To help you estimate how much yarn to buy or how far your leftover yarns will go, figure about 60 yards per ounce.

See materials listed under specific animal you want to make before starting.

CROCHET TIPS: Tip 1: When working in rounds, the right side of work is always facing you.

Unless otherwise specified, do not join rounds, but work around in spiral fashion and mark beg of each new round. Use safety pin or paper clip as a marker. Move it from rnd to rnd as you work.

Tip 2: If you are making more than 1 animal, label small sections as you work to simplify assembly.

Tip 3: Stuff all sections firmly before last dec rnd.

Tip 4: Finishing: Sew pieces together with matching yarn. Whenever possible, when breaking yarn, leave long enough end for sewing.

Tip 5: To Make Pompon: Wrap yarn about 40 times around 1″-wide strip of cardboard. Break off. Clip yarn along 1 edge of cardboard to produce bundle of 2″ strands. Tie strands tightly together in middle and clip to form pompon.

To inc 1 sc: Work 2 sc in 1 st.

To dec 1 sc: Insert hook in next st, y o and draw up lp; insert hook in next st, y o and draw up lp (3 lps on hook), y o and draw through all 3 lps on hook.

See Abbreviations and Terms, page 30.

MOUSE WITH CHEESE
SIZE: 7½" tall.
See General Directions.

MATERIALS: Knitting-worsted-weight yarn (Orlon acrylic), 1 oz. gray (color G), about 10 yds. each baby pink (P) and yellow (Y); 6-strand embroidery floss in white and black; aluminum crochet hook size F (or international size 4.00 mm) **or the size that will give you the correct gauge;** stuffing; tapestry needle.

GAUGE: 4 sc = 1"; 4 rnds = 1".

HEAD: Starting at center of nose with G, ch 2. **1st rnd:** Work 6 sc in 2nd ch from hook. **2nd rnd:** Inc 1 sc in every other sc around (9 sc). **3rd rnd:** Sc in each sc around. **4th rnd:** Inc in every 3rd sc around (12 sc). **5th rnd:** Inc in every 4th sc around (15 sc). **6th rnd:** Repeat 4th rnd (20 sc). **7th rnd:** Inc 3 sc evenly around (23 sc). **8th rnd:** Work even in sc. **9th rnd (dec rnd):** *Sc in each of next 2 sc, dec 1 sc. Repeat from * around, ending with sc in each of last 3 sc.

Stuff head firmly and dec as follows, stuffing as you work. **10th rnd:** * Sc in next sc, dec 1 sc. Repeat from * around. **11th rnd:** * Dec 1 sc. Repeat from * around. Break off. Sew opening closed. This is back of head.

BODY: Starting at neck edge with G, ch 12. Join with sl st to form ring. **1st rnd:** Ch 1, sc in same ch as sl st, sc in each remaining ch around (12 sc). **2nd rnd:** Sc in each sc around. **3rd rnd:** Inc 1 sc in every 3rd sc around (16 sc). **4th rnd:** Inc 2 sc evenly around (18 sc). **5th rnd:** Inc 4 sc evenly around (22 sc). **6th rnd:** Sc in each sc around. **7th and 8th rnds:** Inc 3 sc evenly around (28 sts at end of 8th rnd).

9th rnd (1st dec rnd): * Sc in each of next 5 sc, dec 1 sc. Repeat from * around (24 sc). **10th rnd:** Dec 4 sc evenly around (20 sc). **11th rnd:** Dec 2 sc evenly around (18 sc). **12th rnd:** Sc in each sc around, sl st in next sc. Continue as follows for 1st leg. **13th rnd (1st Leg Opening):** Ch 3, skip next 8 sc, sl st in next sc for 1st leg opening; ch 1, but do not turn.

1st Leg: 1st rnd: Sc in each of next 8 sc, sc in each of 3 ch sts. Working on these 11 sc, work even for 6 more rnds. **8th rnd:** (Sc in next sc, inc in next sc) twice (mark this inc section for front of leg); sc in each sc around. **9th rnd:** Inc 2 sc above those on last rnd, sc to end of rnd. **10th rnd:** Sc in each sc around (15 sc). Stuff body and leg. **11th rnd:** Work in back lp only of each sc, * dec 1 sc. Repeat from * around; sc in last sc, sl st in next st. Break off. Sew opening closed.

2nd Leg: Attach G at leg opening and starting with 1st rnd, complete as for 1st leg.

EAR: Front (make 2): Starting at center with P, ch 2. **1st rnd:** Work 6 sc in 2nd ch from hook. **2nd rnd:** Work 2 sc in each sc around (12 sc). **3rd rnd:** * Sc in next sc, 2 sc in next sc. Repeat from * around. **4th rnd:** * 2 sc in next sc, sc in each of next 2 sc. Repeat from * around (24 sc); sl st in next sc. Break off. Set piece aside.

Back (make 2): With G, work same as for front of ear, ending with sl st in next sc; do not break off. **Joining:** Hold 1 front piece and 1 back piece, wrong sides together. With front piece facing you and working through both thickness of last rnd with G, * sc in each of next 2 sc, 2 sc in next sc. Repeat from * around, stuffing lightly before completing rnd; join with sl st in 1st sc Break off.

ARM (make 2): With G, ch 2. **1st rnd:** Work 6 sc in 2nd ch from hook. Work even on 6 sc for 3 more rnds. Stuff arm, flatten out arm and work through both thicknesses at same time for hand, as follows: **1st row:** Sc across, inc 1 sc (4 sc); ch 1, turn. **2nd row:** Sc in each sc across, sl st in last st, ch 2, sc in 2nd ch from hook, then sl st into sts at side of hand for thumb. Break off. On 2nd arm, reverse thumb placement.

TAIL: With G, ch 25. Sl st in 2nd ch from hook and in each remaining ch. Break off.

CHEESE: Main Section: With Y, ch 2. **1st row:** Work 1 sc in 2nd ch from hook; ch 1, turn. **2nd row:** Work 2 sc in sc; ch 1, turn. Always ch 1 and turn at end of each row. **3rd row:** Sc in each sc (2 sc). **4th row:** Work 2 sc in each sc. Work even on 4 sc for 1 more row. **6th row:** Inc in 1st sc, sc in each of next 2 sc, inc in last sc. Work even on 6 sc for 1 more row. **8th row:** Working in back lp only of each st, sc in each sc across for turning ridge. Working in both lps, work even in sc for 3 more rows. **12th row:** Repeat 8th row. (The last 4 rows between ridges form the base of triangle; mark ends of these rows.)

13th row (1st dec row): Dec 1 sc at beg and end of row. Work even on 4 sc for 1 more row. **15th row:** (Dec 1 sc) twice. Work even on 2 sc for 1 more row. **17th row:** Dec 1 sc. Break off.

Side Section: With Y, ch 16. Sc in 2nd ch from hook and in each remaining ch; ch 1, turn. Work even in 15 sc for 3 more rows. Break off.

Joining: Sew ends of side section to marked ends of rows of main section. Folding main section on ridge rows, pin to long edges of side section. With Y, sc both sections together, stuffing as you go.

FINISHING: Stuff body again, if necessary,

through neck opening, then sew head in place. Sew ears on each side of head. Sew arms to body about ½″ below neck seam.

Embroidery: See Stitch Diagrams, page 30. Using black, work large French knot for nose, running st for mouth. For eyes, work white satin stitch, then use black for pupil of eye. Outline eye in black. With black, work short stitches on hands and front of feet.

Sew tail on back of body. Sew cheese between hands.

POLAR BEAR

SIZE: 9″ tall (without hat).
See General Directions.

MATERIALS: Knitting-worsted-weight yarn (Orlon acrylic), 2 oz. white (color W), about 5 yds. baby pink (P) and 10 yds. red (R); 6-strand embroidery floss in black, dusty pink and brown; aluminum crochet hook size F (or international size 4.00 mm) **or the size that will give you the correct gauge;** stuffing; tapestry needle.

GAUGE: 4 sc = 1″; 4 rnds = 1″.

HEAD: Starting at center of nose with W, ch 2. **1st rnd:** Work 6 sc in 2nd ch from hook. **2nd rnd:** Inc 1 sc in every other sc around (9 sc). **3rd rnd:** Inc 3 sc evenly spaced around. Repeat last rnd 3 more times (21 sc at end of 6th rnd). Inc 5 sc on each of next 2 rnds (31 sc at end of 8th rnd). **9th rnd:** Sc in each sc around.

10th rnd (dec and inc rnd): (Sc in each of next 2 sc, dec 1 sc) 4 times for bottom of head; then (sc in each of next 4 sc, inc in next sc) 3 times for top of head. Work even on 30 sc for 1 more rnd. **12th rnd:** (Sc in each of next 2 sc, dec 1 sc, 3 times for bottom of head, sc in each remaining sc around. **13th rnd:** Dec 4 sc around (23 sc). **14th rnd:** Dec 7 sc around. Stuff head. **15th rnd:** *Dec 1 sc. Repeat from * around. Break off. Sew opening closed.

BODY: Starting at neck edge with W, ch 18. Join with sl st in 1st ch to form ring. **1st rnd:** Ch 1, sc in same ch as sl st, sc in each remaining ch around (18 sc). **2nd rnd:** Sc in each sc around. **3rd rnd:** Inc 1 sc in every 3rd sc around. **4th rnd:** Inc 1 sc in every 4th sc around. **5th rnd:** Inc 5 sc evenly around. Work even on 35 sc for 4 more rnds. **10th rnd:** Inc 5 sc evenly around. Work even on 40 sc for 3 more rnds.

14th rnd (dec rnd): Dec 5 sc evenly around. **15th rnd:** Dec 7 sc evenly around, sl st in next sc (28 sc). Continue as follows for 1st leg.

16th rnd (1st Leg Opening): Ch 3, skip next 13 sc of last rnd, sl st in next sc for 1st leg opening; ch 1, but do not turn.

1st Leg: 1st rnd: Sc in same st as sl st and in each of next 13 sc of last rnd, sc in each of 3 ch sts. Working around on these 17 sc, work even for 6 more rnds. **8th rnd:** (Sc in each of next 3 sc, inc in next sc) twice (mark this inc section for front of leg), sc in each sc around. **9th and 10th rnds:** Inc 2 sc above increases made on last rnd on front of leg, sc to end of rnd. Work even on 23 sc for 1 more rnd. Stuff body and leg. **12th rnd:** Work in back lp only of each sc. * Dec 1 sc, sc in next sc. Repeat from * around, ending dec 1 sc. **13th rnd:** Working in both lps, * dec 1 sc. Repeat from * around, ending with sl st in last sc. Break off. Sew opening closed.

2nd Leg: Following 1st leg, work as follows: Starting with 1st rnd, attach W at leg opening with sc in same sc as sl st on 16th rnd (1st leg opening), and complete as for 1st leg, being sure to work increases on 8th, 9th and 10th rnds at front of leg.

EAR: Front (make 2): Starting at center with P, ch 2. **1st rnd:** Work 6 sc in 2nd ch from hook. **2nd rnd:** Work 2 sc in each sc around (12 sc); sl st in next sc. Break off.

Back (make 2): With W, work same as for front of ear, ending with sl st in next sc; do not break off. **Joining:** Hold 1 front piece and 1 back piece tog with wrong sides facing; with front piece toward you and working through both thicknesses of last rnd, with W, * sc in each of next 3 sc, 2 sc in next sc. Repeat from * around, stuffing ear lightly before completing rnd; join with sl st in 1st sc. Break off.

ARM (make 2): With W, repeat 1st and 2nd rnds of front of ear. Do not sl st or break off. Work even on 12 sc for 7 rnds. Stuff arm. **10th and 11th rnds:** *Dec 1 sc. Repeat from * around. Break off. Sew opening closed.

TAIL: With W, ch 2. Work 6 sc in 2nd ch from hook. Work even in sc for 1 rnd; sl st in next sc. Break off.

SCARF: With R, ch 41. **1st row:** Sc in 2nd ch from hook and in each remaining ch; ch 1, turn. Work even in sc for 2 more rows; ch 1, turn. **Border:** Sl st in each st around all edges of scarf, inc at each corner. Break off. Cut R yarn into about twelve 2″ lengths and knot along ends of scarf for fringe.

HAT: With R, ch 2. Repeat 1st and 2nd rnds of front of ear (12 sc). **3rd rnd:** Inc in every 3rd sc around (16 sc). **4th rnd:** Working in front lps only, sl st in each st around. **5th rnd:** Working in back lps only of sl st, sc in each sl st around. **6th rnd:** Sl st in each sc around.

Break off. Make small pompon with R (see General Directions) and sew to top of hat.

FINISHING: Embroidery: See Stitch Diagrams, page 30. **Head:** Embroider eyes in outline st with brown thread. For nose, work a large black French knot or use satin st. Work mouth in outline st with dusty pink.

Sew head in place. Sew ears in place on each side of head. Pinch top ends of arms together, then sew to body about ½″ below neck seam. Stuff and sew tail on back of body. Sew hat in place. Fold scarf around neck and tack at neck seam and at free end.

PENGUIN

SIZE: 7″ tall (including hat).
See General Directions.

MATERIALS: Knitting-worsted-weight yarn (Orlon acrylic), 1 oz. black (color B), ½ oz. royal blue (R), about 10 yds. white (W) and 5 yds. orange (O); aluminum crochet hook size F (or international size 4.00 mm) **or the size that will give you the correct gauge;** stuffing; tapestry needle.

GAUGE: 4 sc = 1″; 4 rnds = 1″.

HEAD AND BODY: Starting at top of head with B, ch 2. **1st rnd:** Work 6 sc in 2nd ch from hook. **2nd rnd:** Work 2 sc in each sc around (12 sc). **3rd rnd:** Inc 1 sc in every 3rd sc around. **4th rnd:** Inc in every 4th sc around. Work even on 20 sc for 2 more rnds.

7th rnd (dec rnd): * Sc in each of next 3 sc, dec 1 sc. Repeat from * around. **8th rnd:** * Sc in each of next 2 sc, dec 1 sc. Repeat from * around. **9th rnd:** Work on 12 sc. Stuff head.

Continue as follows for body: **10th rnd:** Inc in every 3rd sc around (16 sc). **11th rnd:** Inc 3 sc evenly around. Work even on 19 sc for 1 more rnd. **13th rnd:** Inc 4 sc evenly around. Work even on 23 sc for 1 more rnd. **15th rnd:** Inc 5 sc evenly around. Work even on 28 sc for 1 more rnd. **17th rnd:** Inc 4 sc evenly around. Work even on 32 sc for 1 more rnd.

19th rnd (dec rnd): * Sc in each of next 6 sc, dec 1 sc. Repeat from * around. **20th and 21st rnds:** Sc in each sc around, decreasing 5 sc on each rnd. Stuff body.

22nd rnd: Work in back lp only of each sc. * Dec 1 sc, sc in next sc. Repeat from * around. **23rd rnd:** Working in both lps, * dec 1 sc. Repeat from * around; sl st in next st. Break off. Sew opening closed.

BIB: Starting at top edge with W, ch 7. **1st row:** Sc in 2nd ch from hook and in each remaining ch (6 sc); ch 1, turn. **2nd row:** Inc 1 sc at beg and end of row; ch 1, turn. Work even on 8 sc for 4 rows. Dec 1 sc at beg and end of each next 2 rows; ch 1, turn. **Border:** Sl st around all edges. Break off.

WING AND FOOT (make 2 with B for wings and 2 with O for feet): With B (or O) ch 6. **1st row:** Work as for 1st row of chest (5 sc); ch 1, turn. **2nd row:** Dec 1 sc at beg end of row; ch 1, turn. Work even on 3 sc for 1 row. **4th row:** Draw up lp in each of next 3 sc, y o and draw through all 4 lps on hook; ch 1, turn. **Border:** Work same border as for bib.

HAT: Starting at lower edge with R, ch 25. Join with sl st to form ring. **1st rnd:** Ch 1, sc in same st as sl st and in each remaining ch around (25 sc). **2nd rnd:** Sc in each sc around. **3rd rnd:** Working in front lp only, sl st in each sc around. **4th rnd:** Working in back lp only of same sc of 2nd rnd, sc in each sc around. Work even on 25 sc for 1 more rnd.

6th rnd (1st dec rnd): Dec 5 sc evenly around. **7th rnd:** Sc in each sc around. Repeat 6th and 7th rnds once more. **10th rnd:** Dec 3 sc evenly around. Work even on 12 sc for 2 more rnds. **13th rnd:** Dec 4 sc evenly around. Work even on 8 sc for 3 rnds. **17th rnd:** * Dec 1 sc. Repeat from * around. Break off. Sew opening closed. Make a small pompon (see General Directions) with R and sew to top of hat.

SCARF: With R, ch 35. Sc in 2nd ch from hook and in each remaining ch, but work 3 sc in last ch; then, working across opposite edge of foundation ch, sc in each st, working 2 sc in last st. Break off. Cut R yarn into about six 2″ lengths and knot along ends for fringe.

BEAK: with O, ch 3. Sl st in 2nd ch from hook, sc in last ch, then sl st around entire piece. Break off.

FINISHING: Embroidery: See Stitch Diagrams, page 30. **Eyes:** Use yarn for embroidery. With W, work eyes in satin st. Split B yarn and with 1 strand, work outline st across eye.

To Assemble: Sew bib to front of body. Sew wings in place on each side of body. Sew feet in place at bottom of body; tack feet together at front edge. Sew beak on face. Sew hat in place. Fold scarf around neck and tack in place.

WOLF

SIZE: 10½″ tall.
See General Directions.

MATERIALS: Knitting-worsted-weight yarn (Orlon acrylic), 2 oz. dark brown (color B), 15 yds. taupe (T), 20 yds. each white (W) and light orange (O), 10 yds. pink (P) and 1 oz. dark turquoise (D), few yds. black for nose; black embroidery floss; small piece of red and white felt; aluminum crochet hook size F (or international size 4.00 mm) **or the size that will give you the correct guage;** stuffing; tapestry needle.

GAUGE: 4 sc = 1″; 4 rnds = 1″.

HEAD: Back Section: With B, ch 21. Join with sl st to form ring. **1st rnd:** Ch 1, sc in same st as sl st, sc in each remaining ch around (21 sc). Do not join rnds. **Note:** It is very important to mark beg of each rnd when shaping head. Place markers opposite center 11 sc as follows: Put 2 markers on foundation ch, mark 6th ch and mark 16th ch. The 2 marked sts plus the 9 sts between are for top of head. **2nd rnd:** Sc in each of first 8 sc, * inc in next sc, (sc in next sc, inc in next sc) twice; * sc in each of last 8 sc of rnd (24 sc). **3rd rnd:** Sc in each of first 9 sc, inc in next sc, sc in each of next 5 sc, inc in next sc, sc in each of last 8 sc (26 sc). **4th rnd:** Sc in each of first 11 sc, repeat between *'s on 2nd rnd, sc in each of last 10 sc of rnd (29 sc). **5th rnd:** Inc 6 sc evenly around. Work even on 35 sc for 1 more rnd. **7th rnd:** * Sc in each of next 3 sc, dec 1 sc. Repeat from * around. **8th rnd:** * Sc in next sc, dec 1 sc. Repeat from * around, ending with sc in last sc. Stuff head. **9th rnd:** * Dec 1 sc. Repeat from * around, sc in last sc. Break off. Sew opening closed.

Front Section: Top Half: Working across opposite edge of foundation ch and working in 11 sts marked for top half only, with T, sc in marked sc, sc in each of next 9 sc between markers, sc in next marked sc. Do not work in remaining sts; ch 1, turn. Working in rows, work even on 11 sc for 3 rows more. Dec 1 sc at beg and end of next row. Work even on 9 sc for 1 row.

Next row: (Dec 1 sc) 3 times; dec 1 sc over last 3 sc. Break off.

Lower Half: Working across foundation ch of head, with T, sc in each of 10 free sts; ch 1, turn. Dec 1 st at beg and end of next row. Work even on 8 sc for 2 rows. Dec 1 st at beg and end of next row. Sl st around outer edge of lower half and top half of front section. Break off.

Mouth: With P, ch 4. **1st row:** Sc in 2nd ch from hook and in each of next 2 ch (3 sc); ch 1, turn. **2nd row:** Sc in 1st sc, 2 sc in next sc, sc in last sc; ch 1, turn. Work even on 4 sc for 1 more row. **4th row:** Inc at beg and end of row. Work even on 6 sc for 3 more rows. **8th row:** Dec at beg and end of row. Work even on 4 sc for 3 more rows. **Border:** Ch 1, sl st around entire mouth; join and break off P. With T, sl st in each sl st

around; join and break off.

Stuffing head as you go, with T, sew mouth piece to head.

EAR: Front (make 2): With P, ch 7. **1st row:** Sl st in 2nd ch from hook, sc in each of next 2 ch, h dc in each of last 3 ch; ch 2, turn. **2nd row:** H dc in each of 1st 3 h dc, sc in each of next 2 sc, sl st in last st. Break off.

Back (make 2): With B, work same as for front of ear, but do not break off. Holding 1 front piece and 1 back piece tog, with front piece toward you and working through both thicknesses, sc both pieces tog. Break off.

BODY: Striped Top Section: Starting at neck edge with O, ch 17. Join with sl st to form ring. **1st rnd:** Ch 1, sc in same ch as sl st, sc in each remaining ch around (17 sc). Drop O; attach W. **2nd rnd:** With W, sc in each sc around. Always change color on last st of rnd, drawing lp of new color through last 2 lps on hook. **3rd rnd:** With O, repeat last rnd. Continue to work 1 rnd each W and O and work as follows: **4th and 5th rnds:** Inc 4 sc evenly around. **6th rnd:** Inc 3 sc evenly around. Work even on 28 sc for 1 rnd. **8th rnd:** Inc 2 sc evenly around. **9th rnd:** Inc 3 sc evenly around. Continue in stripe pattern and work even on 33 sc for 4 rnds more. At end of 13th rnd, join with sl st in next sc. Break off W and O; change to D.

Bottom Section: With D, work even on 33 sc for 2 rnds. **3rd rnd:** * (Inc in next sc, sc in each of next 2 sc) twice; inc in next sc *, sc in each of next 17 sc for front. Repeat from * to * once; sc in each of last 2 sc (6 sc inc in all across back). Work even on 39 sc for 2 more rnds.

6th rnd (dec rnd): Dec 5 sc evenly around. **7th rnd:** Dec 6 sc evenly around; sl st in next sc (28 sc). Continue as follows for 1st leg.

1st Leg Opening: Ch 3, skip next 13 sc of last rnd, sl st in next sc for 1st leg opening; ch 1, but do not turn. **1st Leg: 1st rnd:** Sc in same st as sl st and in each of next 13 sc, sc in each of 3 ch sts. Working around on these 17 sc, work even for 9 more rnds. Break off D; attach B. **11th rnd:** With B, sc in each sc around. Mark front section of leg. **12th and 13th rnds:** inc 2 sc on front of leg only. Work even on 21 sc for 2 more rnds. Stuff body and leg. **16th rnd:** Working in back lp of each sc, * dec 1 sc. Repeat from * around, ending with sc in last sc. **17th rnd:** Working in both lps of each sc, repeat last rnd; sl st in next sc. Break off. Sew opening closed.

2nd Leg: Work as for 1st leg, being sure to work

See page 106

See page 102

See page 40

See page 39

See page 27

See page 25

See page 31

See page 32

See page 48

See page 56

See page 65

See page 66

See page 66

See page 75

See pages 69, 70, 71, and 72

See page 62

See page 112

See page 111

See page 43

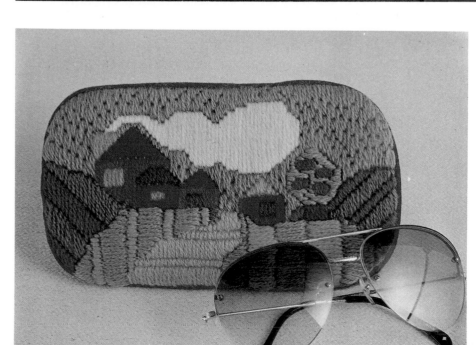

See page 114

See page 105

See page 117

See page 68

See page 23

See page 106

93

See page 56

See page 35

See page 109

See page 34

See page 133

increases on 12th and 13th rnds at front of leg.

ARM (make 2): Striped Top Section: With O, ch 2. Work 8 sc in 2nd ch from hook. With W, inc 2 sc evenly on next rnd. Working 1 rnd each O and W, work even on 10 sc for 5 rnds more. **8th rnd:** With W, dec 2 sc evenly around. **9th rnd:** With O, inc 3 sc evenly around. Break off O and W; attach B. **10th rnd:** With B, inc 3 sc evenly around. Stuff arm. Work even on 14 sc for 2 more rnds. **13th rnd:** * Sc in next sc, dec 1 sc. Repeat from * around, ending dec 1 sc; sl st in next st. Break off. Sew opening closed.

TAIL: With B, crochet 3″ chain. Break off. Cut B yarn into 3″ lengths. Tie 10-strand bunches of cut yarn closely along chain. Trim ends. Brush yarn until it looks furry.

FINISHING: Stuff body again, if necessary, through neck opening, then sew head in place. Sew ears on each side of head. Sew arms to body about 1″ below neck seam. Sew tail on back of body.

Embroidery: See Stitch Diagrams, page 30. Work eyes with white yarn in satin stitch. With black thread, outline each eye. Work eyebrows with short straight sts and work fly st across white of eyes. For nose, make small pompon (see General Directions, using ½″-wide cardboard and winding yarn 20 times) with black yarn. With black thread, work outline st for mouth and French knots near nose. With T, work 3 straight sts on each arm and leg.

Cut teeth from white felt and tongue from red felt and sew in place.

THREE LITTLE PIGS

SIZE: About 6½″ tall.
See General Directions.

MATERIALS: Knitting-worsted-weight yarn (Orlon acrylic): **For pig A,** 6 yds. each green and white for top; 16 yds. turquoise for bottom and 30 yds. pink; **for pig B,** 10 yds. orange for top, 18 yds. royal blue for bottom and 30 yds. pink; **for pig C,** 10 yds. medium blue for top, 16 yds. red for bottom and 30 yds. pink; **for all pigs,** 6-strand embroidery floss in brown and white; aluminum crochet hook size F (or international size 4.00 mm) **or the size that will give you the correct gauge;** stuffing; tapestry needle.

GAUGE: 4 sc = 1″; 4 rnds = 1″.

HEAD: Starting at center of nose with pink, ch 2. **1st rnd:** Work 6 sc in 2nd ch from hook. **2nd rnd:** Work 2 sc in each sc around (12 sc). **3rd rnd:** Working in back lp only of each sc, sc in each sc around. **4th rnd:** Inc in every 4th sc around. **5th rnd:** Inc in every 3rd sc

around (20 sc). **6th rnd:** Inc 3 sc evenly around. **7th rnd:** Inc 2 sc evenly around. **8th rnd:** Inc 5 sc evenly around. Work even on 30 sc for 2 more rnds.

11th rnd (dec rnd): * Sc in next sc, dec 1 sc, sc in each of next 2 sc, dec 1 sc. Repeat from * around, ending with dec 1 sc (9 sc dec). Stuff head. **12th rnd:** * Sc in next sc, dec 1 sc. Repeat from * around. **13th rnd:** * Dec 1 sc. Repeat from * around. Break off. Sew opening closed.

BODY: Top Section: Follow directions in next paragraph, using these colors: *For pig A,* alternate 1 rnd green with 1 rnd white; *for pig B,* use orange; *for pig C,* use medium blue.

Starting at neck edge, ch 17. Join with sl st to form ring. **1st rnd:** Ch 1, sc in same ch as sl st, sc in each remaining ch around (17 sc). **2nd rnd:** Sc in each sc around. **3rd rnd:** Inc 3 sc evenly around. Work even on 20 sc for 1 more rnd. **5th rnd:** Inc 3 sc evenly around (23 sc); sl st in next st. Break off top color.

Bottom Section: Make lp on hook with turquoise for pig A, royal blue for pig B or red for pig C. Continue working in rnds of sc as follows with new colors: **6th rnd:** Inc 3 sc evenly around. Work even on 26 sc for 2 more rnds. **9th rnd (dec rnd):** * Sc in each of next 2 sc, dec 1 sc. Repeat from * around, ending with sc in next sc; sl st in last sc (20 sts). Continue as follows for first leg. **10th rnd (1st Leg Opening):** Ch 3, skip next 9 sc, sl st in next sc for 1st leg opening; ch 1, but do not turn.

1st Leg: 1st rnd: Sc in same st as sl st and in each of next 9 sc, sc in each of 3 ch sts. Working around on these 13 sc, work even in sc for 4 more rnds. **6th rnd:** Working in back lp of each sc, sc in each sc around; sl st in next sc. Break off.

Make lp on hook with pink and continue in sc rnds as follows: **7th rnd:** Sc in each sc around. Mark front section of leg. **8th rnd:** Sc in each sc, inc 2 sc at front section of leg. Work even on 15 sc for 1 more rnd. Stuff leg and body. **10th rnd:** Work in back lp of each sc around. **11th rnd:** * Dec 1 sc. Repeat from * around, ending with sl st in next st. Break off. Sew opening closed.

2nd Leg: Working as for 1st leg, start with 1st rnd, attach yarn at leg opening with sc in same sc as sl st and complete as for 1st leg.

ARM (make 2): Using same color as for top, ch 2. Work 6 sc in 2nd ch from hook. Inc 3 sc evenly around next rnd. Work even on 9 sc for 2 rnds; sl st in next sc. Break off. With pink, continue in sc for 3 rnds more. Stuff arm. * Dec 1 sc. Repeat from * around; sl st in last st. Break off. Sew opening closed.

EAR (make 2): With pink, ch 4. Work 1 row sc (3 sc); ch 1, turn. Dec 1 sc at beg of next 2 rows; ch 1, turn. Sc evenly around entire ear. Break off.

TAIL: With pink, ch 6. Draw up lp in 2nd ch from hook and in each remaining ch, y o and draw through all lps on hook; ch 1 tightly. Break off.

FINISHING: Stuff body again, if necessary, through neck opening, then sew head in place. Sew ears on each side of head. Sew arms to body about ½″ below neck seam. Sew tail in place.

Embroidery: See Stitch Diagrams, page 30. For features on face and trim on arms and legs, use embroidery thread. With white, work eyes in satin st. Use brown for all of the following: Work fly st across each eye. Work 1 fly st on each arm and leg. Outline each eye, work mouth in outline st and work 2 fly sts for nose. Work straight st for each eyebrow.

TRIM: *For pig B only,* make 2 shoulder straps as follows: With royal blue, ch 13. Work even in sc for 1 row. Break off. Sew in place. With orange yarn, work a French knot below each strap. *For pig C only,* with red yarn, work 3 French knots down center front of top section.

LLAMA

SIZE: 10″ tall.
See General Directions.

MATERIALS: Knitting-worsted-weight yarn (Orlon acrylic), 4 oz. beige (color B), 25 yds. rust (R) and 3 yds. pink (P); aluminum crochet hook size F (or international size 4.00 mm) **or the size that will give you the correct gauge;** ½ yd. ¼″-wide pink ribbon; stuffing; tapestry needle.

GAUGE: 4 sc = 1″; 4 rnds = 1″.

HEAD: Starting at center of nose with B, ch 2. **1st rnd:** Work 8 sc in 2nd ch from hook. **2nd rnd:** Inc in every other st around (12 sc). **3rd rnd:** Inc in every 3rd st around (16 sc). **4th rnd:** Inc 5 sc evenly around. **5th rnd:** Inc 3 sc evenly around. Work even on 24 sc for 3 more rnds. **9th rnd:** Inc 3 sc evenly around. Work even on 27 sc for 1 more rnd. Mark last rnd for beg of fur.

11th rnd (1st dec rnd): * Sc in each of next 7 sc, dec 1 sc. Repeat from * around. Stuff head. **12th and 13th rnds:** Dec 5 sc evenly around. **14th rnd:** * Dec 1 sc. Repeat from * around; sl st in next st. Break off. Sew opening closed. **Note:** Neck and body will look very small until fur is added.

NECK: Starting at top edge with B, ch 15. Join with sl st to form ring. **1st rnd:** Ch 1, sc in same st as sl st, sc in each remaining ch around. Work even on 15 sc for 2 more rnds. **4th rnd:** Working in sc, inc 1 sc on rnd. **5th rnd:** Work even in sc. Repeat last 2 rnds twice more. **10th rnd:** Inc 2 sc evenly around. **11th rnd:** Work even in sc. Repeat last 2 rnds once more (22 sc). **14th rnd:** Inc 3 sc evenly around (25 sc); sl st in next st. Break off. Stuff neck.

BODY: With B, work same as for head through 3rd rnd (16 sc). **4th rnd:** Work 2 sc in every other sc around (24 sc). **5th rnd:** Inc 7 sc evenly around. Work even on 31 sc for 3 more rnds. **9th rnd:** Inc 2 sc evenly around. Work even on 33 sc for 3 more rnds.

13th rnd (1st dec rnd): * Sc in each of next 9 sc, dec 1 sc. Repeat from * around. Stuff body. **14th rnd:** * Sc in each of next 3 sc, dec 1 sc. Repeat from * around. **15th rnd:** * Sc in next sc, dec 1 sc. Repeat from * around. **16th rnd:** * Dec 1 sc. Repeat from * around; join with sl st in next sc. Break off. Sew opening closed.

LEG (make 4): Starting at bottom with B, ch 2. **1st rnd:** Work 8 sc in 2nd ch from hook. **2nd rnd:** Inc 3 sc evenly around. Work even on 11 sc for 6 more rnds. **9th rnd:** Inc 1 sc on rnd. **10th rnd:** Work even in sc. **11th rnd:** Inc 1 sc on rnd. Repeat last 2 rnds twice more (15 sc). Break off. Stuff leg.

EAR: Front (make 2): With P, ch 6. **1st row:** Sc in 2nd ch from hook and in each remaining ch; ch 1, turn. **2nd row:** Sc in each sc across (5 sc). Break off.

Back (make 2): With B, work same as for front of ear, but do not break off. **Joining:** Holding 1 front piece and 1 back piece together with front piece facing you and working through both thicknesses with R, sc around; join with sl st. Break off.

FINISHING: Sew head to top neck. Sew lower edge of neck to body. Sew legs to underside of body.

Fur: Cut a piece of cardboard 1¼″ x 6″. Wind yarn (mostly color B and a small amount of color R) around cardboard. Cut yarn at one side into 2½″ lengths. Hold 3 strands of same color yarn tog and fold in half. Sew folded end to body. Sew strands in this manner all over body and head, using color R in patches of various sizes as shown in photograph. Trim fur with scissors and brush ends to make fur fuzzy if desired. Sew ears in place on head.

Embroidery: See Stitch Diagrams, page 30. Use yarn for embroidery on face. For eyes and nose, work fly st with R. Work a few straight sts with P for mouth.

Tie ribbon around neck.

BROWN BEAR

SIZE: 6½".

See General Directions.

MATERIALS: Knitting-worsted-weight yarn (Orlon acrylic), 1 oz. taupe (color T), about 20 yds. rust (R), 15 yds. each orange (O) and white (W), 3 yds. each pink (P) and beige (B); black embroidery floss; aluminum crochet hook size F (or international size 4.00 mm) **or the size that will give you the correct gauge;** stuffing; tapestry needle.

GAUGE: 4 sc = 1"; 4 rnds = 1".

HEAD: Starting at center of nose, with R, ch 2. **1st rnd:** Work 8 sc in 2nd ch from hook. **2nd rnd:** Inc in every other st around (12 sc). **3rd rnd:** Sc in each sc around. **4th rnd:** Inc in every 3rd sc around. **5th rnd:** Inc 3 sc evenly spaced around (19 sc). Break off R; attach T. **6th rnd:** Inc 2 sc evenly around. **7th rnd:** Inc 4 sc evenly around. Work even on 25 sc for 1 more rnd. **9th rnd:** Inc in every 5th sc around. Work even on 30 sc for 2 more rnds.

12th rnd (dec rnd): * Sc in each of next 4 sc, dec 1 sc. Repeat from * around. Stuff head. **13th rnd:** * Sc in each of next 2 sc, dec 1 sc. Repeat from * around, ending with sc in last sc. **14th rnd:** * Sc in next sc, dec 1 sc. Repeat from * around, ending with sc in last sc. **15th rnd:** * Dec 1 sc. Repeat from * around; sl st in next st. Break off. Sew opening closed.

BODY: Striped Top Section: Starting at neck edge with T, ch 17. Join with sl st to form ring. **1st rnd:** Ch 1, sc in same ch as sl st, sc in each remaining ch around (17 sc). Break off T; attach W. **2nd rnd:** With W, sc in each sc around. Always change colors on last st of rnd, drawing lp of new color through last 2 lps on hook. **3rd rnd:** With O, repeat last rnd. Continue to work 1 rnd each W and O and work as follows: **4th and 5th rnds:** Inc 4 sc evenly around. **6th rnd:** Inc 3 sc evenly around. Work even on 28 sc for 1 more rnd. **8th rnd:** Inc sc evenly around. **9th rnd:** Inc 3 sc evenly around. Work even on 33 sc for 2 rnds. Join last rnd with sl st in next sc. Break off W and O, change to T on last sc.

Bottom Section: The 1st 3 rnds are worked with T and B as follows: **1st rnd:** Work in back lp of each sc on this rnd only. With T, sc in each of 1st 13 sc; with B, sc in each of next 7 sc; with T, sc in each of last 13 sc. **2nd rnd:** Working in both lps and using same colors as last rnd, sc in each sc around. **3rd rnd:** With T, work 14 sc; with B, work 5 sc; with T, work 14 sc.

Break off B. With T, work even on 33 sc for 2 more rnds.

6th rnd (dec rnd): * Sc in each of next 4 sc, dec 1 sc. Repeat from * around, ending with sc in each of last 3 sc. Stuff body. **7th, 8th and 9th rnds:** Repeat 13th, 14th and 15th rnds of head. Complete as for head.

EAR (make 2): With P, ch 4. Sc in 2nd ch from hook and in each of next 2 ch. Work even on 3 sc for 1 row. Break off P; attach T. With T, work even in sc for 2 rows. Fold ear in half with P on one side and T on other side. Working through both thicknesses, sc around all edges. Break off.

ARM (make 2): Striped Top Section: With O, ch 2. Work 8 sc in 2nd ch from hook. **2nd rnd:** With W, inc 2 sc evenly around. Working 1 rnd each O and W, work even on 10 sc for 5 more rnds, ending with an O rnd. Join sl st in last st. Break off O and W. With T, work even in sc for 2 more rnds. Stuff arm. **10th rnd:** * Dec 1 sc. Repeat from * around; sl st in last st. Break off. Sew opening closed.

LEG (make 2): Starting at bottom with R, ch 4. **1st rnd:** Sc in 2nd ch from hook, sc in next ch, 3 sc in last ch (mark center sc of this 3-sc group); working along opposite edge of chain, sc in each of next 2 sts, 3 sc in turning ch (mark center sc). **2nd rnd:** Sc in each sc around, working 4 sc in each marked sc (6 sc inc). **3rd rnd:** Sc in each sc around, increasing 2 sc at each end above increases of last rnd; join with sl st in next sc. Break off R.

4th rnd: With T, sc in back lp only of each sc around (20 sc). Mark 1 end of oval for front of leg. Work in both lps of each sc from now on. **5th rnd:** Sc around and dec 2 sc at marked end. **6th rnd:** Sc around, and dec 1 sc at marked end. **7th rnd:** Repeat 5th rnd. Work even on 15 sc for 1 more rnd; join with sl st in next sc. Break off. Mark sc at center front of leg (above dec). **1st row:** With T, sc in marked sc and in each of next 7 sc (this is center back of leg). Do not work remaining sts; ch 1, turn. Work in rows from now on. **2nd row:** Sc in each sc across (8 sc); ch 1, turn. **3rd row:** Inc 2 sc evenly across (10 sc).

4th row (dec row): Dec 3 sc evenly across. Work even on 7 sc for 1 row. Dec 1 sc at beg and end of each of next 2 rows. Break off. Stuff leg.

For 2nd leg, reverse leg shaping. Start 1st row of leg shaping at center back of leg, working last 7 rows on opposite side of leg.

TAIL: With T, ch 2. Work 6 sc in 2nd ch from

hook, then work even on 6 sc for 2 rnds. Break off. Stuff tail.

FINISHING: Stuff body again, if necessary, through neck opening, then sew head in place. Sew ears on each side of head. Sew arms to body about ½" below neck seam. Sew legs at lower edge of body on each side of color B section. Sew tail on back of body.

Embroidery: See Stitch Diagrams, page 30. For eyes, work satin st with white yarn. With black, work 1 fly st across each eye and work outline st around edge of eye. For nose, work in black satin st. Work mouth and eyebrows in black outline st.

LAMB

SIZE: 6½" from head to back.
See General Directions.

MATERIALS: Knitting-worsted-weight yarn (Orlon acrylic), 2 oz. natural (color N), small amount of pink (P) and rust (R); aluminum crochet hook size F (or international size 4.00 mm) **or the size that will give you the correct gauge;** ½ yd. ¼"-wide pink ribbon; stuffing; tapestry needle.

GAUGE: 4 sc = 1"; 4 rnds = 1".

HEAD: Starting at center of nose with N, ch 2. **1st rnd:** Work 8 sc in 2nd ch from hook. **2nd rnd:** Inc in every other st around (12 sc). **3rd rnd:** Inc in every 3rd sc around. Work even on 16 sc for 1 more rnd. **5th rnd:** Inc in every 4th sc around. Work even on 20 sc for 4 more rnds, marking 8th rnd for beg of fur.

10th rnd (1st dec rnd): * Sc in each of next 2 sc, dec 1 sc. Repeat from * around. Stuff head. **11th rnd:** * Sc in next sc, dec 1 sc. Repeat from * around. **12th rnd:** * Dec 1 sc. Repeat from * around. Break off. Sew opening closed.

Note: Neck and body will look very small until fur is added.

NECK: With N, ch 15. Join with sl st to form ring. **1st rnd:** Ch 1, sc in same ch as sl st, sc in each remaining ch. Work even on 15 sc for 2 rnds more. Sl st in next sc. Break off.

BODY: With N, work same as for head through 1st rnd (8 sc). **2nd rnd:** Work 2 sc in each sc around (16 sc). **3rd rnd:** Inc 5 sc evenly spaced around. Work even on 21 sc for 1 more rnd. **5th rnd:** Inc 4 sc evenly around. Work even on 25 sc for 7 more rnds.

13th rnd (1st dec rnd): * Sc in each of next 3 sc, dec 1 sc. Repeat from * around. Work even for 1 more rnd. Stuff body. **15th rnd:** Dec 6 sc evenly around. **16th rnd:** * Dec 1 sc. Repeat from * around; sl st in next st. Break off. Sew opening closed.

LEG (make 4): With N, ch 2. **1st rnd:** Work 8 sc in 2nd ch from hook. **2nd rnd:** Working in back lp of each sc on this rnd only, sc in each sc around. Work even on 8 sc for 4 more rnds. **7th rnd:** Inc in every other st around. Work even on 12 sc for 1 more rnd; sl st in next st. Break off. Stuff leg.

EAR: Front (make 2): With P, ch 4. Sc in 2nd ch from hook, sc in next ch, work 3 sc in last ch; working on opposite edge of chain, sc in each of next 2 sts, work 2 sc in turning ch; join with sl st in 1st sc. Break off.

Back (make 2): With N, work same as for front of ear, but do not break off. **Joining:** Holding 1 front piece and 1 back piece together with front piece facing you and working through both thicknesses with N, sc around; join with sl st. Break off.

FINISHING: Complete as for finishing on Llama, working in same manner for fur (using color N only) and for embroidery.

Colorful Coat Hangers

Gift-tie yarn finger-woven over two wire hangers.

MATERIALS: For each hanger: 1 plain wire hanger and 1 wire hanger with cardboard tube on bar; 2 (6-yard) cards bulky gift-wrap yarn (available in greeting-card stores); masking tape.

Cut 3" length of yarn and reserve. Hold hangers together. Place 1 yarn end from each of 2 cards against 1" tips of hanger hooks with yarn extending from tips. Starting at tips, tightly bind yarn ends to hooks with masking tape (diagram 1). To make 1 sturdy hanger, continue to tape hangers together, covering them (including tube) completely. Make ½" loop with each of the strands extending from tip and tie together tightly, as in diagram 2, with 3" reserved strand (shown in black on diagram).

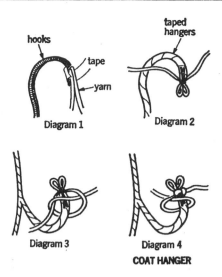

Holding 1 arm of hanger between your knees with hook pointing up, follow diagram 3: Loop right-hand strand around hook as shown; pull tightly to cover knot on tied strand. Following diagram 4, repeat procedure with left-hand strand. Alternate diagrams 3 and 4, covering ends of tied strand. (**Note:** do not wrap yarn around left strand, as in diagram 3, after first time.) Continue to cover hanger in this manner, working along hook and around hanger back to base of hook. Tie ends tightly and clip; hide ends in stitches. Cover joining with strand of yarn tied in bow.

Mad Money Purses

A crocheted apple and gift-box double as necklaces.

SIZES: Box purse, 2″ square; apple, 1½″ x 2″.

MATERIALS: For both purses: Coats & Clark's Speed-Cro-Sheen, 1 (100-yard) ball Spanish red No. 126 and small amount hunter's green No. 48; steel crochet hook No. 1 (or international size 2.50 mm) **or the size that will give you the correct gauge.**

GAUGE: 6 sc = 1″.

BOX

SQUARE (make 2): Starting at lower edge with red, ch 13. **1st row:** Sc in 2nd ch from hook and in each ch across (12 sc); ch 1, turn. **2nd row:** Sc in each sc; ch 1, turn. Repeat 2nd row until piece is square. Break off.

TRIM: With green work sl st from center of one edge across square to center of opposite edge (to work sl-st trim, insert hook in crochet and draw up lp of green, insert hook again a short distance away, y o and draw through crochet and through lp on hook), then sl st from center of 3rd edge to center of 4th edge.

Work cross lines on other square in same manner, then sl st 2 triangles on 1 square, as in photograph, for bow.

FINISHING: Place squares with wrong sides together and bow square facing you. Starting at 1 corner with red, sl st squares together along 3 sides. Do not break off. Crochet 27″-long chain (or desired length), then sl st in opposite corner. Break off.

APPLE

Starting at top with red, ch 2. **1st row:** Work 6 sc in 2nd ch from hook; ch 1, turn. **2nd through 4th rows:** Work 2 sc in 1st sc, sc in each sc to last sc, 2 sc in last sc; ch 1, turn. **5th and 6th rows:** Sc in each sc (12 sc); ch 1, turn. **7th through 9th rows:** Draw up lp in each of 1st 2 sc, y o and draw through all 3 lps on hook (1 sc dec), sc in each sc to within last 2 sc, dec 1 sc; ch 1, turn. Break off. Make another piece in same manner.

STEM AND LEAVES (make 2): With green * ch 4, sc in 2nd ch from hook and in each of next 2 ch. (Repeat from * once more, sl st in 1st ch) 3 times to form stem and 3 leaves (4-pronged shape). Break off. Glue or sew to apple pieces as in photograph.

FINISHING: With wrong sides facing and using red, sl st pieces together, leaving top edge open. Do not break off. Crochet 27″-long chain (or desired length), then sl st in opposite corner. Break off.

Show-off Pot Holders

Crocheted kitchen helpers with flaglike motifs.

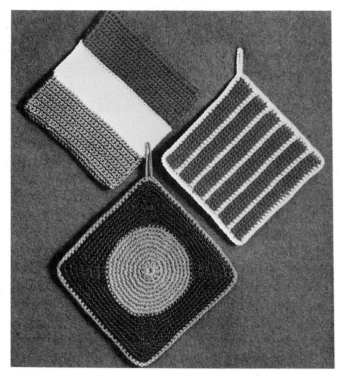

SIZE: About 6" square.

MATERIALS: Coats and Clark's Speed-Cro-Sheen: **Red-and-White-Striped Pot Holder:** 1 (100-yard) ball each white No. 1 (color W) and Spanish red No. 126 (R); **Italian-Flag Pot Holder:** 1 ball each white No. 1 (W), hunter green No. 48 (G) and Spanish red No. 126 (R); **Orange-Circle Pot Holder:** 1 ball each Killarney No. 49-A (dark green, G) and Tango No. 135 (orange, O). **All Pot Holders:** steel crochet hook No. 1 **or the size that will give you the correct gauge.**

GAUGE: 5 sc = 1"; 6 rows = 1".

To Change Colors: Do not ch 1 at end of row or rnd; break off old color, make lp on hook with new color and draw it through lp of old color; ch 1 and turn for piece worked in rows, or continue as specified for piece worked in rnds.

RED-AND-WHITE-STRIPED POT HOLD-ER: Starting at one edge with R, ch 31 to measure about 6". **1st row (right side):** Sc in 2nd ch from hook and in each ch across (30 sc); ch 1, turn. **2nd Row:** Sc in each sc across; ch 1, turn. Repeating 2nd row for pattern, work 3 more rows with R. Break off. (Work 1 row W, 5 rows R) 5 times. Break off. Work another piece in same manner, reversing colors.

With wrong sides facing, using W, join pieces through both lps of matching scs as follows: Sc in sc next to any corner, * sc in each sc to next corner, ch 1, sc in corner, ch 1, sc over side of each sc to next corner, ch 1, sc in corner, ch 1. Repeat from * once more, ending repeat with ch 15 for lp, sl st in 1st sc. Break off.

ITALIAN-FLAG POT HOLDER: Using R, work as for red-and-white pot holder for 5 rows. Continue with R for 7 more rows. Break off. Change to W and work 12 rows. Break off. Change to G and work 12 rows. Break off. Work another piece in same manner.

Join pieces as for red-and-white pot holder, changing colors to match stripes.

ORANGE-CIRCLE POT HOLDER: Starting at center with O, ch 4. Join with sl st to form ring. **1st rnd (right side):** Ch 3, work 11 dc in ring (12 dc, counting ch 3 as 1 dc); join with sl st to top of ch 3. **2nd rnd:** Ch 1, work sc in same place as sl st, work 2 sc in each dc around (24 sc, counting ch 1 as 1 sc); sl st in ch 1 to join. **3rd rnd:** Ch 1, sc in each sc around, increasing 10 sc as evenly spaced as possible (34 sc); join. **4th rnd:** Ch 1, sc in each sc around; join. **5th rnd:** Ch 1, sc in each sc around, increasing 15 sc as evenly spaced as possible (49 sc); join. **6th rnd:** Repeat 4th rnd. **7th rnd:** Repeat 5th rnd (64 sc). **8th rnd:** Ch 1, sc in each sc around, increasing 4 sc evenly spaced (68 sc); join. **9th rnd:** Repeat 4th rnd. Break off. Circle should measure 4" across.

10th rnd (right side): With G sc in any sc on circle edge and in each of next 6 sc; * h dc in next sc, dc in next sc, 2 dc in next sc, dc in next sc, h dc in next sc, sc in each of next 11 sc. Repeat from * 3 times more, ending last repeat with sc in each of remaining 4 sc; join to 1st sc. **11th rnd:** Ch 1, sc in each of next 6 sc, * sc in next h dc, sc in next dc; for corner work 2 dc in each of next 2 dc (corner completed); sc in next dc, sc in next h dc, sc in each of next 11 sc. Repeat from * 3 times more, ending last repeat with sc in each of remaining 4 sc; join. **12th rnd:** Ch 1, * sc in each sc to next dc, sc in next dc, work corner, sc in next dc. Repeat from * 3 times more; sc in each remaining sc; join. **13th rnd:** Repeat 12th rnd. **14th rnd:** Ch 1, * sc in each sc to within 3 sc of corner, h dc in each of next 3 sc, sc in next dc, work corner, sc in next dc, h dc in each of next 3 sc. Repeat from * 3 times more; sc in each remaining sc; join. **15th rnd:** Ch 1, sc in each st around, working 2 sc in each of the center 2 dc at each corner; join. **16th rnd:** Ch 1, sc in each sc around, working 2 sc in each of the center 2 sc at each corner; join. Break off. Work another piece in same manner.

With wrong sides facing, using O, join pieces by working as for 16th rnd through both lps of matching sc along side edges; at last corner, before working sl st to join, ch 15 for lp, then join. Break off.

Petal-and-Pear Neck Warmer

A shapely design crocheted in glowing colors.

SIZE: About 33″ long.

MATERIALS: Knitting-worsted-weight yarn, 1 ounce in each of the following colors: copper (color C), gold (G), lilac (L), aqua (A) and medium blue (B); aluminum crochet hook size F (or Canadian hook No. 10) **or the size that will give you the correct gauge;** tapestry needle.

GAUGE: 4 sts = 1″.

Note: When working rnds, always work with same side (right side) facing you.

SECTION 1: See diagram. **1st rnd:** Starting at

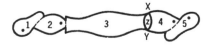

dot with C, ch 2, work 6 sc in 2nd ch from hook; join with sl st to first sc. Mark beg of rnds, moving marker on each rnd. **2nd rnd:** Work 2 sc in each sc around (12 sc); join. **3rd rnd:** Repeat 2nd rnd (24 sc); join. **4th**

rnd: Ch 11 for foundation chain; being careful not to twist chain, sc in 2nd ch from hook and in each ch across to marker, dc in marked sc on 3rd rnd and in each of next 7 sc, h dc in each of next 8 sc, sc in each of next 8 sc; working along opposite side of foundation chain, sc in each ch across, working 3 sc in last ch for corner. **5th rnd:** Continuing around, sc in each sc to first dc, ch 2 (counts as 1 dc), dc in each of next 7 dc, h dc in each of next 2 h dc, 2 h dc in next h dc, h dc in each of next 5 h dc, sc in each of next 2 sc, (2 sc in next sc, sc in each of next 2 sc) twice; sc in each sc to corner; join. Break off.

Edging: With G work sc in back lp of each st around, working 3 sc in corner. Break off.

SECTION 2: 1st row: Starting at dot with G, ch 3, sc in 2nd ch from hook and in next ch; ch 1, turn. **2nd row:** Work 2 sc in each of 2 sc (4 sc); ch 1, turn. **3rd row:** Sc in each sc across; ch 1, turn. **4th row:** Work 2 sc in first sc, sc in each sc to within last sc, 2 sc in last sc; ch 1, turn. Repeat last 2 rows twice more (10 sc at end of 8th row). Work 2 rows even. **11th (dec) row:** Draw up lp in each of first 2 sc, y o and draw through all 3 lps on hook (1 sc dec), sc in each sc to within last 2 sc, dec 1 sc (8 sc); ch 1, turn. Repeat dec row every other row until 2 sc remain. Break off.

Edging: 1st rnd: With C, sc evenly around entire section, working 3 sc at each end for corners; join. Break off. **2nd rnd:** Starting in center st of one corner with L, sc in back lp of each sc to within center st of next corner, 3 sc in center st for corner, sc in each sc to end; join. **3rd rnd:** Sc in each sc around, working 3 sc in center sc of corner; join. Break off.

SECTION 3: Starting along center of section with L, ch 28 to measure about 7″. **1st rnd:** Work 2 dc in 4th ch from hook, dc in each of next 23 ch to within last ch, 5-dc shell in last ch; working along opposite side of foundation chain, dc in each of next 23 ch to within last ch, 2 dc in next ch (5-dc shell completed, counting turning ch as 1 dc); join to top of turning ch. **2nd rnd:** Ch 3, 2 dc in same st (center st of shell), * dc in next dc, 2 dc in next dc, dc in each dc to within next shell, 2 dc in next dc, dc in next dc *, 3-dc shell in next dc. Repeat from * to * once more; join. Break off. **3rd rnd:** With A * work sc in first dc of shell (mark this st), 3 sc in next dc, sc in next dc, 2 sc in next dc, sc in each dc across to within 1 dc of next shell, 2 sc in next dc. Repeat from * once more; join. Break off.

1st short row: With B make lp on hook, y o and work dc in a marked sc, dc in each of next 4 sc; ch 3, turn. **2nd short row:** Skip first dc, dc in each dc across

(5 dc, counting turning ch as 1 dc); ch 3, turn. Repeat 2nd short row twice more. Break off. Attach B to other marked st on 3rd rnd; work opposite end to correspond.

Edging: 1st rnd: With B, working in back lps only, sc evenly around entire outer edge, working 2 sc over posts of dc along sides of short rows and 2 sc in each corner; join. Break off. **2nd rnd:** With A, working in back lps only, sc in each sc around, working 2 sc in 2nd st of each corner. Break off.

SECTION 4: Work same as for Section 2 through 6th row. Work even on 8 sts until piece measures 3½" from beg, marking last row for top edge. Break off.

Edging: 1st rnd: With C, sc evenly around section, working 3 sc at narrow end. Break off. **2nd rnd:** Omitting sts on top edge, with L, sc in back lp of each sc around, working 3 sc in center st at pointed end. Break off.

SECTION 5: Work as for Section 1.

FINISHING: With wrong side facing you, following diagram and using tapestry needle and matching-color yarn, whipstitch Sections 1, 2 and 3 together and Sections 4 and 5 together along dotted lines. Then stitch Sections 3 and 4 together at X and Y (Z is open). With A work 1 rnd sc evenly around entire piece, working 3 sc in corners. Break off.

To wear, slip end of Section 1 through Z.

Bandoliers Vest

Crocheted in two pieces, each with a pocket.

SIZE: Adjustable to fit sizes 8 to 18.

MATERIALS: Bear Brand Win-Knit (knitting-worsted-weight yarn), 2 (4-oz.) skeins each green No. 481 and magenta No. 425; aluminum crochet hook size H for sizes 8—10, I for sizes 12—14 or J for sizes 16—18 (or international sizes 5:00 mm, 5:50 mm or 6:00 mm) **or the size that will give you the correct gauge.**

GAUGE: Size H hook: 3½ st = 1"; size I hook: 3 st = 1"; size J hook: 2½ st = 1".

FIRST BANDOLIER: Starting at 1 end (shoulder) with green, ch 11. **1st row:** Dc in 3rd ch from hook, h dc in next 7 ch, sc in last ch; ch 1, turn. **2nd row:** Sc in sc, h dc in each h dc, dc in dc; ch 1, turn. **3rd row:** Work 1 sc, h dc in each h dc, work 1 dc; ch 2, turn. **4th row:** Work 1 dc, h dc in each st to last st, work 1 sc; ch 1, turn. **5th row:** Repeat 3rd row. **6th row:** Repeat 4th row. **7th row:** Work 1 sc, h dc in each h dc, 2 dc in last dc; ch 2, turn. **8th through 12th row:** Repeat 4th and 3rd rows twice, then 4th row once again. **13th row:** Repeat 7th row. Repeat 8th through 13th rows 4 times more (15 st).

38th row: Dc in each dc, h dc in each h dc to last 3 st, work 3 sc; ch 1, turn. **39th row:** Sc in each sc, h dc in each h dc, dc in each dc; ch 2, turn. **40th row:** Dc in each dc, h dc in each h dc, sc in each sc; ch 1, turn. **41th row:** Sc in each sc, h dc in each h dc, dc in each dc to last dc, 2 dc in last dc; ch 2, turn. **42nd through 49th row:** Repeat 38th through 41st rows twice (18 st).

50th row: Dc in each dc, h dc in each h dc to last 5 st, work 5 sc; ch 1, turn. **51st row:** Sc in each sc, h dc in each h dc, dc in each dc, working 2 dc in last dc; ch 2, turn. **52nd through 55th row:** Repeat 50th and 51st rows twice (21 st).

56th row: Dc in each dc, h dc in each h dc to last 7 st, work 7 sc; ch 1, turn. **57th row:** Repeat 39th row. **58th through 61st row:** Repeat 56th and 57th rows twice. At end of last row do not ch 1; turn. **62nd row:** Sl st in 1st dc, ch 1, dc in each remaining dc, h dc in each h dc and in 1st 2 sc, work 5 sc (20 st); ch 1, turn.

63rd row: Sc in each sc, h dc in each h dc, dc in each dc; turn. **64th row:** Sl st in 1st dc, ch 1, dc in each remaining dc, h dc in each h dc, sc in each sc (19st); ch 1, turn. **65th and 66th rows:** Repeat 63rd and 64th rows (18 st).

67th row: Work 3 sc, h dc remaining 2 sc and in each h dc, dc in each dc; ch 2, turn. **68th row:** Repeat 40th row. **69th through 73rd row:** Repeat 63rd and 64th rows twice, then repeat 63rd row once more (16 st). **74th row:** Sl st in 1st dc, ch 1, dc in next st, h dc in each h dc and in 1st 2 sc, sc in last sc (15 st); ch 1, turn. **75th through 79th row:** Repeat 3rd and 4th rows twice, then repeat 3rd row once more. **80th through 120th row:** Repeat 74th through 79th row 6 times more, then repeat 74th through 78th row once more (8 st).

121st and 122nd rows: Work 1 dc, h dc in each h dc to last st, work 1 sc; ch 2, turn. **123rd row:** H dc in each st across; ch 1, turn. **124th row:** Y o, insert hook in 1st st, y o and draw lp through, y o and draw up lp in next st, y o and draw through all lps on hook (1 st dec), h dc to last 2 st, dec 1 st (6 st); ch 1, turn. **125th and 126th rows:** Repeat 123rd and 124th rows (4 st).

Edging: Work 2 rnds sc with green and 1 rnd sc with magenta around entire piece, keeping edges flat and working 3 sc in each corner; join and break off.

Lap last rows (narrow end) over 1st rows so that piece fits when worn looped over one shoulder and under opposite arm. Sew flap along this line.

Pocket: Starting at bottom with green, ch 11. **1st row:** Work 2 h dc in 2nd ch from hook, h dc in next 8 ch, 2 h dc in last ch; ch 1, turn. **2nd row:** 2 h dc in 1st h dc, h dc across row, working 2 h dc in last h dc (14 h dc); ch 1, turn. Work 7 rows h dc, 2 rows sc. Break off. With magenta, work 1 row sc. Break off. Sew pocket to widest part of bandolier slightly on diagonal as shown in photograph.

SECOND BANDOLIER: Work as for 1st bandolier, reversing colors. Loop over opposite shoulder as shown so that pieces crisscross.

Toddler's Corduroy Pinafore

Made in two pieces for easy on and off.

SIZE: 2 to 4.

MATERIALS: ⅔ yard 36″-wide print corduroy; 3 yards cotton seam binding; matching threads.

Enlarge diagram (see To Enlarge Patterns, page 30), and cut paper pattern for pinafore. Cut four pieces, adding ½″ seam allowance all around. With right sides facing, pin 2 pairs of pinafore pieces together; stitch seams indicated on pattern. Press seams open. To bind raw edges, with edges matching, pin wrong side of corduroy edge to right side of cotton seam binding; stitch. Trim corduroy seam. Fold and press to right side so that binding edges corduroy; topstitch.

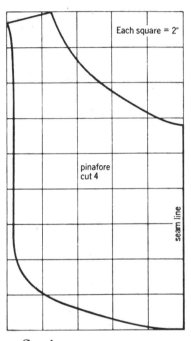

Each square = 2″

pinafore cut 4

seam line

Picnic Place Settings

Each packs a napkin, holds cutlery in a special pocket.

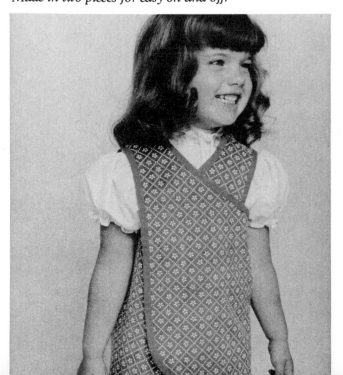

SIZE: Each place mat measures 11″ x 15½″.

MATERIALS: For Each Place Mat: ⅜ yard 45″-wide quilted fabric (we used Mariello's cotton/polyester/nylon tricot bandanna-print fabric); 4½″ x 7″ piece contrasting quilted fabric for cutlery pocket; 1½ yards 1½″-wide matching grosgrain ribbon; purchased napkins; matching sewing threads.

From quilted fabric cut 2 mat pieces measuring 12″ x 16½″.

Fold one edge (top) of cutlery pocket rectangle under 1″; fold other edges under ½″ and press. Place pocket on 1 mat piece so that top edge of pocket is 5″ from top edge and 2½″ from left edge of mat. Topstitch in place close to fold, leaving top edge open.

Pin mat pieces together with right sides facing. Fold ribbon length in half and place between mat pieces with folded end at raw edge of mat near top of pocket. Catching folded end of ribbon in stitching, stitch mat pieces together, using ½″ seam and leaving 5″ open along one edge for turning. Turn right side out. Fold raw edges under and blindstitch opening closed. Clip ends of ribbon as in photograph.

Pincushion Whatnot Holders

Safekeeping for all kinds of oddments.

MATERIALS: Plastic or glass jar with screw-on lid; square of cotton fabric at least 2″ larger than lid diameter; assorted pieces of trim such as ribbon, lace, rickrack, etc.; cardboard; small amount Dacron polyester or absorbent cotton for stuffing; heavy thread; glue.

To Make Dome: Cut fabric circle 2″ larger than lid diameter. Work running stitch around circle ⅜″ from edge. Pull threads to gather the fabric, then stuff to form dome shape. Cut cardboard circle same size as lid and slide into bottom of pincushion dome. Tighten and knot threads to prevent cardboard from slipping.

Glue pincushion to top of lid and hold in place with rubber bands until dry.

Cut trims into strips ½″ longer than lid circumference. Glue trim in place (see photograph), overlapping ends and covering edge of fabric pincushion.

Gingerbread Hanging and Pillows

A boy, a girl, a candy-sweet house; appliqué and embroidery.

SIZE OF HANGING: 24″ x 30″.

MATERIALS: 36″-wide cotton fabrics, 1¼ yds. rust-brown, ¾ yd. blue-and-white gingham, ½ yd. caramel-brown; scraps of peach, dusty-pink, rust, light-blue, light-green and white cotton; ½ yd. thin, iron-on, nonwoven interfacing; 1 skein each yellow, green and natural 6-strand embroidery floss; white sewing thread for appliqué; black felt-tipped marker; dressmaker's carbon paper.

From rust-brown fabric cut 25″ x 31″ lining, two 3″ x 23″ top and bottom borders, two 2″ x 31″ side borders and four 5″ x 6″ tabs. From gingham cut 23″ x 27″ background.

Enlarge pattern, (See To Enlarge Patterns, page 30). With felt-tipped marker outline directly on pattern the following: caramel-brown house in 1 piece, roof but not tiles (they will be indicated with stitching later), white scalloped "icing" around house, brown scalloped trim on gable, strip of brown trim below gable window, brown door in 1 piece, brown

shutters and brown step unit under house in 1 piece. Also outline 1 each: heart, lollipop circle, candy cane, flower (2 sizes), leaf and star.

Place interfacing on top of pattern, adhesive side up, and trace all heavily outlined shapes (they will show through the interfacing). Repeat all identical shapes as many times as necessary (5 candy canes, etc.). Cut out pieces roughly and laminate them by ironing them onto *wrong side* of fabrics (see photograph for colors). Cut out laminated fabric pieces carefully without seam allowance.

Using dressmaker's carbon paper, transfer all remaining details marked on pattern to house, roof and steps.

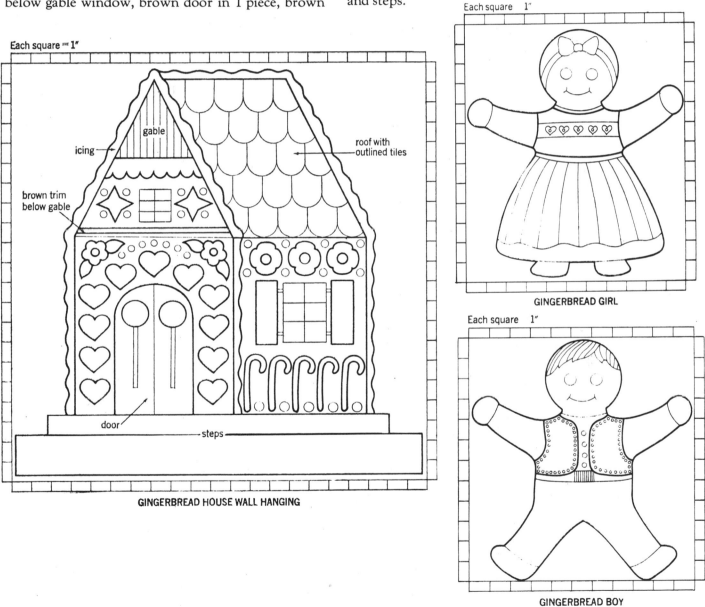

GINGERBREAD GIRL

GINGERBREAD HOUSE WALL HANGING

GINGERBREAD BOY

Baste all appliqué pieces except icing and steps to house. Using zigzag stitch, appliqué pieces in place. (**Note:** If you don't have a zigzag attachment on your sewing machine, you can simulate the effect with narrow rows of satin stitch worked by hand.) Following Stitch Diagrams, page 30, and photograph for color and using 3 strands floss, embroider small circles on house in satin stitch and outline circles on gable in chain stitch.

Placing steps 2½″ up from lower edge of gingham, baste steps, house, roof, and icing to gingham background. Zigzag-stitch along all transferred details and over all remaining raw edges.

Making ½″ seams, stitch top and bottom borders to gingham, then stitch side borders in place. Fold tabs in half lengthwise wrong side out. Seam long edge and turn. Pin tabs on right side of hanging along top edge with raw edges matching. With right sides facing, stitch lining to hanging (tabs are sandwiched between), leaving 8″ open at lower edge for turning. Turn; close opening.

GINGERBREAD-BOY AND -GIRL PILLOWS

SIZE: 14″ square without ruffle.

MATERIALS: For 2 pillows: 36″-wide cotton fabrics, 1 yd. blue-and-white gingham, ⅜ yd. caramel-brown; scraps of rust-brown cotton; ½ yd. 45″-wide blue-and-white polka-dot cotton for ruffles; 6-strand embroidery floss, 4 skeins natural, 1 skein pink; crewel embroidery needle; 1 yd. 36″-wide muslin for pillow lining; Dacron polyester for stuffing; two 9″ or 12″ zippers (optional).

Enlarge patterns, (see To Enlarge Patterns, page 30). Following heavy lines, cut out patterns, cutting complete outline of each doll, 2 vest pieces, 1 bodice and 1 turban (light lines are embroidery indications). Trace patterns lightly onto right side of fabrics (see photograph for fabric colors), leaving at least 1½″ space between shapes. Cut out, adding ¼″ seam allowance to all edges. Turn under seams, clipping curves; press.

Appliqué vest, bodice and turban to dolls. Following patterns, lightly indicate embroidery details with pencil (transfer with dressmaker's carbon paper if desired). For embroidery use all 6 strands floss unless otherwise specified (see photograph for colors). Following Stitch Diagrams, page 30, work as follows: **Gingerbread Girl:** Work hearts on bodice and lines around neck in chain stitch and lines above and below

hearts in running stitch with 3 strands floss. Work a French knot at each dot. Work satin-stitch eyes and outline-stitch mouth with 3 strands. Work lower edge of bodice, apron lines and skirt lines over feet in outline stitch; turban, armhole, top edge of apron and wrist lines in chain stitch. **Gingerbread Boy:** Work dots on vest in French knots. Outline vest and belt in chain stitch with 3 strands floss. Work satin-stitch buckle, eyes and buttons. Work hair and mouth and vertical stitches on belt in outline stitch with 3 strands. Work wrist lines in outline stitch, ankle and neck lines in chain stitch.

FINISHING: For each pillow cut 2 gingham pieces 15″ square. Baste, then appliqué a doll to center of a square. With 3 strands floss outline doll in chain stitch.

To Make Pillows: For each pillow cut 2 muslin pieces 15″ square. Stitch together, leaving 8″ opening. Turn and stuff softly. Close opening. Cut two 5″ x 45″ strips polka-dot fabric and stitch ends together to form ring. Fold strip in half, right side out, to form 2½″-wide ring. Gather raw edges to fit around pillow. With raw edges matching, pin to right side of gingham pillow top. With right sides facing, stitch 2nd gingham square to pillow top (ruffle is sandwiched between), leaving 1 side open; turn. Insert zipper if desired. Insert pillow and close opening.

"Family Hands" Appliquéd Apron

Gay cotton imprints of favorite hands.

MATERIALS: 1 yard 45"-wide cotton broadcloth; small amounts assorted cotton prints.

For apron, cut 22" x 27½" rectangle from broadcloth. Cut 4"-wide strips for waistband and ties, piecing them to measure 72".

Make ½" finished hem along each 22" side of apron. Gather waist edge to measure about 21". Fold under ½" across long edges of waistband-tie strip and press. Fold in half length-wise. Insert ½" seam allowance of gathered waist edge between folded edges of band, centering apron. Pin in place. Cut tie ends diagonally and turn in edges.

Topstitch across band and ties, joining band to apron. Hem apron.

Trace seven different hands on paper. Using tracings as patterns, cut hands from assorted cotton prints (do not add seams). Following photograph for placement and using zigzag stitch, appliqué hands to apron.

Mother Pig and Piglets Toy

Mama's tummy holds up to five beanbag babies.

MATERIALS: ½ yard 54"-wide vinyl; small amounts of cotton batting or nylon stockings cut in strips for stuffing; five scrap lengths of assorted colors and widths of rickrack trim; 7" skirt zipper; felt scraps to trim pigs; 16" x 16" piece of felt or cotton-print fabric for each piglet; dry beans or rice; matching thread.

MOTHER PIG: See To Enlarge Patterns, page 30, and enlarge patterns for body, handle, tail, ears

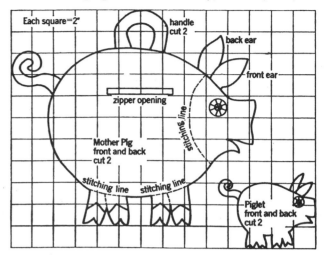

and hooves. Using patterns, cut body and handle from vinyl, adding ½" seam allowance to ends of handle pieces only. Cut one each front and back ears, two tail pieces and four hooves from scrap felt, adding seam allowance to end of ears and tail to be inserted into body. Referring to body patterns, cut opening for zipper and insert, following manufacturer's directions. Topstitch rickrack to body as in photograph. Topstitch felt hooves to feet. For eye cut two felt circles as in pattern and, using an overcast stitch, attach as shown. With right sides out, topstitch tail and handle pieces, leaving lower edge open. Stuff both loosely. Following photograph for placement, pin tail, handle and ears to wrong side of pig front. Matching raw edges, topstitch pig back and front together with tail, handle and ears sandwiched between. Leave opening by legs and head; stuff legs and head within stitching lines as indicated. Close openings and topstitch lines for head and legs.

PIGLETS: Enlarge pattern for piglet on brown wrapping paper. Cut two body pieces and one tail piece from felt for each piglet and do not add seam allowance. If making fabric piglets, allow ½" for seams all around and cut one felt tail piece. For all piglets, following pattern, cut two pieces of felt for eye and attach as described for mother pig. For felt piglets, matching edges, insert felt tail as in photograph and topstitch all around, leaving 2″ opening for filling. For fabric piglets pin body with right sides together; stitch, leaving opening to turn at tail area. Turn, fill piglets with beans or rice. Insert tail and close opening.

Hearts-and-Flowers Necklaces

Tiny-print fabrics puffed into heart shapes.

SIZE: Heart measures 2¾″ wide.

MATERIALS: For each necklace: Scrap of floral-print cotton fabric; one yard matching rattail cord; small amount Dacron polyester for stuffing.

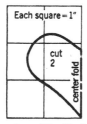

Enlarge pattern (see To Enlarge Patterns, page 30), adding ¼″ seam allowance all around. Cut 2 pieces from fabric.

LOOP: From fabric cut a ½″ x 1¾″ strip. Fold in half lengthwise wrong side out and stitch together up on circle; slide carbon paper between tracing and with ⅛″ seam. Turn; fold in half crosswise and press.

With right sides facing, pin heart-shaped pieces together. Insert loop at top center of heart between pieces so that raw edges match. Stitch together, leaving 1″ opening. Turn, stuff and blindstitch opening closed.

Thread rattail through loop, knotting ends to prevent raveling.

Satin Evening Pouch

A lace-edged oval with dainty tassel.

SIZE: About 7″ deep, without lace.

MATERIALS: ¼ yd. each quilted satin and lining fabric; 1 yd. 1¼″-wide lace, 2 yds. woven cord for strap; tassel.

CUTTING: From satin cut two 8½″ squares. Repeat with lining. Cut 2 rounded corners on all 4 pieces for bottom of bag.

ASSEMBLING: Hold quilted pieces together with right sides facing; place pin at each side edge 2″ below top. Making ½″ seam, stitch pieces together from 1 pin, along side, around shaped bottom, along other side to 2nd pin (2″ flaps at top of bag will form casings). Turn right side out. Repeat with lining pieces, but don't turn. Insert lining in bag. Turn in seam allowance at side ends of top flaps; topstitch seams separately.

Fold flaps over ¼″, then fold again 1″; topstitch to form casings.

Gather 1 long edge of lace to fit around bag seam; blindstitch to bag.

Cut cord in half. Run 1 piece through both casings and sew ends together. Hide joining in a casing. Starting at opposite edge of bag, run other cord through both casings and sew ends. Pull cord loops at each side to close bag. Sew tassel to bottom of bag.

Long Scarf and Matching Cap

It's a glorious 82", the cap a seamed triangle.

SIZE: Scarf measures about 19" x 82" without fringe. Cap will fit all.

MATERIALS: Spinnerin Germantown Deluxe (Orlon acrylic knitting-worsted-weight yarn), 3 (4-ounce) skeins turquoise No. 3216 (color T), 1 skein each hunter green No. 3222 (G), cherry No. 3262 (C), bronze No. 3207 (B), aqua No. 3214 (A), burnt orange No. 3256 (O) and purple No. 3235 (P) (if using leftover yarns, 1 ounce of each color except turquoise is sufficient); knitting needles, 1 pair each No. 5 and No. 8 (or English needles No. 8 and No. 5) **or the sizes that will give you the correct gauge;** tapestry needle.

GAUGE: Cap: 4 sts = 1"; 8 rows = 1". **Scarf:** 5 sts = 2"; 4 rows = 1".

CAP: Cap is worked in vertical rows of garter stitch throughout. Starting at seam edge with No. 5 needles and T, cast on 34 sts. K 12 rows. Drop T but do not break off. With A k 2 rows. Break off A; pick up T. K 14 rows T, 2 B, 14 T, 2 C, 14 T, 2 P, 14 T, 2 G, 14 T, 2 O, 14 T, 2 A, 14 T, 2 C, 2 T. Bind off.

FINISHING: Sew ends together to form tube, then weave yarn through sts at one end of tube and draw up tightly for crown. Break off.

SCARF: Starting at one end with No. 8 needles and T, cast on 50 sts. **1st row (right side):** * Insert right needle into st as if to k, y o twice and draw through st, letting st drop from left needle. Repeat from * across (100 lps on needle). **2nd row:** * To work each st, k in first lp of st, letting 2nd lp drop from left needle. Repeat from * across (50 lps on needle). Repeating last 2 rows for pattern, work 4 rows more with T. Break off T. **1st Color Band:** With B work in pattern for 2 rows, then work 2 rows A, 2 G, 8 P, 6 C, 4 O, 4 C, 2 G, 4 A, 2 G and 2 B. With T work in pattern for 28", ending with a wrong-side row. **Center color band:** Work 6 rows O, 6 P, 2 G, 2 C, 6 P and 6 O. With T work in pattern for 28", ending with a wrong-side row. **Last color band:** Work 2 rows B, 2 G, 4 A, 2 G, 4 C, 4 O, 6 C, 8 P, 2 G, 2 A, 2 B, and 6 T. Bind off.

FRINGE: Work 19 T tassels 1" apart along each short edge as follows: Cut four 12" strands T. Holding strands together, fold in half. Draw folded end through a st and draw ends through fold. Pull tight.

"Stop" and "Go" Mittens

Playful warmers for young traffic directors.

SIZE: 4- to 6-year-old child.

MATERIALS: 4-ply sports yarn, 2 ounces each red and green, small amounts white for letters; dp knitting needles, 1 set (4) No. 5 (or English needles No. 8) **or the size that will give you the correct gauge;** tapestry needle.

GAUGE: 6 sts = 1"; 15 rounds = 2".

RIGHT MITTEN: Starting at cuff with green, cast on 36 sts, placing 18 on first needle and 9 each on 2nd and 3rd needles. Join into ring and work in ribbing of k 2, p 2 for 2¼". K around even until piece measures 3½" from beg. **Next rnd:** With a strip of contrasting-color yarn, k first 7 sts; transfer the 7 sts just worked back onto left-hand needle and k them again with green yarn (yarn strip will be removed later to form thumb opening); k to complete rnd. K even until mitten measures 7" from beg, or 1" less than desired length.

To Shape Tip: 1st rnd: K 1, sl 1, k 1, psso, k to last 3 sts on first needle, k 2 tog, k 1; k 1, sl 1, k 1, psso, k to end of 2nd needle; k to last 3 sts of 3rd needle, k 2 tog, k 1. **2nd rnd:** K around. Repeat last 2 rnds 3 times more (20 sts). Break off, leaving 8" end. Place sts from 2nd and 3rd needles onto one needle and weave together with sts from first needle (see Kitchener stitch, below).

KITCHENER STITCH: Divide remaining stitches equally on 2 needles. Break off yarn, leaving a 15" end. Thread in tapestry needle and work as follows: Hold 2 knitting needles even and parallel, with end of yarn coming from right end of back needle. * Draw tapestry needle through first stitch of front knitting needle as if to knit and slip stitch off; draw needle through second stitch as if to purl but leave stitch on knitting needle; draw needle through first stitch of back needle as if to purl and slip stitch off; draw needle through second stitch of back needle as if to knit, leaving stitch on knitting needle. Repeat from * until all stitches are joined. Break off.

Thumb: Carefully remove strand of contrasting yarn from thumb sts and divide the 14 sts (around both edges of opening) onto 3 needles. Attach green and k around until thumb measures 2", or ¼" less than desired length. **To Shape Tip:** K 2 tog around (7 sts). Break off, leaving 6" end. Draw yarn through sts, pull up and fasten on wrong side.

LEFT MITTEN: With red, work as for right mitten to thumb opening. **Next rnd:** K to last 7 sts on first needle, k next 7 sts with contrasting yarn; transfer the 7 sts just worked back onto left-hand needle and k them again with red yarn; k to complete rnd.

Finish as for right mitten.

TO DECORATE: Place a pin as marker, ¾" down from ribbing on back of green mitten. Following "Go" chart and using duplicate stitch diagram, work letters with white yarn and tapestry needle. Start the

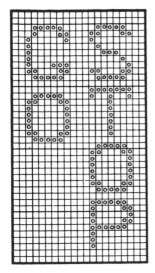

Duplicate stitch

word "STOP" directly below ribbing on back of red mitten.

Mini Floral Rounds

To decorate a wall, a dresser or a pretty neck.

SIZES: 2½" and 3½" diameter.
MATERIALS: Small pieces linenlike fabric; assorted colors 6-strand embroidery floss; embroidery needle; 2½" and 3½" macramé rings; ribbon, scraps of felt for backing; dressmaker's carbon paper.

Trace around ring on fabric. Add ¾" all around for seam allowance. Choose a full-size bouquet pattern and trace on tracing paper. Place tracing right side up on circle; slide carbon paper between tracing and circle. Mark over design with semisharp stylus such as knitting needle or dried-out ballpoint pen.

Cut out circle. Wrap and baste circle over ring. Blanket-stitch over rim (see Stitch Diagrams, page 30). Following photograph for colors and key for stitches, embroider with 1, 2 or 3 strands floss, depending upon the effect you want. Trace around ring on felt. Cut out felt circle and glue to back of ring. Trim with ribbon.

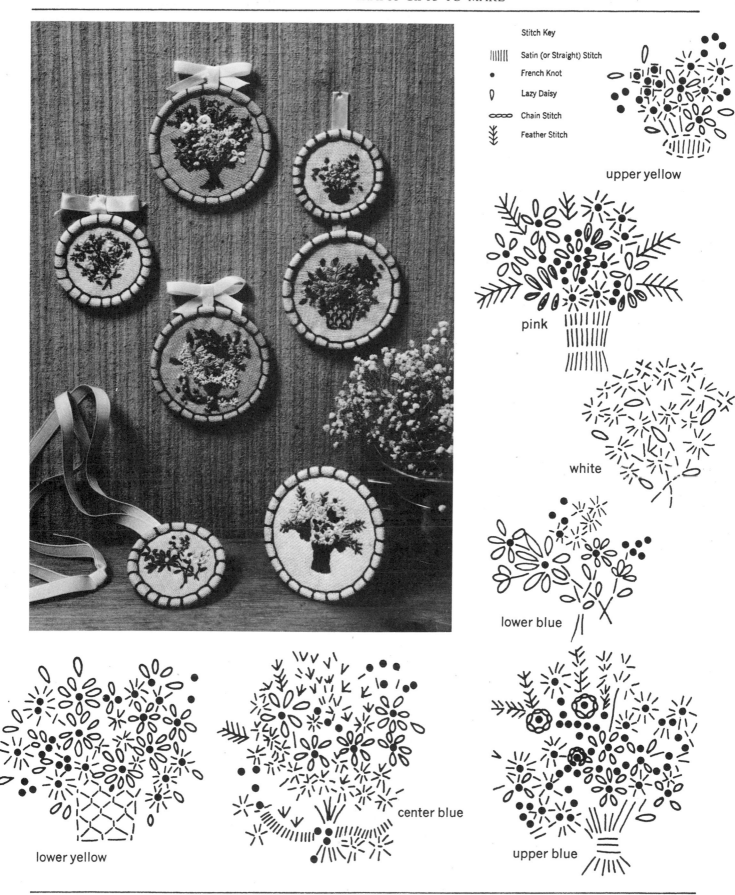

Stitch Key

|||||| Satin (or Straight) Stitch

• French Knot

◊ Lazy Daisy

∞∞∞ Chain Stitch

⅄ Feather Stitch

upper yellow

pink

white

lower blue

lower yellow

center blue

upper blue

Tennis Tie

A bought tie embroidered with rackets and balls.

MATERIALS: Purchased tie; 6-strand embroidery floss, 1 skein each red (R) and white (W); embroidery needle; dressmaker's carbon.

Enlarge pattern, (see To Enlarge Patterns, page 30). Using dressmarker's carbon, transfer pattern to tie (see photograph for placement).

Using 3 strands of the 6-strand floss and working satin stitch (see Stitch Diagrams, page 30), embroider

Each square=1"

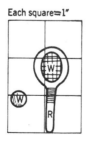

tie. **Note:** The lines on pattern show direction in which to work stitches. For tennis racket work strings as follows: Work 7 vertical straight stitches spaced evenly across. Work 7 horizontal straight stitches spaced evenly across, weaving under and over vertical stitches.

Big Bargello Eyeglass Case

Charming countryside scene; extra-wide size.

SIZE: About 4¼" x 7¼".

MATERIALS: 5¼" x 8¼" piece mono (single-mesh) needlepoint canvas with 12 meshes per inch; 3-ply Persian-type needlepoint and crewel yarn, 10 yards sky blue (color S), 5 yards each aqua (A), royal blue (B), light green (C), medium green (G), white (W) and yellow-gold (Y); small amounts each lavender (L), orange (O), bright pink (P), red (R), and brown (T), 6" x 17" piece red lining fabric; 6" x 9" piece blue velveteen backing; ¾ yard red piping; tapestry needle.

TO PREPARE CANVAS: Fold masking tape over edges to prevent raveling.

With pencil or marker made especially for needlepoint, copy outline of case on canvas (each square on chart equals 1 space on canvas). Follow chart for color placement and sample stitches on chart for stitch direction and length (for sky, work stitches at various lengths as shown). Use all 3 strands of the 3-ply yarn and make sure that the end of 1 st occupies the same space as the end of the st directly above it to completely cover canvas (see sample stitches on chart).

FINISHING: Block canvas, if necessary. With raw edges facing outward, sew piping to right side of canvas around edges of needlepoint. Trim canvas to ½" seam allowance. Cut 2 lining pieces and backing piece to size of canvas. With right sides facing and piping sandwiched between, sew backing piece to needlepoint between dots on chart, stitching in direction of arrows. Trim seams, clip curves and turn.

Sew lining pieces together in same manner; turn. Insert lining in case, fold in all raw edges and blind-stitch around open edges of case.

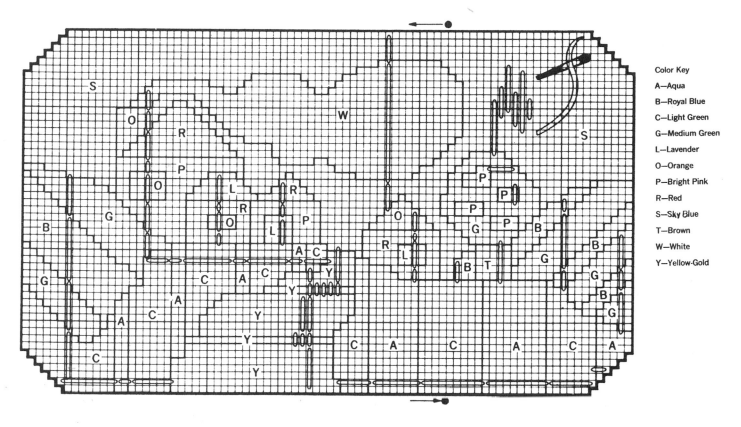

Color Key

A—Aqua
B—Royal Blue
C—Light Green
G—Medium Green
L—Lavender
O—Orange
P—Bright Pink
R—Red
S—Sky Blue
T—Brown
W—White
Y—Yellow-Gold

Early American Planter

Pine, with its own "fence" to set off a plant.

MATERIALS: 1½′ of ½ x 10 clear pine stock; 3′ of ¼″-diameter dowel; white wood glue; ¾″ brads or wire nails; pine stain; clear satin-finish polyurethane.

See To Enlarge Patterns, page 30, and enlarge

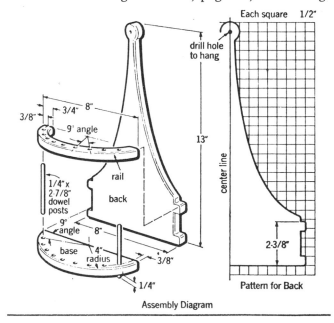

Each square   1/2″

drill hole to hang

13″

center line

2·3/8″

Pattern for Back

3/4″   8″

3/8″

9° angle

1/4″ x 2·7/8″ dowel posts

rail

back

9° angle   8″

base   4″ radius

3/8″

1/4″

Assembly Diagram

pattern for shaped back on brown wrapping paper. Transfer pattern for back on pine piece; cut out. Drill hole at top to hang as indicated. Cut two 5" x 9" pine pieces and temporarily nail together. Mark and cut two 8"-diameter semicircles for base and rail as in the Assembly Diagram. Mark and drill nine equally spaced ¼" holes for dowel posts in both semicircular pieces. Separate pieces, round edges and mark inner edge of rail; cut out. Cut nine 3" dowel posts and round both ends as shown.

Round other edges of all pieces as shown and sand smooth. Attach base and rail to back with glue and brads. Glue posts in place. To finish, apply pine stain, wiping away excess. When dry, apply two coats of polyurethane; let dry.

Key Rack Organizer

Other simple shapes can substitute for car, house or boat.

SIZE: 24¼" long.
MATERIALS: 12" x 18" piece ¼" hardboard; 2' of ¼" x 1⅛" pine lattice; white glue; 4 screw-in-type cup hooks; pigmented-shellac primer; high-gloss red, dark-blue and yellow enamel; white semigloss enamel; hanger plate.

Enlarge patterns for 2 cars, house and boat (see To Enlarge Patterns, page 30) on brown wrapping

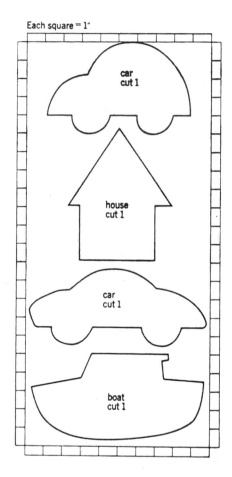

Each square = 1"

car
cut 1

house
cut 1

car
cut 1

boat
cut 1

paper; cut out. Using patterns, cut car, house and boat shapes from ¼" hardboard. Sand all cut edges smooth. Apply primer to 2' length of lattice and all hardboard shapes; let dry. Paint lattice white, boat and one car blue, one car red, house yellow; let dry.

Assemble four shapes centered and equally spaced down 2' lattice; glue in place. When dry, turn a cup hook centered through each shape and into lattice. File end of cup-hook screw flush to back of lattice.

Hang rack with hanger plate.

Fabric-covered Message Boards

Complete with pinch clips and note pads.

SIZE: 6½″ x 7¼″.

MATERIALS: Scrap 1 x 8 pine stock or ¾″ plywood; scrap of heavy-textured cotton, duck or canvas; white glue; scrap of leather; ½″ brads; ½″ picture hook; 1″ pinch clip; ⅞″ decorative hanger; 3″ x 5″ note pad.

Cut pine or plywood to 6½″ x 7¼″; sand all cut edges smooth. Cut fabric to cover message board, using pinking shears and allowing 2″ all around. Brush glue on one side of board, then center and press onto wrong side of fabric. Brush glue on side edges and onto back; pull and wrap excess fabric to back. Smooth any wrinkles. Pull up top and bottom edges and cut away excess fabric so that corners lie flat. Brush on glue and wrap top and bottom edges with fabric.

Cut a ¼″ x 3½″ leather strip and position ¾″ down from top and ½″ in from one side. Tack strip in place with brads. Slip cardboard backing of note pad over strip. Nail picture hook into other half of board as in photograph and hook pinch clip on it. Turn decorative hanger into center of top edge of board.

Decorated Frames

Plain bought frames transformed with bright paint and fabrics.

SIZES: Red Wood: 8¾″ x 10½″, Green Calico: 8″ x 10″ and Blue Calico: 9″ x 11″.

MATERIALS: For Red Wood: 8¾″ x 10½″ frame with glass; high-gloss red enamel; turpentine; 12″ x 12″ piece red plaid lightweight wool fabric; 1 yd. black jumbo rickrack. **For Green Calico:** 8″ x 10″ frame without glass; 12″ x 24″ piece green calico cotton fabric; 1 yd. ½″-wide woven trim. **For Blue Calico:** 9″ x 11″ frame with glass; 8″ x 10″ piece mirror-glass; 9″ x 11″ piece blue and white cotton gingham; 12″ x 12″ piece blue and white calico cotton fabric; 1 yd. 1″-wide eyelet trim; matching thread; small amount of Dacron polyester batting. **For all frames:** 3-ply Bristol board; spray adhesive; screw eyes; picture wire.

RED WOOD FRAME

Remove glass and backing from picture frame. **To finish frame:** Thin a small amount of enamel 50 percent with turpentine. Brush mixture on frame to prime it; let dry. Apply full strength enamel; let dry.

To cover mat: Using ruler, pencil and mat knife, mark and cut mat for your picture from Bristol board. Cut four strips of plaid fabric wide enough to cover and wrap around sides of mat. Apply spray adhesive to mat, following manufacturer's directions. Cover two opposite sides of mat first, centering fabric strips and pressing them in place. Slit fabric at inside corners, wrap around to back and glue down. Trim away any excess. Cover remaining two sides of mat, folding under ends of each strip to form mitered corners. (You will have to spray a little adhesive on fabric where corners overlap.) Repeat procedure for finishing edges. Glue rickrack strips to back of mat to decorate edge as in photograph.

Assemble frame with glass, mat, picture and backing; hold in place with glazier tips or small escutcheon pins. Add screw eyes and picture wire to hang.

GREEN CALICO FRAME

Remove backing from picture frame. **To cover frame:** Cut strips of calico fabric sufficient to cover and wrap around each side of frame. Use adhesive to attach centered strips on two opposite sides; press in place. Slit inside corners, than wrap fabric around inside edges and glue. Slit fabric at outside corners, wrap fabric around back and glue. Cover remaining two sides, folding ends under to form mitered corners, then repeat procedure for finishing edges. **To make and cover mat:** Mark and cut Bristol board mat as described for red wood frame. Then cut a rectangle of remaining fabric somewhat wider and longer than mat (for overlap). Spray mat with adhesive, center fabric on mat and press in place. Cut out center, leaving some overlap to wrap around back. Slit fabric at inside corners, then wrap fabric to back and glue. Cut woven trim strips to decorate mat, glue to mat as in photograph, folding under ends of top and bottom strips to form miter.

Assemble frame and add hanger as described for red wood frame.

BLUE CALICO FRAME

Remove glass and backing from picture frame. **To make padded frame:** Cut two strips of batting for each frame side. Using spray adhesive tack double layers of batting to frame. Cut calico fabric strips to cover and wrap around sides of frame. Cover two opposite sides first by wrapping fabric lightly around frame. Slit inside corners and glue fabric along inside and outside edges. Repeat to cover remaining two sides, first folding under fabric ends to form mitered corners, then sewing in place.

To make and cover mat: Mark and cut Bristol board mat as described for the red wood frame. Then cover mat with gingham as described for the green calico frame, above. Finish inside edge of mat with eyelet as in photograph.

Assemble frame and add hanger as described for red wood frame.

GIFTS FROM YOUR KITCHEN

To share food is one of the oldest acts of love known to us, a gesture so simple and familiar and yet so profound in its intention to nourish and sustain the lives of others. Some of the fondest memories of Christmas for us all are created in the kitchen and around the table: the shining eyes of children passing cookies they've made themselves, the bubbling appreciation of your family and guests as the noble Christmas roast and trimmings are laid on, the expectant smiles when the special candies and cakes are revealed, the surprised "How nice!" of a friend or neighbor when you deliver a carefully prepared and wrapped homemade treat. Gifts from your kitchen can be an answer to many of the question marks on your Christmas list. They're appropriate for all ages and sizes and both genders! Moreover, they bring distinct human satisfactions both to you and the recipient—the wonderful sensory pleasures of tasting, of touching, of sniffing the sweet and savory aromas.

Inexpensive Packaging and Wrapping

A welcome aspect of giving food gifts is that you can use simple, low-cost (sometimes free) packaging and wrapping. Ideas for containers that you may already have on hand or can save up:

• Coffee or shortening can covered with attractive self-stick vinyl, heavy-duty foil, leftover wallpaper, felt or other fabric. Makes a sturdy mailer for steamed puddings, breads, cookies, candy or nuts. If desired, top the lid with a colorful big bow.

• Plastic basket (from berries or cherry tomatoes) lined with colorful paper napkin or doily. Or weave ribbon around basket. Great for cookies, candy or nuts.

• Egg carton with each compartment cushioned with colorful tissue paper or paper grass. If lid has printing, cover with self-stick vinyl or gift wrap. Tie with ribbon. Good for pieces of fudge or other candy wrapped individually in plastic wrap. Also a good mailer.

• Glass jar from instant coffee, fruits, jams, pickles and nuts. If there's printing on lid, cover with a bow or self-stick vinyl cut to fit. If desired, attach label.

• Apothecary-type jar from vitamins or spices. Good for seasoning and beverage mixes, your own spice or herb blends.

• Plastic container from delicatessen, margarine or soft cheeses. Top with bow and attach label.

• Long plastic basket (from tomatoes). Line with paper napkin or overlapping small doilies. Great for cookies, lined up on edge.

• Plastic bags—super for seasoned popcorn, nuts, beverage or seasoning mixes. Secure with colorful ribbon and, if desired, place in colorful miniature shopping bag.

• Small foil pan—especially good for gifts that need molding, baking or refrigerating, such as brownies and other bar cookies, fudge, pâtés. Cover with plastic wrap; top with bow and label.

• Sturdy cardboard (cut to fit) covered with foil makes good carrier-server for breads, cakes and coffee cakes. Wrap all in plastic wrap, gather ends and tie with ribbon or heavy yarn.

• Canning jar, especially one of the fancier type with designs and decorated lids—good for jams, relishes, marmalades, sauces, nuts and beverage mixes.

Other packages you may have around the house or can pick up inexpensively at a variety store are: small plastic or decorated metal boxes, breadboards or large square tiles, assorted baskets, plastic or clay flowerpots (lined with napkins), interesting glass jars, small trays, muffin pans, mugs, custard cups, small bowls, plastic glasses, crocks, holiday-decorated paper plates, dishes and sturdy gift boxes. When there is no lid or cover, wrap in clear plastic so you can see contents yet keep food fresh or crisp.

If you have any scraps of gay calico or printed cotton fabric, cut strips for ribbon with pinking shears. Use fabric also for wrapping—makes a lovely, personalized, coordinated wrap for bread, coffee cake or steamed pudding.

For decorative edges on napkins, tissue or wrapping paper, use pinking shears to cut to necessary size.

Appetizers
including savories, spreads, pâtés, cheeses

CHEESE-SESAME STICKS
1   cup packed coarsely shredded sharp Cheddar cheese (about 4 ounces)
1½ cups flour
½   cup butter or margarine, softened
½   cup (2¼ ounce can) sesame seed, toasted

Work with hands cheese, flour and butter to form stiff dough. Shape in 1½-inch thick log and cut crosswise in ¼-inch slices. With hands roll slices of dough in 5- or 6-inch sticks, then roll in sesame seed. Bake on greased cookie sheets in preheated 350° oven until golden and crisp, 15 minutes. Cool on rack. Store airtight in cool dry place; keeps 3 weeks. Makes about 3 dozen.

ROASTED ROSEMARY WALNUTS
Water
4   cups walnut halves (about 1 pound)
¼   cup butter or margarine, melted
1   tablespoon rosemary, crushed
1   to 2 teaspoons salt
¼   teaspoon cayenne

Fill large saucepan about three fourths full with water; bring to boil. Add walnuts and bring to boil again; boil 1 minute. Drain in colander, then rinse with hot water; drain well. Spread in single layer in ungreased 15 x 10-inch jelly-roll pan. Bake in preheated 275° oven until dry to the touch, 30 minutes, stirring occasionally. Drizzle with butter. Sprinkle with rosemary, salt and cayenne; mix well. Roast until lightly browned and crisp, 20 to 30 minutes longer, stirring occasionally. Cool in pan. Store airtight in cool place. Will keep about 1 month. Makes 4 cups.

GARLIC-LEMON GREEN OLIVES

1 jar (2 to 2½ ounces) pitted green olives
1 tablespoon olive oil
1 medium clove garlic, peeled (optional)
1 lemon

Drain olives, reserving all but 1 tablespoon brine. Add olive oil and garlic to brine; set aside. With vegetable parer cut thin 2-inch strips of yellow zest from peel of lemon. Fold each in quarters and stuff olives. Return olives to jar and add brine mixture. Cover and chill overnight. Allow to stand at room temperature about 1 hour before serving. Will keep 2 weeks in refrigerator. Makes 15 to 20 appetizers.

SHRIMP BUTTER

¼ pound sweet butter or margarine, softened
1 can (4½ ounces) shrimps, drained and chopped
¼ teaspoon dillweed
2 teaspoons lemon juice
Freshly ground pepper to taste

Mix well all ingredients. Pack in glass jar, crock or plastic container; refrigerate. Allow to stand at room temperature about 30 minutes before serving. Use on assorted crackers or breads. Makes 1 cup.

HAM-NUT SPREAD

8 ounces cooked ham, ground
½ cup toasted almonds or cashews, ground
¼ cup mayonnaise
2 tablespoons sweet-pickle liquid
1 teaspoon each dry mustard and Worcestershire

Mix well all ingredients, Pack in glass jar, crock or plastic container; refrigerate. Will keep 1 week. Makes about 1½ cups.

LIVER PÂTÉ

1 egg
¾ cup milk
¼ cup flour
1 teaspoon salt
½ teaspoon sugar
¼ teaspoon each allspice, ginger and pepper
½ pound calf's liver, cubed
3 slices bacon, diced
1 small onion, chopped coarse
Olive Garnish and Glaze (optional)

With fork beat together egg, milk, flour and seasonings until smooth and well blended. Put about a third each of egg mixture, liver, bacon and onion in blender and whirl until smooth; repeat twice. Pour into 4 greased 4 x 2 x 1-inch foil pans or 10-ounce custard cups, filling about ⅔ full. Cover tightly with foil and bake in pan of water halfway up foil pans in preheated 325° oven 1 hour or until knife inserted in center comes out clean. Cool, wrap airtight and refrigerate; will keep up to 1 week. Can be frozen.

OLIVE GARNISH AND GLAZE (Prepare shortly before giving.) Garnish pâté (in pans or cups) with sliced stuffed or ripe olives. Combine 1½ teaspoons unflavored gelatin with ¼ cup beef broth in small saucepan. Stir over low heat until dissolved. Stir in ¾ cup broth, then chill until consistency of unbeaten egg whites. Spoon ¼ cup over each pâté to glaze. Chill until set.

MOLDED TUNA PÂTÉ WITH BRANDY

1 can (3 or 4 ounces) chopped mushrooms
1 envelope unflavored gelatin
½ cup boiling water
2 cans (7 ounces each) tuna, undrained
½ cup green-goddess salad dressing or mayonnaise
¼ cup parsley leaves
1 tablespoon brandy
¼ teaspoon hot-pepper sauce

Drain liquid from mushrooms into blender. Sprinkle gelatin over liquid and allow to soften. Add boiling water. Whirl at low speed until gelatin is dissolved. Add mushrooms, tuna, dressing, parsley, brandy and pepper sauce. Whirl at high speed until smooth. Pour into small foil pans or large custard cups. Cover with plastic or foil and chill until firm. Will keep in refrigerator 4 to 5 days. To serve, unmold. Good with toast or crisp crackers. Makes about 4 cups.

MINI CHEDDAR-CHEESE BALLS

1 package (8 ounces) cream cheese, softened
8 ounces Cheddar cheese, shredded (2 cups)
1 teaspoon each dry mustard and Worcestershire
⅛ teaspoon cayenne
Garnish (see Note): dried parsley flakes, finely chopped nuts (walnuts, pecans, almonds, peanuts) and/or toasted sesame seed

Beat together cheeses, mustard, Worcestershire and cayenne until smooth. Refrigerate until easy to handle. Shape rounded tablespoonfuls in balls. Roll in garnish until well coated. If desired, place in small foil baking cups or in 2-inch rounds of foil folded up. Serve at room temperature to spread on crackers. Store airtight in refrigerator; will keep 4 weeks. Makes about 18. **Note** About ½ cup garnish coats 18 balls.

MINI BLUE-CHEDDAR BALLS Prepare as above, but substitute 4 ounces crumbled blue cheese for mustard, Worcestershire and cayenne pepper. Makes about 24.

SAVORY CHEESE CUP

1 Gouda or Edam cheese (10 to 15 ounces) in red wax casing
¾ to 1 teaspoon each dry mustard and Worcestershire
Dash of hot-pepper sauce
2 to 3 tablespoons mayonnaise
2 to 3 tablespoons dry white wine

Carefully cut about ½ inch off top of cheese and reserve to use as lid. Let cheese soften at room temperature. With small knife and teaspoon cut and scoop out cheese from both pieces. Chop cheese and put with seasonings into small bowl of mixer. Gradually add mayonnaise and wine and beat until smooth and fluffy. Pack firmly into cheese cup. (Pack any remaining cheese into crock or small jar.) Replace lid and wrap airtight in plastic wrap or foil. Chill at least 2 days before giving or serving. Serve at room temperature. Will keep 2 weeks. Makes 8 to 12 appetizer servings.

YOGURT CHEESE WITH SALTED PECANS

1 quart plain yogurt
¾ to 1 cup toasted buttered salted pecan halves

Line colander with several layers of cheesecloth wrung out in cold water. Spoon in yogurt. Tie corners of cheesecloth together to form pouch. Set in bowl and allow to drain in refrigerator 2 days, occasionally pouring off liquid that accumulates in bowl. Stretch 3 large squares of rinsed cheesecloth over pie plate. Add yogurt cheese (about 1¾ cups) and shape in mound about 5 inches in diameter. Decorate sides and top with toasted pecans. Tie corners of cheesecloth together. Return to refrigerator and let mellow 2 days, draining off liquid occasionally. Place on serving plate, remove cheesecloth and serve yogurt cheese with crackers. Will keep in refrigerator up to 1 week. Makes about 1¾ cups.

PORT-WINE YOGURT CHEESE To unmolded yogurt cheese add 4 tablespoons tawny port wine, 1 teaspoon sugar and generous dash of salt. Stir just until blended. Spoon into 10-ounce crock or soufflé dish and refrigerate. Just before serving, decorate top

with whole blanched almonds, toasted and cooled. Will keep in refrigerator up to 1 week.

FRUITED CHEESE LOG

½ cup dried apricots
1 pound Monterey Jack (or mild Cheddar) cheese, shredded (4 cups)
1 package (8 ounces) cream cheese, softened
⅓ cup dry sherry
1 teaspoon poppy seed
½ teaspoon seasoned salt
⅓ cup golden raisins
⅓ cup chopped dates
Chopped walnuts
2 tablespoons chopped red candied cherries

Soak apricots in 1 cup water 2 hours, then drain and chop. Blend cheeses. Add sherry, poppy seed and salt; mix well. Add apricots, raisins and dates and mix thoroughly. Turn out onto sheet of foil, waxed paper or plastic wrap and shape in 9-inch log. Wrap securely. Chill until firm. Roll in chopped nuts and candied cherries to coat, then cover again; store in refrigerator until ready to use. Serve with crackers. Makes one 2-pound log.

Candies and Confections

CANDY-MAKING TIPS

Preparation Allow plenty of time when making most candies. Many, such as caramels, take long cooking and stirring. For best results, don't double any of the recipes or make substitutions in ingredients.

Weather In humid or rainy weather, cook candies 2° higher than the recipe directions specify.

Utensils Use a heavy saucepan that will accommodate a volume four times greater than that of the original ingredients. Use an asbestos mat (if available) for candies made with milk or cream, since they burn easily. A candy thermometer is almost a necessity for candy making. There are several types available at reasonable prices. An electric beater is convenient too.

Cooking Watch candy carefully, especially during the last few minutes of cooking. Temperatures rise quickly at end. When boiling, wash sugar crystals from side of pan with pastry brush dipped in water.

Storing Different kinds of candies should be stored separately. Brittles soften if stored with creamy candies. Airtight storage in a cool place is best for all candies unless otherwise indicated in recipe.

NUTTY PEPPERMINT BRITTLE

1½   cups graham-cracker crumbs
1   cup finely crushed peppermint candies or candy canes (6 ounces)
6   tablespoons butter or margarine, melted
1   cup nuts (walnuts, pecans, peanuts), chopped coarse

In bowl mix well crumbs and crushed candies. Add butter and toss until well mixed. Stir in nuts. Spread evenly in greased 15 x 10-inch jelly-roll pan and press firmly. Bake in preheated 375° oven 10 to 12 minutes or until melted and bubbly. Cool completely; break in pieces. Store in open container. Will keep 2 months. Makes about 1 pound.

PEANUT BRITTLE

2   cups sugar
1   cup light corn syrup
⅓   cup water
2   tablespoons butter or margarine
¼   teaspoon salt
2   cups roasted blanched peanuts
1   teaspoon baking soda
1   teaspoon vanilla

In large heavy saucepan mix well sugar, corn syrup, water, butter and salt. Cook and stir over medium heat until sugar dissolves. Continue cooking, stirring occasionally, until candy thermometer registers 300° (hard-crack stage). Stir in peanuts. Mix soda and vanilla and quickly stir into candy (mixture will foam). Quickly turn out into greased 15x10x1-inch jelly-roll pan. Cool completely, then break in pieces. Store airtight in cool dry place up to 4 weeks. Makes about 2 pounds.

ALMOND-PASTE CONFECTIONS

8   ounces (2 cups) slivered blanched almonds
1½   tablespoons lemon juice
1   cup sugar
½   cup water
¼   teaspoon almond extract
4   to 6 drops red, green or yellow food coloring (to make pastel color)
Semisweet chocolate pieces or squares, melted

Whirl almonds in blender or food processor to make fine crumbs. Put in mixing bowl and sprinkle with lemon juice; set aside. In small heavy saucepan over medium heat, cook sugar and water *without stirring* until candy thermometer registers 240° (soft-ball stage). Pour over almond mixture; add almond extract and mix well. When cool enough to handle, sprinkle

with food coloring and knead until smooth and even-colored. Wrap airtight and store in refrigerator about 2 days to ripen. Shape in small fruits, vegetables or ¾-inch balls and dip tops in chocolate (good to eat as is or for decorating cakes). Or shape in logs and cut in slices. Store airtight in cool dry place. Makes about 1 pound.

DATES STUFFED WITH ALMOND PASTE

8   ounces almond paste (see Almond-Paste Confections recipe preceding)
48   (15 to 18 ounces) pitted dates or ready-to-eat pitted prunes
Confectioners' sugar (optional)

Pinch off small pieces (about rounded ½ teaspoon measure) of almond paste and shape in rolls the length of dates. Slit dates lengthwise and insert paste. (With prunes make an indentation in center and fill with small balls of paste.) Sift confectioners' sugar over fruit. Store airtight in single layers between sheets of waxed paper in cool dry place. Makes about 48.

CANDIED CITRUS PEEL

Peel with white pith from 2 large grapefruits or 5 large thick-skinned oranges, cut in 2½ x ⅜-inch strips (3 cups)
Water
Sugar
6   squares (1 ounce each) semisweet chocolate (optional)

In 4-quart heavy saucepan bring peel to boil with 6 cups water. Boil uncovered 10 minutes; drain and rinse well with cold water. Repeat process; drain peel and set aside. In same saucepan bring to boil 2 cups sugar with 1¾ cups water; boil 1 minute. Add well-drained peel and simmer briskly until almost all syrup has been absorbed, 30 to 40 minutes; stir frequently to avoid scorching. Drain well in colander, about 10 minutes. Toss peel with ⅓ cup sugar until coated. Spread on jelly-roll pan lined with waxed paper; let stand overnight or until very crusty. Melt chocolate over hot water and dip ends of peel about ½ inch deep in chocolate. Place on rack in cool place to harden. Store in airtight container in cool place up to 3 weeks. Makes about 1 pound.

CANDIED PUFFED RICE AND PEANUTS

4   cups puffed-rice cereal
2   cups shelled peanuts
1   cup sugar
½   cup water

1   teaspoon cider vinegar
3   tablespoons molasses
½   teaspoon salt

In greased bowl stir cereal and peanuts together; set aside. In medium saucepan stir sugar, water and vinegar together; bring to boil. Cover and boil 2 minutes. Stir in molasses and salt. Gently boil without stirring until candy thermometer registers 290° (soft-crack stage). Pour over cereal mixture and quickly toss until well coated. Immediately spread in well-greased jelly-roll pan. Cool completely, then break in pieces. Store in closed container in cool place. Will keep 6 weeks. Makes 1 pound.

POPCORN CONFECTIONS

4   cups salted popcorn
½   cup sugar
⅓   cup light corn syrup
2   tablespoons butter or margarine
Red and green gumdrops, cut in pieces with kitchen
    shears

Keep popcorn warm in large bowl in 300° oven. In small saucepan cook and stir sugar, syrup and butter until sugar dissolves. Continue cooking, without stirring, until candy thermometer registers 254° (hard-ball stage). Slowly pour hot syrup on popcorn, tossing well with wooden spoon to coat kernels evenly. On foil with spoon quickly pack popcorn into large well-buttered holiday-shape cookie cutters. Cool. Unmold. Decorate while still slightly sticky. Firmly press cut side of gumdrop pieces onto confections, forming a design. Wrap separately in plastic wrap and store in cool place; will keep a few weeks. Makes 4 or 5 confections about 3 to 4 inches in diameter. **Note** Use cookie cutters that are open at both ends so popcorn shapes can be pushed out easily.

DATE-NUT SQUARES

2½   cups sugar
1   cup undiluted evaporated milk
¼   teaspoon salt
2   cups chopped nuts
1½   cups finely cut pitted dates
1   teaspoon vanilla extract

In heavy saucepan bring to boil sugar, milk and salt, stirring until sugar is dissolved. Cook, stirring occasionally, until candy thermometer registers 236° (soft-ball stage). Remove from heat and add remaining ingredients. Let stand until lukewarm, then beat until mixture is creamy and loses its gloss. Spread in 9 x 9 x 2-inch pan and let stand until firm. Cut in squares. Store closely covered. Makes about 2 pounds.

Note Walnuts, pecans or filberts are all good to use.

CHOCOLATE-WALNUT CRUNCH

1   pound (2 cups) butter or margarine
2   cups sugar
¼   cup water
2   tablespoons light corn syrup
2   cups coarsely chopped walnuts
1   package (6 ounces) semisweet chocolate pieces,
    melted
½   cup finely chopped walnuts

In large heavy saucepan over low heat melt butter. Add sugar, stirring until sugar is dissolved. Add water and corn syrup. Continue cooking over low heat, without stirring until candy thermometer registers 290° (soft-crack stage). This takes about 45 minutes. Remove from heat; stir in coarsely chopped walnuts. Spread in greased 15 x 10 x 1-inch pan and let stand until firm. Spread chocolate evenly over candy. Sprinkle with finely chopped walnuts. Let stand until chocolate is firm; break in pieces. Store airtight; keeps up to 3 weeks. Makes about 2 pounds.

BOURBON BALLS

1   package (7¼ ounces) vanilla wafers, finely crushed
1   cup finely chopped walnuts
1   package (6 ounces) semisweet chocolate pieces
Sugar
3   tablespoons light corn syrup
⅓   cup bourbon

In large bowl mix well wafer crumbs and walnuts; set aside. In top of double boiler over hot water or heavy saucepan over low heat, melt chocolate. Remove from heat, stir in ½ cup sugar and the corn syrup, then bourbon; add to crumb-nut mixture. Stir until well blended. Shape quickly in 1-inch balls and roll in additional sugar. Store airtight. Let ripen at room temperature several days before serving. Makes about 4½ dozen.

COCONUT KISSES

4   egg whites
½   teaspoon salt
1¼   cups very fine granulated sugar
1   teaspoon vanilla
2   cups shredded coconut
24   candied cherries, halved

In large bowl of mixer beat whites and salt until stiff but not dry. Gradually add sugar, beating until granules are dissolved. Stir in vanilla and coconut until blended. Drop by teaspoonfuls onto ungreased brown paper on cookie sheets. Bake in preheated 350° oven 20 minutes. Slip paper onto wet table or board.

Let stand for 1 minute. Loosen kisses with spatula; remove to racks to cool. Top each with cherry half. Store airtight. Makes about 48.

DIVINITY

2½ cups sugar
½   cup light corn syrup
½   cup water
¼   teaspoon salt
2   egg whites at room temperature
½   cup chopped walnuts, lightly toasted, if desired
¼   cup candied cherries, chopped
1   teaspoon vanilla

In heavy medium saucepan mix sugar, corn syrup, water and salt. Stir over medium heat until sugar is dissolved. Cook syrup over low heat without stirring until candy thermometer registers 250° (hard-ball stage). Meanwhile in large bowl of mixer beat egg whites until stiff, but not dry, peaks form. Slowly pour in hot syrup, beating at high speed until mixture begins to lose its gloss and holds its shape when beaters are raised. Quickly stir in walnuts, cherries and vanilla. Drop by heaping teaspoonfuls onto cookie sheets covered with waxed paper. Cool completely. Store airtight in cool dry place. Makes about 1½ pounds.
Note If mixture becomes too firm before all candy is shaped, stir in 2 drops of hot water.

CHOCOLATE FONDANT

2   cups sugar
2   tablespoons light corn syrup
½   cup water
2   squares (1 ounce each) unsweetened chocolate, melted and cooled
About 18 pecan halves
About 3 ounces white chocolate

In heavy medium-deep saucepan mix sugar, corn syrup and water. Bring to boil over medium heat stirring to dissolve sugar. Boil syrup without stirring until candy thermometer registers 242° (hard-ball stage). Rinse large platter in cold water but do not dry. Pour syrup on platter but do not scrape pan. Let stand 5 minutes or until surface feels just warm, moving platter a few times to cool surface. Work candy with spatula or wooden spoon, scraping to center of platter until white and firm. Scrape from platter into heavy or doubled plastic bags. Add melted unsweetened chocolate. Close bag and knead candy until it clings together and is smooth. Shape in 1-inch balls. Press pecan halves into half the balls. Coat remaining balls: Melt white chocolate in small saucepan over very low

heat, stirring occasionally. (Do not overheat—chocolate will separate.) Spear fondant balls on fork and dip in white chocolate. Tap fork against rim of pan to knock off excess chocolate. Place balls on waxed paper to cool. Store airtight in cool dry place. Keeps about 1 month. Makes about 36.

ALMOND NOUGAT

2   cups sugar
1½ cups light corn syrup
¼   cup water
¼   teaspoon salt
2   egg whites
½   teaspoon almond extract
Green food coloring
¼   cup butter or margarine, softened
1   cup toasted unblanched almonds

In heavy saucepan, mix well sugar, corn syrup, water and salt. Cook and stir until sugar is dissolved. Cook without stirring until candy thermometer registers 250° (hard-ball stage). In large bowl of mixer beat whites until stiff but not dry. Gradually beat in about one fourth (not more) of the syrup and continue beating until mixture holds its shape. Cook remaining syrup until candy thermometer registers 300° (hard-crack stage). Gradually beat into white-syrup mixture and continue beating until mixture begins to hold its shape. Add almond extract and food coloring to tint a delicate green. Beat in butter and continue beating until very thick and satiny. Stir in almonds. Press into greased 8-inch square pan, smoothing top. Let stand until firm, then turn out and cut in 1-inch squares. Wrap each piece in waxed paper or plastic wrap. For best flavor, store airtight in cool place several days to ripen. Makes about 1½ pounds.

NO-COOK CHOCOLATE CHEWS

2   tablespoons butter or margarine
½   cup corn syrup
2   squares (1 ounce each) unsweetened chocolate, melted
1   teaspoon vanilla
3   cups confectioners' sugar
¾   cup nonfat dry milk powder

Mix well butter and corn syrup, then stir in chocolate and vanilla. Mix sugar and milk powder. Gradually stir into chocolate mixture. Knead until thoroughly blended. Roll ¾ inch thick. Cut in 1-inch pieces. Makes about 1½ pounds.

WHITE LIME FUDGE

2 tablespoons butter or margarine
2 cups sugar
¾ cup milk
Grated peel of 1 lime
¾ cup chopped pecans

In medium heavy saucepan melt butter. Stir in sugar and milk until sugar dissolves. Bring to boil. Cover; boil 1 minute. Cook syrup gently without stirring until candy thermometer registers 236° (soft-ball stage). Cool to 110° to 120° (warm), about 45 minutes. Stir in lime peel and pecans. Beat vigorously until mixture just starts to lose its gloss. Pour immediately into well-greased 8 x 8 x 2-inch pan. Cool; cut in squares. Store in plastic bags or airtight container. Will keep about 3 weeks. Makes about 1 pound.

SWEDISH CREAM FUDGE

1½ cups sugar
2 tablespoons butter or margarine
1 cup heavy cream
3 tablespoons cocoa
¼ teaspoon salt
1 teaspoon vanilla
About ⅓ cup toasted blanched whole filberts (optional)

In large heavy saucepan mix sugar, butter, cream, cocoa and salt. Bring to boil over medium heat, stirring to dissolve sugar. Cook over low heat *without stirring* until candy thermometer registers 234° (soft-ball stage). Remove from heat and stir in vanilla. Cool until mixture is lukewarm to touch. Beat vigorously until mixture mounds when dropped from spoon. Pour onto small carving board and pat into 8 x 4-inch rectangle. Cover loosely with waxed paper and let stand overnight in cool dry place. Cut only as many squares as you plan to serve; top each with a filbert. Store remaining fudge loosely covered in cool dry place. Makes about 1 pound.

NUT CARAMELS

1 cup heavy cream mixed with ½ cup milk
½ cup granulated sugar
½ cup packed light-brown sugar
¾ cup light corn syrup
Dash of salt
½ teaspoon vanilla
½ cup chopped almonds, lightly toasted (optional)
2 tablespoons butter or margarine

In large heavy saucepan mix ¾ cup cream mixture, sugars, corn syrup and salt. Bring to boil over medium heat, stirring to dissolve sugars. Cook syrup, stirring occasionally, until candy thermometer registers 234° (soft-ball stage). Very slowly stir in remaining ¾ cup cream mixture so that syrup mixture continues to boil. Cook, stirring occasionally, until candy thermometer registers 244° (firm-ball stage). Remove from heat; stir in vanilla, almonds and butter. Pour into greased 9 x 5 x 3-inch loaf pan. Cool completely at room temperature. Turn out of pan onto board. Using knife or kitchen scissors dipped in hot water, cut in pieces or squares. Wrap each in plastic wrap. Store airtight in cool dry place. Makes about 1¼ pounds.

PECAN-CARAMEL CHEWS

3 cups pecan halves (¾ pound)
1 recipe Nut Caramels (recipe preceding; omit almonds)
1 cup or 1 package (6 ounces) semisweet chocolate pieces, melted

On greased cookie sheet, for each candy arrange 4 pecan halves in 4-point star (overlapping slightly in center). Spoon about 2 teaspoonfuls hot caramel mixture over nuts almost to cover. Let stand until caramel is set. Spread about 1 teaspoon chocolate on center of each. Let stand until set. Store airtight in single layers between sheets of waxed paper in cool dry place. Makes about 36.

BUTTERSCOTCH-NUT DROPS

2 cups granulated sugar
1 cup packed light-brown sugar
¾ cup water
¼ cup light corn syrup
1 teaspoon vinegar
½ teaspoon salt
1 package (6 ounces) butterscotch pieces
¾ cup coarsely chopped nuts

In large heavy saucepan bring to full boil over high heat, stirring, the sugars, water, corn syrup, vinegar and salt. Boil 3 minutes without stirring. Remove from heat, add butterscotch pieces and stir until melted (mixture will be thin). Add nuts and drop by teaspoonfuls on ungreased foil. Let stand until set. Makes about 1¾ pounds. **Note** If mixture becomes too thick to drop, stir in about 1 teaspoon hot water.

PEPPERMINT PATTIES

2 cups sugar
2 tablespoons light corn syrup
Water
⅛ teaspoon peppermint extract or 2 drops oil of cinnamon

Green or red food coloring
Prepared cake-decorating icing in tube (optional)

In large deep saucepan mix sugar, corn syrup and ½ cup water. Bring to boil over medium heat, stirring to dissolve sugar. Boil syrup without stirring until candy thermometer registers 242° (firm-ball stage). Rinse large platter in cold water but do not dry. Pour syrup on platter but do not scrape pan. Let stand 5 minutes or until surface feels just warm, moving platter a few times to cool surface. Work candy with spatula or wooden spoon, scraping to center of platter, until white and firm. Scrape from platter into heavy or doubled plastic bags. Close bag and knead candy until it clings together and is smooth. Let ripen at room temperature 1 to 3 days. To make mints, melt fondant in top of double boiler over simmering water. Add about 1 tablespoon hot water to thin to syrup consistency. Stir in extract and coloring. Form 1- to 1½-inch patties, pouring about a fourth of fondant at a time from warmed glass measuring cup or dropping by teaspoonfuls onto waxed paper. (Keep remaining fondant over hot water. If fondant hardens, stir in a few drops of hot water.) Let patties set. If desired, decorate with icing. Let set. Store airtight in cool dry place. Makes about 36.

CREOLE PRALINES

3 cups packed light-brown sugar
1 cup heavy cream
¼ cup butter or margarine
2 tablespoons light corn syrup
¼ teaspoon salt
1 teaspoon vanilla
1½ cups pecan halves, lightly toasted

In large heavy saucepan mix sugar, cream, butter, corn syrup and salt. Bring to boil over medium heat, stirring to dissolve sugar. Cook syrup, stirring occasionally, until candy thermometer registers 234° (soft-ball stage). Remove from heat; let stand 5 minutes. Stir in vanilla and pecans. Beat with spoon until mixture begins to thicken and loses its gloss. Drop by ½ tablespoonfuls onto waxed paper and spread to form patties about 2 inches in diameter. Let stand until firm, then wrap individually in plastic wrap. Store in airtight containers in cool dry place. Makes about 1¾ pounds.

ORANGE SPICED PECANS

1 cup sugar
1 teaspoon cinnamon
⅛ teaspoon nutmeg
½ cup orange juice
1 teaspoon butter or margarine
1 teaspoon vanilla
2 cups pecan halves

In medium saucepan cook, stirring occasionally, sugar, cinnamon, nutmeg and orange juice until candy thermometer registers 236° (soft-ball stage). Remove from heat; stir in butter; let stand 5 minutes. Stir in vanilla and pecans until mixture is thick. Immediately turn out and separate on waxed paper. Cool completely. Store in airtight container or plastic bag; will keep 1 to 2 months. Makes about 2 cups.

Cookies

COOKIE-MAKING TIPS

Mixing Dough Give cookie dough your undivided attention when measuring, mixing and baking. Measure exactly, using standard measuring cups and spoons. Don't make substitutions in ingredients.

Rolling and Cutting For easier rolling, make use of a pastry cloth or canvas and a stockinet rolling-pin cover. If specific instructions aren't given, roll out a small amount of dough at a time, keeping remainder chilled. Use a light hand to flour your working surface. Cut out cookies with lightly floured cutter, using a fairly plain one if dough is soft and short.

Cookie Sheets Be sure they are at least two inches narrower and shorter than the oven rack so heat can circulate. Sheets need not be greased unless specified in recipe.

Baking Because ovens vary, watch cookies closely. Many ovens tend to overheat; your second, third and subsequent sheets of cookies may take a shorter time to bake than specified in recipe. Check for doneness just before minimum baking time is up. If some cookies are thinner than others, you may have to remove them sooner.

Cooling Unless otherwise specified in your recipe, remove baked cookies from sheet to rack as soon as baked. Cool thoroughly.

Storing Store bar cookies in tightly covered baking pan and other soft cookies in tightly covered container in cool place. If cookies tend to dry out, put a piece of bread or a wedge of apple in container with them to maintain moisture. Store crisp cookies in container with loose-fitting cover in cool place. If cookies soften, put on cookie sheet in slow oven about five minutes to recrisp. Store soft and crisp cookies separately.

Freezing Cookie dough and baked cookies can be frozen. To freeze cookie dough, shape stiff dough in rolls or bars and wrap carefully. Put soft dough in freezer container and cover tightly. Label. Before baking, thaw stiff dough just until it can be sliced. (Cooking time may be longer.) Thaw soft dough until easy to handle. To freeze baked cookies, cool them and pack carefully in freezer containers. Thaw at room temperature 15 to 20 minutes. Dough and cookies can be stored in freezer six months to one year.

Mailing Select cookies that keep fresh at least two weeks under average conditions and are thick and firm enough not to break easily. Wrap separately in transparent plastic wrap or foil. Pack in crumpled tissue paper in a coffee can or firm box so cookies can't slide around. Gift-wrap; cover box with corrugated cardboard, put in a slightly larger box and mark it "Fragile."

LEMON SUGAR COOKIES

1   cup butter or margarine, softened
1   cup sugar
1   teaspoon vanilla
1/2   teaspoon salt
1   whole egg
1   egg, separated
3   tablespoons lemon juice
4   cups flour
1   tablespoon water
Colored sugar or chopped nuts

In large bowl of mixer, cream butter, sugar, vanilla and salt until fluffy. Beat in whole egg, egg yolk and lemon juice. Stir in flour until well blended. Divide dough in fourths and wrap each airtight; chill overnight. On lightly floured surface roll out each 1/8 inch thick. With floured small holiday cookie or doughnut cutters cut in desired shapes (reroll scraps). Place 1/2 inch apart on lightly greased cookie sheets. Brush with egg white slightly beaten with water; sprinkle with sugar. Bake in preheated 350° oven until golden, 8 to 10 minutes. Remove to racks to cool. Store airtight in cool dry place. Makes 96 to 120.

YUGOSLAVIAN PECAN CRESCENTS

About 2 cups flour
1   envelope active dry yeast
Dash of salt
1/2   cup butter or margarine, softened
2   eggs, separated
1/2   cup sour cream
1/2   cup packed light-brown sugar
1   cup finely chopped pecans
1   teaspoon vanilla
Confectioners' sugar

In large bowl mix well 2 cups flour, yeast and salt. Cut in butter until mixture resembles coarse crumbs. Stir in egg yolks and sour cream until well blended. Gather in ball. On lightly floured surface knead until smooth, 8 to 10 minutes. Divide in thirds, wrap each in waxed paper and chill 2 to 3 hours. To make filling, in small bowl of mixer beat egg whites until foamy. Gradually add 1/4 cup sugar and beat until stiff. Combine remaining 1/4 cup sugar with pecans and vanilla; fold into egg-white mixture; set aside. On lightly floured surface roll each piece of dough in 9-inch circle; cut in 8 wedges. Spoon about 1 tablespoon filling along wide end of each wedge. Carefully roll up from wide end to point (filling is light and some will ooze out). Press dough where point overlaps. Shape in crescent. Place about 2 inches apart on greased cookie sheet, point side down. Bake in preheated 375° oven until golden brown, 20 to 25 minutes. Sprinkle with confectioners' sugar while warm. Remove to rack to cool. Makes 24.

PINEAPPLE BARS

2 1/2   cups flour
1/3   cup sugar
1/4   teaspoon salt
1   cup butter or margarine, softened
1   egg, separated
2/3   cup pineapple, peach or apricot preserves
1/2   cup chopped nuts

In bowl mix well flour, sugar and salt. Cut in butter until mixture resembles coarse crumbs. Stir in egg white until well blended. Gather in ball. Cut off a third; wrap and chill. Press remaining dough on bottom of 13 x 9 x 2-inch baking pan. Bake in preheated 375° oven until dry to touch, about 12 minutes. Cool in pan on rack. Spread with thin layer preserves. Sprinkle with nuts. On lightly floured surface roll out remaining chilled dough 1/8 inch thick. With pastry wheel or sharp knife cut 1/2-inch-wide strips. Arrange crisscross over preserves, leaving about 3/4 inch between strips. (Pinch strips together if they break or are not long enough.) Brush strips with slightly beaten egg yolk. Bake in preheated 375° oven until golden brown, 15 minutes. Cool on rack before cutting. Store airtight in cool dry place. Makes about 32.

Clockwise from top left: *Mexican Wedding Cookies, Light Pfeffernuesse, Divinity, Pecan-Caramel Chews, Dates Stuffed with Almond Paste, Yugoslavian Pecan Crescents, Pineapple Bars, Lemon Sugar Cookies, Swedish Cream Fudge and Peppermint Patties.*

CHOCOLATE-ALMOND SPRITZ COOKIES

½ cup butter or margarine, softened
1 cup sugar
1 egg
2 squares (1 ounce each) unsweetened chocolate, melted and cooled
2 teaspoons milk
1 teaspoon vanilla
1¼ cups flour
½ cup ground roasted almonds
½ teaspoon salt
Confectioners' sugar (optional)

In large bowl of mixer, cream butter and sugar until fluffy. Beat in egg until light and fluffy. Add chocolate, milk and vanilla until well blended. Gradually stir in flour, almonds and salt until well blended. Chill at least 2 hours. Press through cookie press in desired shapes about 1 inch apart on ungreased cookie sheets. Bake in preheated 350° oven until top springs back when pressed lightly with fingertips, 8 to 10 minutes. Cool on cookie sheets 1 minute; remove to racks to cool completely. Sprinkle with confectioners' sugar. Store in airtight container in cool, dry place. Will keep about 2 weeks. Makes about 87.

LIGHT PFEFFERNUESSE

3 eggs
1 cup sugar
3 cups flour
Grated peel of 1 medium lemon
1 teaspoon cinnamon
¼ teaspoon each baking powder, salt and pepper
¼ teaspoon ground cardamom (optional)
¼ cup minced blanched almonds
1 container (4 ounces) candied lemon peel, chopped fine
Red candied pineapple or red candied cherries, cut in small thin wedges (optional)
Green citron or green candied cherries, cut in pieces (optional)
Confectioners' sugar
1 apple wedge

In large bowl of mixer, beat eggs and sugar until light and frothy. Combine flour, lemon peel, cinnamon, baking powder, salt, pepper and cardamom; stir into egg mixture until well blended. Stir in almonds and candied lemon peel until well blended. On lightly floured surface roll ¼ inch thick (reroll scraps). With 1¼-inch round cutter, cut out cookies. Place about 1 inch apart on greased cookie sheet. Decorate each with piece of pineapple and citron. Bake in preheated 350° oven 15 minutes until light brown on bottom. Sprinkle with confectioners' sugar while warm.

Remove to racks to cool. Store with apple in airtight containers at least 1 week to permit mellowing. Keeps about 3 weeks. Makes about 84.

COCONUT-PECAN BARS

½   cup butter or margarine, softened
1½ cups packed brown sugar, divided
1   cup plus 2 tablespoons flour
2   eggs
½   teaspoon salt
1   teaspoon vanilla
1   cup each chopped pecans and flaked coconut
Confectioners' sugar (optional)

In large bowl of mixer, cream butter and ½ cup sugar until fluffy. Gradually stir in 1 cup flour until well blended. Pat evenly in greased 9 x 9 x 2-inch baking pan. Bake in preheated 350° oven until firm to touch, 12 minutes. Remove from oven. Meanwhile in small bowl of mixer beat eggs until light-colored. Add remaining 1 cup brown sugar, the salt and vanilla and beat until well blended. Fold in remaining 2 tablespoons flour, the pecans and coconut. Spread over crust. Bake until light brown, 20 to 25 minutes. Cool completely in pan on rack. Cut in 2 x 1-inch bars. Store airtight in cool dry place. Before serving, sprinkle with confectioners' sugar. Will keep about 2 weeks. Makes about 32.

MEXICAN WEDDING COOKIES

1   cup butter or margarine, softened
Confectioners' sugar
1   teaspoon vanilla
¼   teaspoon salt
2   cups flour

In large bowl of mixer, cream butter, ½ cup sugar, vanilla and salt until fluffy. Stir in flour until well blended. Chill 30 minutes or until firm enough to handle. Shape in 1-inch balls. Place 1 inch apart on ungreased cookie sheet. Bake in preheated 375° oven until light golden, 12 to 15 minutes. Remove to rack (close to each other). Sprinkle heavily with confectioners' sugar while warm. Cool completely. Store airtight in cool dry place. Before serving, sprinkle with more confectioners' sugar. Will keep about 2 weeks. Makes about 48. **Note** If desired, stir in 1 cup very finely chopped pecans with flour. However, these cookies will not be as tender as plain cookies.

DECORATED GINGER COOKIES

5   cups flour
1   tablespoon ground ginger
1   teaspoon each cinnamon and baking soda
½   teaspoon salt
1   cup butter or margarine, softened
1   cup each sugar and molasses
½   cup strong coffee
Decorator Icing (recipe follows)
Colored candies (optional)

Stir together flour, ginger, cinnamon, soda and salt; set aside. In large bowl of mixer, cream butter and sugar until light. Beat in molasses until light and fluffy. Stir in flour mixture alternately with coffee until well blended. Chill several hours or overnight until firm. On well-floured surface with floured rolling pin roll out a fourth of dough at a time ⅛ inch thick. Keep remaining dough chilled. With cutters cut out ginger men or holiday shapes (reroll scraps). With 2 wide spatulas transfer to ungreased cookie sheets. Bake in preheated 350° oven until slightly browned around edges, 13 to 17 minutes. With spatulas remove to racks to cool. Decorate with icing and candies. Store in airtight containers in cool, dry place. Will keep about 2 weeks. Makes about twenty-five 8-inch cookies or seventy-five 2½-inch cookies.

DECORATOR ICING   In small bowl of mixer at high speed beat 1 egg white, 1¼ cups confectioners' sugar, ¼ teaspoon cream of tartar and about 1 tablespoon water until stiff peaks form, 10 minutes. Fill pastry tube or paper cone with icing and decorate cookies as desired.

CHOCOLATE REFRIGERATOR COOKIES

1   cup butter or margarine, softened
¼   cup sugar
1   teaspoon vanilla
¼   teaspoon salt
1   egg
2   cups flour
½   cup cocoa
1   cup chopped walnuts
4   squares (1 ounce each) sweet cooking chocolate, melted

In large bowl of mixer, cream butter, sugar, vanilla and salt until light. Beat in egg. Stir in flour and cocoa until well blended. Chill dough in bowl about 2 hours or until firm enough to handle. Form 2 rolls 1½ inch in diameter. Roll in walnuts until well coated. Wrap airtight and chill overnight. Cut in 3/16-inch slices and place 1 inch apart on lightly greased cookie sheet. Bake in preheated 400° oven until crisp, 8 to 10 minutes. Remove to rack to cool. Spoon about ½ measuring teaspoon chocolate on center of each cookie, then spread to within ¼ inch of edge. Let chocolate harden. Store airtight in cool dry place. Makes about 72.

LIZZIES

1½   cups raisins
¼   cup bourbon or orange juice
¾   cup flour
¾   teaspoon baking soda
¾   teaspoon cinnamon
¼   teaspoon nutmeg
¼   teaspoon ground cloves
2   tablespoons butter or margarine
¼   cup packed light-brown sugar
1   egg
½   pound (2 cups) pecan halves or broken walnut halves
¼   pound citron, diced
½   pound candied cherries
Confectioners' sugar (optional)

Stir together raisins and bourbon; let stand 1 hour. Stir together flour, baking soda and spices; set aside. In large bowl of mixer, cream butter until fluffy; beat in sugar, then egg. Stir in flour mixture. Add raisin-bourbon mixture, pecans and fruits; mix well. Drop by teaspoonfuls about 1 inch apart on greased cookie sheets. Bake in preheated 325° oven about 15 minutes. Remove cookies at once to racks to cool. Before serving, sprinkle with confectioners' sugar. Store airtight in cool dry place at least two weeks to permit mellowing. Makes about 60. **Note** Recipe can be doubled.

ORANGE-NUT BARS

2⅓   cups flour
1   teaspoon each baking soda and cinnamon
½   teaspoon each nutmeg and salt
½   cup butter or margarine, softened
1   cup sugar
¼   cup molasses
2   eggs
1   cup thick applesauce
1   tablespoon grated orange peel
½   cup chopped walnuts
Orange Glaze (recipe follows; optional)
Additional chopped walnuts for garnish (optional)

Stir together flour, soda, cinnamon, nutmeg and salt; set aside. In large bowl of mixer, cream butter and sugar until light and fluffy. Beat in molasses until well mixed. Add eggs and beat until light. Add flour mixture, applesauce and orange peel. Gently stir with spoon just until blended. Stir in ½ cup walnuts. Pour into 3 greased 8 x 8 x 2-inch pans (can be foil). Bake in

preheated 350° oven 30 minutes or until pick inserted in center comes out clean. Cool completely on racks. Frost with Orange Glaze. Garnish with chopped walnuts. To serve, cut each cake in 18 bars. Wrap tightly with foil. Store in cool, dry place. Keeps about 1 week. Makes 54.

ORANGE GLAZE In small bowl beat 3 cups confectioners' sugar and 3 to 6 tablespoons orange juice until smooth and of glaze consistency. Makes enough for 3 cakes.

PECAN BUTTER BALLS

2½   cups finely chopped pecans, divided
2   cups flour
1   cup butter or margarine, softened
¼   cup sugar
2   teaspoons vanilla
¼   teaspoon salt
1   egg white, slightly beaten
½   cup very fine sugar

Beat 2 cups pecans, flour, butter, sugar, vanilla and salt until well blended. Gather in ball. Divide in fourths. With lightly floured hands roll 1 inch thick. Cut in ¾-inch slices. Shape each in 1-inch balls, brush with egg white then roll in mixture of ½ cup of pecans and very fine sugar. Bake in preheated 325° oven until lightly browned, about 15 to 20 minutes. (Do not overbake.) Remove to rack to cool; store airtight. Makes about 66. **Note** Walnuts, almonds or filberts can be used in place of pecans.

VANILLA-CHOCOLATE CLOVERS

1   cup butter or margarine, softened
¾   cup sugar
¼   teaspoon salt
2   teaspoons vanilla
2½   cups flour
2   tablespoons cornstarch
2   tablespoons cocoa
1   egg white, slightly beaten

In large bowl of mixer, cream butter. Add sugar, salt and vanilla and continue creaming until light and fluffy. Mix flour with cornstarch; gradually add to butter-sugar mixture. On lightly floured surface form dough in ball. Divide in half. In one half work in cocoa until well blended. Divide each half in 4 pieces and shape in ¾-inch rolls. Brush each roll with egg white. Put 1 white roll next to 1 cocoa roll, then put 1 cocoa roll on top of white and 1 white roll on top of cocoa. Repeat with 4 remaining rolls, making 2 larger rolls, each consisting of 4 rolls. Wrap each in waxed paper and chill. Cut in ¼-inch slices (pinch rolls together if they separate while cutting) and place on lightly greased cookie sheet. Bake in preheated 350° oven until white part is golden brown, about 8 to 10 minutes. Remove to rack to cool. Store airtight. Makes about 60.

Dessert Sauces and Syrups

QUICK RUMTOPF

1   can (20 ounces) pineapple chunks, drained
1   can (16 ounces) sliced peaches, drained
1   can (16 ounces) pear halves, drained
1   can (11 ounces) mandarin-orange sections, drained
1½   cups dark rum
1   cup sugar
½   cup raisins
½   teaspoon cinnamon

In large bowl, stir together all ingredients. Ladle into clean sterilized jars. Store in cool place. Let age 1 month before serving. Makes about 3 pints. Serve over ice cream or pound cake. **Note** As *rumtopf* is used, add more fruit and rum to syrup in jar. Can be refrigerated to prevent further fermentation.

GINGER-CARAMEL DESSERT SAUCE

2   cups sugar
1½   cups boiling water
½   cup chopped nuts
¼   cup minced preserved ginger

In heavy skillet melt sugar over medium-low heat, stirring constantly, until it becomes a clear brown syrup, about 20 minutes; remove from heat. Carefully stir in water, nuts and ginger. Return to heat. Cook, stirring constantly, until syrup is smooth again. Cool. Pour into clean jars; cover tightly. Store at room temperature. Will keep 5 to 6 months. Serve over ice cream, cake or fruit. Makes 2½ cups.

MARINATED APRICOTS AND LIQUEUR

8   ounces dried apricots (1⅓ cups packed)
8   ounces white rock candy
1½   cups vodka (least-expensive kind)

Layer apricots and candy in wide-mouth 1-quart glass bottle or glass jar. Pour on vodka. Cover airtight (if cork top is used, first wrap cork in plastic wrap or foil). Let stand at room temperature 2 to 3 weeks or until candy is dissolved, stirring twice. Makes about 1¾

cups liqueur, about 2 cups apricots. To serve, drain liqueur into decanter; serve after dinner. Apricots are good with walnuts in the shell or over ice cream. Will keep indefinitely.

RUM SAUCE

2   cups sugar
1¼   cups hot water
⅔   cup rum or brandy
1   tablespoon butter or margarine
Dash of salt

In skillet heat sugar over medium-low heat, stirring constantly, until it becomes a clear brown syrup, about 20 minutes; remove from heat. Carefully stir in water. Cook, stirring, until syrup is smooth again. Stir in rum, butter and salt until well blended. Delicious on ice cream, plum pudding or plain cakes. Will keep in refrigerator up to 2 weeks. To serve, reheat. Makes about 2½ cups.

CHERRY-CINNAMON SAUCE

1   can (15 ounces) sweet pitted cherries
3   tablespoons sugar
¼   cup light corn syrup
1   cinnamon stick
1   tablespoon lemon juice (optional)
1   tablespoon cornstarch blended with 1 tablespoon water

Drain syrup from cherries into saucepan (reserve cherries). Stir in sugar, corn syrup, cinnamon and lemon juice; bring to boil, then simmer 10 minutes. Remove cinnamon stick. Stir in blended cornstarch and cook until thickened. Stir in reserved cherries. Cool. Store in jars in refrigerator; will keep about 1 week. Makes about 2½ cups.

APRICOT SYRUP (for pancakes)

Water
8   ounces dried apricots (1⅓ cups packed)
2   cups light corn syrup
2   tablespoons brandy (optional)

In saucepan pour enough water over apricots just to cover. Bring to boil; reduce heat and simmer about 15 minutes or until tender. Drain, reserving 1 cup liquid (add water if necessary to make 1 cup). Purée apricots and liquid in blender or force through fine sieve until smooth. Stir in corn syrup and brandy until well mixed. Pour into clean jars; cover tightly. Store in cool place. Will keep 2 months. Makes 4 cups. **Note** If thinner syrup is desired, thin with additional water. If thinner and sweeter syrup is desired, thin with additional corn syrup.

Fruitcakes and Steamed Puddings

FRUITCAKE TIPS

Preparation Different combinations of fruits and nuts can be used in any fruitcake, but the total amount should be the same as given in the recipe.

Glazing and Decorating Before serving or gift wrapping, fruitcakes can be glazed and decorated. Melted tart jelly or equal parts of honey or corn syrup and water, boiled 2 minutes, can be brushed warm on cold cakes. Press designs made of candied cherries and nuts, leaves cut from citron, angelica or green candied cherries and slices of red or green candied pineapple into glaze. Brush again with glaze and put in slow oven (300° F.) about 10 minutes to set. Glazed dried fruits such as prunes and apricots make attractive decorations. To prepare, cover fruits with water and simmer, covered, 10 minutes; drain. Bring to boil equal parts of honey, sugar and water. Add fruits and simmer about 15 minutes. Drain on cake rack. Remaining mixture can be used to glaze cake.

Storage Dark fruitcakes keep better than light ones since the larger proportion of fruit to batter adds moisture. Both types keep better if refrigerated. They can also be frozen. When refrigerated, they should be wrapped in foil, waxed paper or plastic wrap and, if possible, put in an airtight container. Dark cakes can be wrapped first with a cloth soaked in brandy, wine or bourbon. Liquor should not be put on white fruitcakes since it may make them soggy. Wrapped and refrigerated, dark cakes will keep several months, light ones about 2 weeks. Dark cakes will ship better.

Serving Fruitcakes, especially dark ones, are better if allowed to age a week or two before eating. Chilled cakes usually cut best. Slice thin with a serrated knife, if available. If not, use a thin sharp knife.

PECAN-BOURBON CAKE

1/2 cup butter or margarine, softened
1 cup plus 2 tablespoons sugar
3 eggs, separated
1/2 cup bourbon
2 teaspoons freshly grated nutmeg
1 1/2 cups flour
1 teaspoon baking powder
1 pound (4 1/4 cups) shelled pecans, coarsely chopped
1 1/4 cups seeded raisins, coarsely chopped

In large bowl of mixer, cream butter. Gradually beat in sugar until light. Add egg yolks one at a time, beating thoroughly after each. Mix bourbon and nutmeg and add alternately to butter-sugar mixture with 1 cup flour stirred with baking powder; blend thoroughly.

Left to right, along the top: *Popcorn Confections.* Top shelf: *Mini Cheddar-Cheese Balls, Decorated Ginger Cookies, Lemon-Parsley Butter Log, Garlic-Lemon Green Olives, Orange-Nut Bars* (in pan), *Seeded Cheese Crackers, Orange-Wine Jelly, Apricot Syrup* (in back), *Louisiana Hot-Pepper Jelly* on *Anne's Fresh-Cranberry Chutney.* Middle shelf: *Chocolate-Almond Spritz Cookies, Candied Puffed Rice and Peanuts, Sourdough Starter* (with *Sourdough Biscuit* recipe), *Coconut-Pecan Bars, Lavash Crackers, Graham Crisps, Roasted Rosemary Walnuts, Orange Spiced Pecans* (in back), *Yogurt Cheese with Salted Pecans, Sweet Carrot Pickles, Ginger-Caramel Dessert Sauce, Cinnamon Apple Slices* (in back), *Preserved Orange Slices.* Bottom shelf (back row): *Chocolate Fondant* (white and dark), *White Lime Fudge, Raisin-Almond Loaf, Holiday Whole-Wheat Wreath, Brandied Mincemeat Banana Bread, Bran Monkey Bread;* (front): *Nutty Peppermint Brittle, Nut-Pumpkin Loaf, Stollen, Armenian-Style Whole-Wheat Lavash, Easy Dark Fruitcake* and *Maple, Whole-Wheat and Raisin Bread.*

Mix well remaining flour, nuts and raisins. Add to batter and mix well to distribute evenly. In small bowl of mixer, beat egg whites until stiff peaks form. Fold into batter. Put in 10-inch tube pan lined on the bottom with waxed paper, then greased. Let stand in pan 10 minutes. Bake in preheated 325° oven about 1 hour and 15 minutes. Cool in pan on rack, then turn out on plate and peel off paper. Invert on another plate so right side is up (handle carefully since cake crumbles easily). Makes 1 cake. **Note** If desired, pour ½ cup bourbon over cake before wrapping.

LIGHT FRUITCAKE

3   cups flour
1¼   teaspoons baking powder
¾   teaspoon salt
1½   cups butter or margarine, softened
2   cups sugar
6   eggs
4   cups golden raisins
½   cup sliced maraschino cherries
1   cup diced citron
1   cup chopped nuts
1   tablespoon grated lemon rind
1   cup heavy cream, whipped

Stir together flour, baking powder and salt; set aside. In large bowl of mixer, cream butter. Gradually beat in sugar until light. Add eggs one at a time, beating thoroughly after each. Mix fruits, nuts, lemon rind and dry ingredients. Add alternately with cream to butter-sugar mixture, blending thoroughly. Put in well-greased 10-inch tube pan. Cover with lid; bake in preheated 325° oven 1 hour. Uncover; bake about 1 hour. Cool in pan on rack. Makes 1 cake.

ECONOMY FRUITCAKE

2   cups flour
½   teaspoon baking soda
1˙   teaspoon baking powder
1   teaspoon cinnamon
¼   teaspoon ground cloves
¼   teaspoon salt
2   cups seeded raisins, chopped
8   ounces dates, pitted
1   cup currants
1   cup packed brown sugar
1   cup strong coffee
½   cup plus 1 tablespoon shortening
¼   cup molasses
1   egg

Mix well flour, soda, baking powder, cinnamon, cloves and salt; set aside. In large heavy saucepan, bring to boil raisins, dates, currants, sugar, coffee, shortening and molasses. Boil 5 minutes; cool. Stir in egg and dry ingredients. Pour in 9x5x3-inch loaf pan lined on the bottom with waxed paper. Bake in preheated 300° oven about 1½ hours. Remove from pan to wire rack. Cool completely. Makes 1 cake.

EASY DARK FRUITCAKES

1   box (1 pound) brown sugar
1   pound (2½ cups) mixed chopped candied fruit
1   package (15 ounces) raisins
1½   cups orange juice
2   tablespoons cocoa powder
2   tablespoons rum or brandy
2   tablespoons butter or margarine
2   teaspoons cinnamon
1   teaspoon salt
¼   teaspoon ground cloves
3   cups flour
1   teaspoon baking soda
1   cup chopped walnuts
Orange Glaze (recipe follows; optional)
Candied fruit (optional)

In heavy saucepan mix well sugar, fruit, raisins, orange juice, cocoa, rum, butter, cinnamon, salt and cloves. Bring to boil and boil, stirring occasionally, 5 minutes. Cool completely. Stir together flour, soda and walnuts. Stir into fruit mixture until well blended. Turn into 3 well-greased and floured 8 x 4-inch loaf pans. Bake in preheated 325° oven 1 hour or until pick inserted in center comes out clean. Remove from pan to rack. Cool completely. Wrap in cheesecloth soaked in brandy or sherry, then wrap in foil. Store in refrigerator. If desired, cheesecloth may be resoaked as it becomes dry. Cakes will keep 2 months. Before giving, drizzle with Orange Glaze and decorate with candied fruit. Makes 3 loaves.

ORANGE GLAZE Mix well 1 cup confectioners' sugar and 1 to 2 tablespoons orange juice until smooth.

STEAMED CHOCOLATE PUDDINGS

1   cup sugar
½   cup butter or margarine, softened
2   eggs
2   squares (1 ounce each) unsweetened chocolate, melted
1   teaspoon vanilla
1½   cups flour
1¼   teaspoons baking powder
¼   teaspoon baking soda
¼   teaspoon salt

½ cup milk
¾ cup chopped walnuts
¼ cup ground walnuts
Peppermint Sauce (recipe follows)

In large bowl of mixer, cream sugar and butter until light and fluffy; beat in eggs until smooth, then chocolate and vanilla. Mix flour, baking powder, soda and salt; add half at a time alternately with milk, beating well after each addition. Stir in chopped walnuts. Grease four 1-pound fruit or vegetable cans or 20-ounce or ½-liter straight-sided canning jars; shake ground walnuts into containers to coat sides. Pour batter into containers. Place double thickness of foil over cans and tie with string, or seal canning jars as directed. Place on rack in kettle and add boiling water to come halfway up sides of containers. Cover and simmer 1 hour. Remove and cool on racks. Wrap *cans* airtight in foil and refrigerate 2 to 3 days or freeze up to 4 weeks. (Sealed *jars* will keep at *room temperature* up to 4 weeks.) To serve, remove from container and reheat in top of double boiler over simmering water 30 to 40 minutes or until hot. (If pudding sticks in container, loosen by dipping container in hot water.) Slice and serve with Peppermint Sauce. Each pudding makes 4 to 6 servings.

PEPPERMINT SAUCE

½ cup water
2 tablespoons cornstarch
⅔ cup ground peppermint candies
¼ teaspoon salt
1 cup heavy or whipping cream

In small saucepan stir water and cornstarch until blended. Add candies and salt; cook and stir over medium heat until thickened and smooth. Cool slightly, then stir in cream. Serve immediately. To store, refrigerate 2 to 3 days; reheat over low heat. Good on Steamed Chocolate Pudding, ice cream or unfrosted cake. Makes about 1½ cups.

INDIVIDUAL STEAMED DATE PUDDINGS

1 package (8 ounces) chopped dates
½ cup brandy
2 cups flour
2 teaspoons baking powder
1 teaspoon cinnamon
½ teaspoon each ginger and cloves
¼ teaspoon salt
½ cup butter or margarine, softened
1 cup honey
2 eggs

½ cup orange juice
1 cup chopped pecans or walnuts
1 teaspoon grated orange peel
Hard Sauce (recipe follows)

Soak dates in brandy several hours. Stir together flour, baking powder, spices and salt; set aside. In large bowl of mixer beat butter and honey until well blended. Add eggs one at a time, beating well after each. Mix in flour mixture alternately with orange juice. Stir in pecans, orange peel and date-brandy mixture. Pour into 8 greased 6-ounce custard cups to about 1 inch from top, cover each with square of greased foil and secure with elastic band. Place wire rack in extra-large skillet at least 2½ inches deep (or in 2 smaller skillets), arrange cups on rack and add enough boiling water to come halfway up sides of cups. Cover skillet and steam 1 hour. Remove cups and cool on rack; remove foil and turn out puddings when cool enough to handle. Will keep in refrigerator about 2 weeks. To serve, reheat and top with Hard Sauce. Makes 8 servings.

HARD SAUCE Cream ⅓ cup softened butter until fluffy. Gradually beat in 1 cup confectioners' sugar. Add ½ teaspoon vanilla. Keep refrigerated.

CRANBERRY-ORANGE STEAMED PUDDING

1 cup flour
½ cup sugar
2 teaspoons baking powder
½ cup raisins
3 medium oranges
½ cup raw cranberries
14 (2-inch each) saltines
2 eggs
¼ cup butter or margarine, melted
½ teaspoon vanilla
Rum or brandy (optional)
Confectioners' sugar (optional)
Whipped cream flavored with brandy or sugar to taste

Mix well flour, sugar, baking powder and raisins; set aside. Grate peel from 1 orange and reserve. Peel remaining oranges and remove pith from all. Cut in quarters, remove seeds and purée in blender (there should be 1 cup). Add cranberries, saltines, eggs, butter and vanilla; whirl until cranberries are chopped coarse. Remove to large bowl and stir in flour mixture and orange peel until well blended. Spoon into well-greased 1-pound coffee can. Cover with foil top, allowing some slack for pudding to rise. Put can on rack in deep pot. Add hot water to pot to 2-inch depth, cover and steam 2 hours or until pudding starts to pull away from sides of can. (Check water in pot occasionally, adding more if necessary.) Remove can from pot, cool on rack 30 minutes, then unmold pudding and cool completely. Return to can for storage or giving; cover with snap-on lid. Will keep in refrigerator about 1 week. To reheat, sprinkle with a few tablespoons rum or brandy and steam as above about 30 minutes or until heated through. To serve, sift with confectioners' sugar, cut in slices and top with flavored whipped cream. Makes 8 to 10 servings.

Pickles and Relishes

Including chutney, pickles and relishes

CURRANT-CORN RELISH

1   cup white vinegar
½   cup sugar
1   teaspoon salt
1   teaspoon whole celery seed
½   teaspoon whole mustard seed
½   teaspoon hot-pepper sauce
2   cans (12 ounces each) whole-kernel corn, drained
¼   cup finely chopped green pepper
3   tablespoons currants
2   tablespoons finely chopped onion
1   jar or can (2 ounces) pimientos, drained and chopped

In saucepan mix vinegar, sugar, salt, celery and mustard seeds and pepper sauce; boil 2 minutes. Remove from heat and add corn, green pepper, currants, onion and pimientos. Pour into clean jars, cover and store in refrigerator. Will keep about 1 week. Makes 4 half-pints.

EASY TOMATO RELISH

1   can (28 ounces) tomatoes
1   cup sugar
1   cup cider vinegar
1   medium tart apple, chopped fine (1 cup)
2   cloves garlic, minced
½   teaspoon ginger
¼   teaspoon cayenne
½   cup golden raisins

In heavy kettle mix well tomatoes, sugar, vinegar, apple, garlic, ginger and cayenne. Cook over medium heat, stirring occasionally, until mixture thickens, about 40 minutes. Stir in raisins and cook 5 minutes longer. Spoon into 3 hot sterilized ½-pint jars and seal at once. Store in refrigerator; will keep about 2 months. Makes 3 half-pints.

PICKLED MUSHROOMS

1   pound small mushrooms
Salt
1   quart water
⅓   cup oil
¼   cup white-wine or cider vinegar
1   small onion, chopped
1   clove garlic, minced
½   teaspoon peppercorns
1   bay leaf

Cut thin slice from bottom of mushroom stems; discard slice. Dissolve 1 tablespoon salt in the water, add mushrooms and soak 10 minutes; drain. In saucepan mix well oil, vinegar, onion, garlic, peppercorns, bay leaf and 1 teaspoon salt. Add mushrooms, bring to boil and simmer 5 minutes or until tender. Cool completely and pour into jars. Will keep in refrigerator 2 weeks. Makes about 2 cups.

PICKLED PINEAPPLE SLICES

1   can (29½ ounces) pineapple slices, reserve 1¼ cups syrup
1   cup sugar
½   cup cider vinegar
Cinnamon stick
Whole cloves

In large skillet bring to boil reserved pineapple syrup, sugar, vinegar and cinnamon stick. Cook and stir 10 minutes. Stick each pineapple slice with a clove and carefully add to skillet. Simmer 20 minutes, basting frequently with syrup. Remove from heat and cool completely. Put in jars or containers; cover tightly and refrigerate. Keeps up to 2 months. Makes 8 large slices.

SWEET CARROT PICKLES

2   pounds carrots, peeled and cut in sticks or coins
1   cinnamon stick
2   tablespoons mixed pickling spices
2   cups white or cider vinegar
1   cup each sugar and water
1   teaspoon salt

Cook carrots until almost tender; drain. Tie cinnamon and spices in cheesecloth. Bring to boil spices, vinegar, sugar, water and salt. Boil gently 8 minutes. Pack carrots in hot sterilized jars. Remove spice bag. Pour hot syrup over carrots, leaving ¼-inch headspace. Seal at once, then process in boiling-water bath 30 minutes. Will keep several months in cool place. Makes about 6 half-pints.

PICKLED CAULIFLOWER

1   head cauliflower, broken in florets
Salt
Water
1   cup oil
½   cup cider vinegar
1   rib celery including top, sliced thin
1   small onion, chopped
1   thick slice lemon
1   clove garlic, minced
¼   teaspoon peppercorns
¼   teaspoon mustard seed
1   bay leaf
⅓   cup chopped pimiento

Cook cauliflorets in ½-inch boiling salted water 10 minutes or until fork-tender; drain and set aside. In saucepan bring to boil oil, vinegar, celery, onion, lemon, garlic, 1 teaspoon salt, peppercorns, mustard seed and bay leaf; pour over cauliflorets. Gently stir in pimiento. Cover and chill. Makes 1½ quarts.

ZUCCHINI PICKLES

4   medium zucchini, sliced thin (1 quart)
1   small green pepper, chopped
2   small onions, sliced thin
4   teaspoons pickling salt
2   trays ice cubes
¾   cup each sugar and white vinegar
1   teaspoon each dillweed and mustard seed
½   teaspoon celery seed

In large mixing bowl mix zucchini, pepper, onions, salt and ice cubes; let stand at room temperature 3 hours; drain well. In kettle bring to boil sugar, vinegar and seasonings; add vegetables and heat just to boiling. Ladle into 4 hot sterilized ½-pint jars, leaving ½-inch headspace; seal at once and process in boiling-water bath 5 minutes. Let stand at least 3 weeks before serving. Makes 4 half-pints.

CAPONATA

2   large green peppers, seeded and chopped (2 cups)
3   small onions, chopped (about 1½ cups)
½   cup olive oil, divided
4   ribs celery, chopped (about 1½ cups)
2   medium eggplants, diced (6 cups)
2   cans (28 ounces each) peeled tomatoes, chopped coarse
1   can (16 ounces) pitted black olives, drained and sliced
1   jar (2 ounces) pitted green olives, drained and sliced
2   tablespoons capers
½   cup vinegar mixed with 2 tablespoons sugar
2   cloves garlic, halved, with wood pick inserted in each piece

In large skillet sauté peppers and onions in ¼ cup oil until crisp-tender, about 10 minutes, stirring frequently. Add celery and eggplant and cook and stir until eggplant is limp, adding remaining ¼ cup oil as needed. Stir in tomatoes, olives, capers and ¼ cup vinegar mixture. Cook uncovered over low heat 15 minutes. Transfer mixture to large bowl; add remaining ¼ cup vinegar and toss lightly. Bury garlic in mixture. Cover tightly and store in refrigerator 24 hours to blend flavors, or until giving. Will keep about 2 weeks. Serve cold. If desired, remove garlic cloves before giving. Makes about 10 cups.

TO CAN Pack in ten ½-pint jars. Seal according to manufacturer's instructions and process in pressure *canner* at 10 pounds pressure 25 minutes or in pressure *saucepan* 50 minutes.

PRESERVED ORANGE SLICES

2   medium oranges
2   cups sugar
1   cup water or orange juice

Wash and dry oranges. Slice about 3/16 inch thick. Discard ends and remove pits; set slices aside. In heavy large saucepan bring to boil sugar and water. Cook without stirring until candy thermometer registers 240° (soft-ball stage), 20 to 25 minutes. Add orange slices, bring to boil and simmer until slices are transparent and tender but do not lose their shape, about 15 minutes. Pack in clean wide-mouth jars and cover with remaining syrup. Cover tightly and store in cool place. Good as relish with roast pork, goose or duck (or as topping for plain cakes or puddings or in drinks). Keeps about 2 months. Makes about 3 cups.

CINNAMON-APPLE SLICES

1   cup light corn syrup
½   cup red cinnamon candies
½   cup cider vinegar
8   whole cloves
1   cinnamon stick
4   medium-size firm tart apples, cored and cut crosswise in ½-inch slices

In heavy 10-inch skillet bring to boil over medium heat corn syrup, candies, vinegar, cloves and cinnamon stick. Cook and stir until candies melt. Add enough apple slices to make a single layer in skillet and simmer just until slices are tender and transparent but do not lose their shape, 10 to 12 minutes. Remove with slotted spoon to clean wide-mouth jars. Cook remaining apple slices, place in jars and pour remaining syrup over slices. Cover tightly and chill at least 1 week before serving. Good as relish with roast meat (or as topping for puddings). Keeps about 3 weeks. Makes about 3 cups.

ANNE'S FRESH-CRANBERRY CHUTNEY

1¾ cups each sugar and water
1 pound fresh or frozen cranberries (4 cups)
1 cup golden raisins
½ cup red-wine vinegar
1½ tablespoons curry powder
2 tablespoons molasses
2 tablespoons grated or minced fresh ginger or 2 teaspoons ginger powder
1 tablespoon Worcestershire
1 teaspoon salt
½ teaspoon hot-pepper sauce

In medium saucepan bring to boil sugar and water; simmer 5 minutes. Add cranberries; cook just until skins pop, about 5 minutes. Stir in remaining ingredients; simmer uncovered 15 minutes or until thickened, stirring occasionally. Ladle into hot sterilized jars. Seal at once, then process in boiling-water bath 5 minutes. Makes about 2 pints. **Note** If desired, omit boiling-water bath. Store airtight in refrigerator. Will keep about 6 weeks.

Quick Breads and Crackers

NUT-PUMPKIN LOAVES

2½ cups flour
½ cup plus 2 tablespoons wheat germ, divided
½ cup chopped nuts
1 tablespoon baking powder
½ teaspoon baking soda
1½ teaspoons salt
1 teaspoon each cinnamon and ginger
¼ teaspoon nutmeg
1½ cups sugar
½ cup oil
2 eggs
1 can (1 pound) pumpkin

Stir together flour, ½ cup wheat germ, nuts, baking powder, soda, salt and spices until well blended; set aside. Beat together sugar, oil and eggs until well blended. Beat in pumpkin until well blended. Stir in flour mixture until well blended (**do not overmix**). Turn into 2 well-greased 8x4x2-inch loaf pans. Sprinkle each with 1 tablespoon wheat germ. Bake in preheated 350° oven 50 to 60 minutes or until pick inserted in center comes out clean. Cool in pans on

rack about 5 minutes. Turn out on rack to cool. Store airtight in cool, dry place. Will keep about 1 week in refrigerator. Makes 2 loaves.

FRUIT-NUT BREAD

1¾ cups flour
1 cup sugar
½ teaspoon salt
4 teaspoons baking powder
1 cup coarsely chopped walnuts
½ cup mixed candied fruit
1 egg, well beaten
Grated peel of 1 lemon (1 tablespoon)
¾ cup evaporated milk
½ cup water
2 tablespoons butter or margarine, melted

In medium bowl mix well flour, sugar, salt and baking powder. Stir in nuts and fruit. Mix well egg, peel, milk, water and butter; pour into dry ingredients. Stir just until dry ingredients are moistened. Put in well-greased 9x5x3-inch loaf pan. Bake in preheated 350° oven 60 to 65 minutes. Cool in pan 10 minutes, then turn out on rack to cool. Wrap in foil and store in refrigerator. Will keep about 1 week. Can be frozen. Makes 1 loaf.

BRANDIED MINCEMEAT BANANA BREAD

1 package (9 ounces) condensed mincemeat
¼ cup brandy
3 cups flour
1 tablespoon baking powder
1 teaspoon salt
1 cup mashed ripe banana
½ cup each dark corn syrup and milk
¼ cup each sugar and oil
1 egg

In small bowl, break up mincemeat; add brandy and soak until brandy is absorbed. Stir together flour, baking powder and salt; set aside. In large bowl beat together banana, corn syrup, milk, sugar, oil and egg. Beat in mincemeat, then flour mixture until well mixed. Turn into five greased and floured 1½-cup soup cans. Bake in preheated 350° oven until pick inserted in center comes out clean, 45 to 50 minutes. Cool in cans 5 minutes; turn out on rack. Cool completely before wrapping or slicing. Store tightly wrapped in refrigerator. Will keep 2 weeks. Makes 5 small round loaves. **Note** Bread may be baked in 9 x 5 x 3-inch loaf pan. Bake in preheated 350° oven 1 hour 15 minutes or until pick inserted in center comes out clean.

RAISIN-ALMOND LOAVES

1 cup boiling water
¾ cup raisins
⅔ cup packed light-brown sugar
⅓ cup each oil and molasses
1 egg
2½ cups flour
1½ teaspoons baking soda
¾ teaspoon cinnamon
½ teaspoon salt
½ cup chopped almonds (plus ¼ cup chopped or slivered for decoration; optional)

In large bowl pour boiling water over raisins. Stir in sugar, oil and molasses; cool to 110° (warm). Beat in egg until blended. Stir together flour, soda, cinnamon, salt and ½ cup chopped almonds. Stir in molasses mixture just until dry mixture is moistened. Turn into 2 greased 7x3x2-inch loaf pans lined with waxed paper. Decorate with remaining almonds. Bake in preheated 350° oven until pick inserted in center comes out clean, 35 minutes. Cool in pans 10 minutes; loosen edges with thin-bladed spatula. Turn out and cool on rack. Wrap airtight in foil. Keeps about 1 week. Makes 2 loaves. **Note** Can be baked in one 9 x 5 x 3-inch loaf pan 1 hour or until pick inserted in center comes out clean.

MAPLE, WHOLE-WHEAT AND RAISIN BREAD

2 cups whole-wheat flour
½ cup all-purpose flour
1 teaspoon baking soda
½ teaspoon baking powder
1½ cups buttermilk
½ cup maple or maple-flavored syrup
1 egg
1 tablespoon butter or margarine, melted
1 cup golden raisins, plumped (see Note)

In bowl mix flours, baking soda and powder; set aside. Beat buttermilk, syrup, egg and butter until well blended. Stir into flour mixture just to moisten. Fold in raisins. Spoon into 2 greased 1-pound coffee cans. Bake in preheated 350° oven until pick inserted in center comes out clean, 35 to 45 minutes. Cool in pan 10 minutes. With knife loosen edges and invert on racks, removing cans. Cool. Wrap airtight and store in cool place. Will keep 3 days. **Note** To plump raisins cover with hot water. Let stand 5 to 10 minutes. Drain well.

ARMENIAN-STYLE WHOLE-WHEAT LAVASH

1 envelope active dry yeast
⅔ cup warm water (115°)
¼ cup sugar
½ teaspoon salt
¼ teaspoon cinnamon (optional)
½ cup butter or margarine, softened
1 egg
1¼ cups whole-wheat flour
About 1¼ cups all-purpose flour, divided
1 egg, beaten
Sesame seed

In bowl sprinkle yeast over warm water, stir until dissolved. Add sugar, salt, cinnamon, butter, egg and whole-wheat flour. Beat until smooth. Gradually beat in 1 cup all-purpose flour to make a stiff dough. Turn out on lightly floured surface, knead until smooth and elastic, using remaining ¼ cup flour. Place in greased bowl; turn to grease top. Cover; let rise in warm, draft-free place until doubled, about 1 hour. Punch down and let rise again until doubled, about 45 minutes. Turn out and knead until smooth. Shape in roll and cut in 16 equal pieces. On lightly floured pastry cloth roll each piece to very thin 8-inch circle. Put 2 on each cookie sheet. Brush with egg and sprinkle with sesame seed. Bake in preheated 350° oven until bread starts to get dry, lightly browned and blistered, 8 to 10 minutes. Turn bottoms up and bake 2 minutes longer. Remove to racks to cool. Store stacked in plastic bag in dry place. Good with butter or cottage cheese and honey. Will keep about 3 weeks. Makes 16.

GRAHAM CRISPS

2 cups whole-wheat flour
¾ cup all-purpose flour
1 teaspoon baking powder
½ teaspoon baking soda
½ cup shortening
1 cup packed brown sugar
½ teaspoon salt
½ cup buttermilk, or ½ cup milk mixed with 1 teaspoon lemon juice

Stir together whole-wheat flour, all-purpose flour, baking powder and soda; set aside. In large bowl of mixer, cream shortening, sugar and salt until light. Stir in flour mixture alternately with buttermilk. Turn out on lightly floured surface and work with hands just until smooth. Cut in quarters. On lightly floured pastry cloth roll each quarter about ⅛ inch thick. Prick with fork. Cut out with 3-inch round cutter and place ¼ inch apart on greased cookie sheet. Bake in preheated 350° oven until crisp and light brown, 10 to 12 minutes. Remove to rack to cool. Good with cheese or jam. Store loosely covered in dry place. Will keep 2 to 3 weeks. Makes about 60.

SEEDED CHEESE CRACKERS

¾ cup flour
¼ cup wheat germ
2 teaspoons caraway seed, lightly crushed
¼ teaspoon salt
Dash of cayenne
⅓ cup butter or margarine, softened
1½ cups (6 ounces) coarsely shredded sharp Cheddar cheese

In large bowl, stir together flour, wheat germ, caraway seed, salt and cayenne. Add butter and cheese and mix with hand to form dough. Divide in half and shape each half in roll about 1½ inches in diameter. Wrap airtight and chill 1 hour. Cut with serrated knife in 3/16-inch slices and place ½ inch apart on greased cookie sheet. Bake in preheated 350° oven until golden brown, 12 to 14 minutes. Remove to rack to cool. Store airtight in cool dry place. Will keep about 2 weeks. Makes about 48.

LAVASH CRACKERS

1 envelope active dry yeast
¾ cup warm water (115°)
1 teaspoon sugar
½ teaspoon salt
About 2½ cups flour

In mixing bowl, sprinkle yeast over warm water; stir until dissolved. Add sugar, salt and 1½ cups flour. Beat until smooth. Gradually beat in enough flour to make a stiff dough. Turn out on lightly floured surface and knead until smooth and elastic. Place in greased bowl; turn to grease top. Cover; let rise in warm, draft-free place until doubled, about 45 minutes. Punch down and let rise again in warm, draft-free place until doubled, about 30 minutes. Turn dough out and knead until smooth. Shape in long thin rope and cut in 24 pieces. On lightly floured pastry cloth roll each piece very thin in round or oblong shape. Put on cookie sheet and bake in preheated 400° oven until crackers start to get dry, lightly browned and blistered, about 7 minutes. Remove to racks to cool. Store loosely covered in dry place. Good with butter and cheese. Will keep 3 to 4 weeks. Makes 24.

Seasonings, Dressings

ZIPPY BARBECUE SAUCE

1 cup chili sauce
½ cup wine vinegar

1 small onion, chopped
1 teaspoon each paprika, chili powder, salt and Worcestershire
Juice and grated peel of ½ lemon

In small saucepan mix well all ingredients. Simmer 15 minutes, stirring often. Pour into bottles and cover. Keeps refrigerated at least 4 weeks. Makes 1¾ cups.

HERBED CROUTONS

¼ cup grated Parmesan cheese
2 tablespoons oregano
2 tablespoons garlic powder
1 tablespoon basil
½ teaspoon salt
½ teaspoon freshly ground pepper
4 to 5 cups dry bread cubes
3 tablespoons oil

In small bowl mix cheese, oregano, garlic powder, basil, salt and pepper; set aside. In large bowl toss bread cubes with oil, then toss with cheese-herb mixture until well mixed. Spread on ungreased cookie sheet. Bake in 225° oven 1 hour or until crisp and light golden, stirring occasionally so all sides toast. Cool. Store in plastic bags secured with tie; will keep about 1 month. Makes 4 to 5 cups.

SAVORY MUSTARD SAUCE

2 tablespoons Dijon-style mustard
2 tablespoons wine vinegar
½ cup oil
1 tablespoon sugar
1 teaspoon dried dillweed, or to taste
¼ teaspoon salt
⅛ teaspoon pepper

In small bowl beat mustard and vinegar until well blended and smooth. Gradually beat in oil until sauce is smooth, shiny and thick; stir in sugar, dillweed, salt and pepper. Store in jar in cool place. Good on seafood. Makes about ¾ cup.

POULTRY SEASONING

Thinly shredded peel of 2 lemons
½ cup parsley flakes
1 tablespoon salt
1 tablespoon each thyme and marjoram
1 teaspoon freshly ground pepper

Spread peel on paper-towel-lined cookie sheet, put in warm dry place (oven with pilot light) and let stand 1 hour, or until dried. Combine with remaining ingredients and store in airtight jar. Sprinkle on roast chicken or pork or use in stuffing or basting sauce. Makes about ¾ cup.

CALIFORNIA SALAD SEASONING

¾ cup grated Parmesan cheese
¼ cup parsley flakes
1 teaspoon garlic powder
½ teaspoon freshly ground pepper
1 teaspoon chives
1 teaspoon bell pepper flakes
1 teaspoon basil
½ teaspoon salt

Mix well all ingredients and store in small airtight jars. Sprinkle on tossed green salad, sliced zucchini or cucumber-tomato salad. Makes about 1 cup.

SHERRY PEPPERS

Slit small hot red or green peppers lengthwise. Pack, but do not crush, in small jug or other small attractive bottle (such as salad-dressing bottle). Pour ½ to 1 cup medium-dry sherry over peppers. Close tightly with cork or screw top and let stand 4 to 5 days. Sprinkle spicy liquid lightly as seasoning over cooked greens, seafood salad, chowder, soup, stew, curry or gravy. Makes ½ to 1 cup.

MILD CURRY SEASONING

½ cup plus 1 tablespoon coriander
¼ cup plus 2 tablespoons turmeric
2 tablespoons salt
1½ tablespoons fenugreek, crushed (see Note)
1 tablespoon each cumin, cardamom and dry mustard
1½ teaspoons each garlic powder, cayenne and dillseed, crushed
¾ teaspoon each cinnamon, ginger, mace, cloves and fennel, crushed

Mix well all ingredients, divide in thirds and pour into spice jars (some vitamins come in reusable jars suitable for spices). Use as specified in favorite curry recipes. Makes enough to fill three 3-ounce jars. **Note** To crush fenugreek, dill and fennel seeds, place in mortar and crush with pestle, or wrap in cloth and crush with hammer or some other heavy object.

HOT CURRY SEASONING Add 1 tablespoon (or more for extra-hot) crushed red pepper to Mild Curry Seasoning.

LEMON-PARSLEY BUTTER LOG

½ cup butter or margarine, softened
2 tablespoons lemon juice
2 teaspoons dried parsley
1 teaspoon finely grated lemon peel

In small bowl of mixer, beat butter until creamy and light. Gradually beat in lemon juice a drop at a time until well blended. Blend in parsley and lemon peel.

Chill in freezer 8 to 10 minutes or in refrigerator 30 minutes (until butter starts to harden but is still soft enough to mold). On waxed paper, plastic wrap or foil, with spatula mold butter in 5-inch log. Chill until firm. Wrap airtight. Store in refrigerator; will keep a few weeks. To use, slice off desired amount and flavor broiled fish or cooked vegetables (especially good on broccoli or asparagus). Or soften and use as a spread on sandwiches and canapés. Makes ½ cup.

TARRAGON BUTTER LOG Reduce lemon juice to 1 tablespoon and substitute 1 teaspoon tarragon for parsley and lemon peel. Good on broiled fish or chicken, toasted Italian or French bread, or use it to cook veal or eggs. Makes ½ cup.

HORSERADISH BUTTER LOG Substitute 2 tablespoons prepared horseradish for the lemon juice, parsley and lemon peel. Good on broiled beef, ham or fish. Makes ½ cup.

Jellies, Jams and Marmalades

ORANGE-WINE JELLY

3½ cups sugar
1 cup dry white wine
½ cup orange juice
2 tablespoons lemon juice
1 tablespoon finely shredded orange peel
½ bottle (6 ounces) liquid pectin

In top of double boiler over hot water or in heavy saucepan over low heat mix well sugar, wine, orange and lemon juices and peel. Cook and stir until sugar dissolves. Remove from heat; stir in pectin. Ladle into hot sterilized jars. If using 2-piece metal caps, leave ⅛-inch headspace. Close tightly, then invert jars a few seconds and stand upright to cool. If using paraffin, leave ½-inch space; pour in ⅛ inch hot paraffin. Cool; cover with loose-fitting lid. Store in cool, dry place. Will keep 3 to 4 months. Makes 3 half-pints. **Note** Check expiration date on bottle to be sure pectin is fresh.

LOUISIANA HOT-PEPPER JELLY

1 cup water
2 teaspoons hot-pepper sauce, or to taste
⅓ cup lemon juice
3 cups sugar
½ bottle (6 ounces) liquid pectin
Red food coloring (optional)

In large saucepan mix well water, pepper sauce, lemon juice and sugar. Bring to boil, stirring. Add pectin and a few drops of food coloring; cook and stir until mixture comes to full rolling boil. Boil hard ½ minute. Remove from heat; skim. Pour into 3 hot sterilized 8-ounce jars; cover with ⅛ inch paraffin. Cool. Will keep several months in cool, dry place. Good with meat and on cream-cheese party sandwiches. Makes 3 half-pints. **Note** Check expiration date on bottle to be sure pectin is fresh.

PRUNE-WALNUT CONSERVE

4   lemons, sliced thin
2   cups sugar
1   package (12 ounces) pitted prunes, each cut in half
1¼   cups coarsely chopped walnuts
¼   to ½ teaspoon nutmeg
¼   cup port

In heavy saucepan cook lemon slices, uncovered, in 4 cups water until slices are tender, 20 minutes. Drain off liquid and measure (you will need 3 cups; add water if necessary to make up amount). Put liquid back in saucepan with lemon slices, sugar and prunes. Cook over medium heat, stirring occasionally until liquid is lightly syrupy, 30 minutes. Remove from heat and stir in remaining ingredients. Ladle at once into hot sterilized jars or glasses and seal. Keeps several months. Makes six ½-pint jars.

EASY STRAWBERRY JAM

2   packages (10 ounces each) frozen sliced strawberries, thawed
2½   cups sugar
¼   bottle (6 ounces) liquid pectin

Combine strawberries and sugar in heavy 4-quart saucepan and mix well. Bring to boil over high heat and boil rapidly 1 minute, stirring constantly. Remove from heat and immediately stir in the pectin. Skim off foam with metal spoon, then stir and skim 5 minutes to cool slightly and to prevent fruit from floating. Ladle into sterilized jars and seal at once with ⅛ inch paraffin. Cool completely. Keeps several months. Makes about 3 cups. **Note** Check expiration date on bottle to be sure pectin is fresh.

PEACH-ORANGE MARMALADE

2   packages (10 ounces each) frozen sliced peaches, undrained (2 cups)
1   small orange, washed, seeded and ground
1½   cups sugar

In 3-quart wide saucepan, bring to boil peaches, orange and sugar. Boil rapidly, stirring often, until syrup is thick, about 15 minutes. Ladle into hot sterilized jars. If using 2-piece metal caps, leave ⅛-inch headspace. Close tightly, then invert jars a few seconds and stand upright to cool. If using paraffin, leave ½-inch space; pour in ⅛ inch hot paraffin. Cool; cover with loose-fitting lid. Will keep several months. Makes about 2½ cups.

LIME MARMALADE

2   large or 3 medium limes
Water
2   cups sugar
Few drops of green food coloring (optional)

With brush scrub limes in warm water. With vegetable peeler remove zest (green portion of peel) in strips, cook in water to cover in small saucepan 10 minutes, then drain and rinse with cold water. Repeat; reserve. Remove all white pith from limes, cut fruit in quarters and remove seeds. In blender whirl limes, 1 cup water and the zest until finely chopped. Pour into large heavy saucepan; add sugar. Bring to boil and cook rapidly about 15 minutes, stirring often. Do not overcook. (Mixture will still be thin but will thicken after chilling. To test, chill small amount on saucer. It should be of marmalade consistency.) Stir in coloring. Ladle into small hot sterilized jars. If using 2-piece metal caps, leave ⅛-inch headspace. Close tightly, then invert jars a few seconds and stand upright to cool. If using paraffin, leave ½-inch space; pour in ⅛ inch hot paraffin. Cool; cover with loose-fitting lid. Will keep several months. Makes 1⅔ cups.

Yeast Breads and Coffee Cakes

APPLE-OATMEAL BREAD

1   cup quick-cooking rolled oats (not instant)
¼   cup packed brown sugar
2   tablespoons butter or margarine
1½   teaspoons salt
¼   teaspoon nutmeg
1½   cups apple juice
1   envelope active dry yeast
About 3½ cups flour, divided
Melted butter or margarine (optional)

In large bowl mix well oats, sugar, butter, salt and nutmeg. Bring juice to boil, pour over oat mixture, stir well and cool to 110° (warm), about 20 minutes. Sprinkle with yeast and mix well. Let stand about 1 minute, then stir in ½ cup flour. Mix well, then stir in 1 cup flour. Cover tightly with plastic wrap and let stand in warm draft-free place until doubled in bulk, about 1 hour. Stir down, add 2 cups remaining flour or enough to make firm dough that leaves sides of bowl. Turn out on lightly floured surface and knead 5 minutes or until smooth and elastic. Shape in loaf and place in greased 9 x 5 x 3-inch loaf pan. Cover loosely and let rise in warm draft-free place until dough comes to top of pan, about 1 hour. Bake in preheated 350° oven 50 minutes or until top is quite brown (it will *not* sound hollow when tapped). Turn out on rack and brush with melted butter. Store in cool dry place; will keep about 1 week. Can be frozen. Makes 1 loaf.

BRAN MONKEY BREAD

About 3¾ to 4¼ cups flour
1½ cups whole-bran cereal
⅓ cup sugar
1 teaspoon salt
2 envelopes active dry yeast
1 cup milk
½ cup water
⅓ cup butter or margarine
1 egg, at room temperature
⅓ cup butter or margarine, melted

In large bowl mix thoroughly 1 cup flour, the bran cereal, sugar, salt and yeast. In saucepan mix well milk, water and ⅓ cup butter. Heat until liquids are very warm (120° to 130°); butter does not need to melt. Gradually add to dry ingredients and beat 2 minutes at medium speed, scraping bowl occasionally. Add egg and ½ cup flour. Beat at high speed 2 minutes, scraping bowl occasionally. Stir in enough remaining flour to make a stiff batter. Cover; let rise in warm, draft-free place until doubled, about 1 hour 15 minutes. Stir down. Turn out onto well-floured surface and roll out to 21 x 12-inch rectangle. Cut in 1½-inch strips, then crosswise in 3-inch pieces. Brush each piece with melted butter, then toss helter-skelter into 10-inch angel-cake pan. Cover; let rise in warm, draft-free place until doubled, about 1 hour 15 minutes. Bake on lowest rack in preheated 400° oven about 30 minutes or until golden brown. Remove from pan and cool on rack. Wrap and store in cool place. Will keep 3 days. Makes 1 "loaf."

DILL-PICKLE RYE BREAD

4 cups all-purpose flour
2 cups rye flour
2 envelopes active dry yeast
1 cup water
½ cup liquid from dill pickles
½ cup buttermilk
¼ cup oil
2 tablespoons sugar
2 teaspoons dillseed
2 teaspoons caraway seed
1 teaspoon salt
1 egg, beaten, or oil

Stir together flours. In large bowl of mixer, mix well 2 cups flour mixture and yeast. In saucepan, heat water, pickle liquid, buttermilk, oil, sugar, seeds and salt until warm (110°); pour over flour-yeast mixture and beat at medium speed about 3 minutes, or until smooth. Add 2 cups flour and beat at low speed about 2 minutes. With wooden spoon, stir in remaining 2 cups flour to make soft dough; turn out on floured surface and knead until smooth and elastic. Cover dough with mixing bowl and let rest 40 minutes. Punch down and knead again until smooth. Divide dough in half and shape in smooth, round balls; place each in greased 1-quart round glass casserole. With sharp knife, cut three slits on top of loaves. Brush with egg for shiny, firm crust or with oil for soft crust. Let rise in warm draft-free place until double, about 40 minutes. Bake in preheated 350° oven 50 minutes, or until bread sounds hollow when lightly tapped with fingers. If browning too quickly, cover loosely with foil last 10 minutes of baking. Cool in pans 10 minutes, then turn loaves out on rack to cool completely. Makes 2 loaves.

SOURDOUGH BISCUITS

Biscuits best eaten hot. Give recipe with Sourdough Starter.

1⅓ cups flour
2 teaspoons baking powder
½ teaspoon each baking soda and salt
⅓ cup shortening
1 cup Sourdough Starter (page 144)
1 tablespoon butter or margarine, melted

In bowl stir together flour, baking powder, soda and salt. Cut in shortening until particles are the size of coarse cornmeal. Add Sourdough Starter and stir only until dry mixture is moistened. Turn out onto lightly floured surface and knead lightly until smooth. Roll or pat dough ½ inch thick. Cut out 2-inch rounds and put on ungreased baking sheet. Brush with butter. Let rise in warm, draft-free place until very light to the touch, about 1 hour. Bake in preheated 425° oven 15 to 20 minutes or until golden brown. Makes 13.

SOURDOUGH STARTER

Give with recipe for Sourdough Biscuits, page 143.

1½ teaspoons active dry yeast
2 tablespoons sugar
2 cups flour
2½ cups warm water (115°)

In large glass or pottery mixing bowl mix well yeast, sugar and flour. Gradually add water while beating until mixture is smooth. Cover with plastic wrap and let stand 2 days in warm, draft-free place, such as unheated oven. Beat before using. After using, add 1 cup each flour and warm water (115°) to remaining starter. Beat until smooth. Pour into glass jar or crock with tight-fitting lid, allowing room for expansion. Store in refrigerator. For best results use often. Makes about 3 cups.

HOLIDAY WHOLE-WHEAT WREATHS

2 envelopes active dry yeast
2½ cups warm water (105° to 115°)
1 tablespoon sugar
2 teaspoons salt
2 tablespoons butter or margarine, softened
3 cups whole-wheat flour
About 4 to 5 cups all-purpose flour
Melted butter or margarine
1 tablespoon sesame seed

In large warm bowl sprinkle yeast over warm water; stir until dissolved. Add sugar, salt, softened butter, whole-wheat flour and 1 cup all-purpose flour; beat until smooth. Add enough remaining all-purpose flour to make a stiff dough. Turn out onto generously floured surface; knead until smooth and elastic, 8 to 10 minutes. Place in greased bowl, turning to grease top. Cover; let rise in warm, draft-free place until doubled, about 1 hour. Grease 2 large baking sheets and the outside of two 6-inch round ovenproof bowls or dishes (or make 6 inch foil collars). Place bowl, upside down, on center of each baking sheet; set aside. Punch dough down and divide in half. From half cut off about one eighth of dough; set aside. Divide remaining dough half in 3 equal pieces. Shape in ropes 28 inches long. Braid ropes together. Place braid flat on baking sheet around outside of bowl. Pinch ends together. Roll reserved eighth of dough into 28-inch rope. Shape in bow. Place bow on braid where seams meet. Make another wreath with remaining dough half. Cover; let rise in warm, draft-free place 30 minutes. Brush melted butter gently over wreaths; sprinkle evenly with sesame seed. Bake in preheated 375° oven 30 to 40 minutes or until wreaths sound hollow when lightly tapped. Remove from baking sheets; cool on racks. Wrap and store in cool place. Will keep 1 week. Makes 2 wreaths.

STOLLEN

¾ cup mixed candied fruit
½ cup raisins
2 tablespoons rum
About 5½ to 6½ cups flour
½ cup sugar
1¼ teaspoons salt
2 envelopes active dry yeast
1¼ cups milk
½ cup butter or margarine
3 eggs, at room temperature
¾ cup chopped almonds
Confectioners'-Sugar Frosting (recipe follows)
Sliced almonds
Candied cherries

Mix well fruit, raisins and rum; set aside. In large bowl of mixer stir together 2 cups flour, the sugar, salt and yeast until well mixed. Heat milk and butter until very warm (120° to 130°); butter does not need to melt. Gradually add to flour mixture and beat 2 minutes at medium speed, scraping bowl occasionally. Add eggs and ½ cup remaining flour or enough to make a thick batter. Beat at high speed 2 minutes, scraping bowl occasionally. Stir in enough remaining flour to make a soft dough. Turn out onto generously floured surface; knead until smooth and elastic, 8 to 10 minutes. Place in greased bowl; turn to grease top. Cover; let rise in warm, draft-free place until doubled, about 1½ hours. Punch down. On floured surface knead in fruit mixture and almonds. Divide in 3 equal pieces and roll each to about 12 x 7-inch oval. Fold each in half lengthwise. Place on greased baking sheets. Cover; let rise in warm, draft-free place until doubled, about 45 minutes. Bake in preheated 350° oven 20 to 25 minutes or until bread sounds hollow when tapped. Cool slightly on racks. Frost with Confectioners'-Sugar Frosting. Decorate with sliced almonds and cherries. Remove from racks and cool completely. Wrap and store in cool place. Will keep 3 days. Makes 3 loaves.

CONFECTIONERS'-SUGAR FROSTING In small bowl stir 1 cup confectioners' sugar and 1 tablespoon water until smooth.

ALMOND-FRUIT BRAID

5 to 5½ cups flour
2 envelopes active dry yeast
½ cup butter or margarine

1¼ cups milk
½ cup sugar
1 teaspoon salt
2 eggs, at room temperature
½ cup golden raisins
½ cup chopped mixed candied fruits
½ cup chopped blanched almonds
1 egg yolk beaten with 1 tablespoon milk

In large bowl of mixer, stir together 2 cups flour and yeast. In saucepan melt butter over low heat; stir in milk, sugar and salt and heat until very warm (120°). Pour slowly over flour mixture and beat at medium speed about 3 minutes, or until smooth. Add eggs and 1 cup flour and beat 2 minutes more. With wooden spoon, stir in raisins, ½ cup fruits, the almonds and remaining 2 to 2½ cups flour to make a soft dough. Turn out on lightly floured surface and knead until smooth and elastic. Cover dough with mixing bowl and let rest 30 minutes. Punch down and knead until smooth. To make 2 braided loaves, divide dough in half. To shape each loaf, take ⅔ of one of the halves and divide in 3 pieces. Roll each piece between hands to form 15-inch rope. Braid the 3 ropes loosely to make a 12-inch braid; place on lightly greased cookie sheet. Divide remaining third of dough in 3 pieces and shape each into thin 18-inch rope; braid and place on top of first braid, pressing in lightly. Tuck ends of top braid under ends of bottom braid. Let rise in warm draft-free place until doubled, about 45 minutes. Brush with egg-yolk mixture and bake in 350° oven until golden, 25 to 30 minutes. Remove to rack, cover with clean kitchen towel and cool. Makes 2 loaves.

POPPY-SEED COFFEE CAKE

1 envelope active dry yeast
2 tablespoons warm water (115°)
1 cup milk
About 4 cups flour
3 egg yolks
½ cup sugar
¼ teaspoon salt
¾ cup butter or margarine, melted and cooled
1 tablespoon grated lemon peel
3 tablespoons butter or margarine, softened
Poppy-Seed Filling (recipe follows)
Confectioners' sugar

In small bowl sprinkle yeast onto water, allow to soften, then stir to dissolve. Heat milk to warm (105° to 115°) and pour into large mixing bowl. Stir yeast mixture into milk until dissolved. Stir in 2½ cups flour. Cover dough with clean towel and let rise in warm draft-free place until almost double in bulk,

about 1 hour. Beat together egg yolks, sugar and salt until thick and light yellow; stir into dough. Stir in melted butter and lemon peel. Gradually stir in 1½ cups flour. Let stand 20 minutes. Turn out on lightly floured surface (dough should be barely firm enough to handle). Knead thoroughly, working in additional flour, until dough is just firm enough to cut without sticking (dough must be soft; add no more flour than necessary). Roll out in 20 x 16-inch rectangle. Spread with softened butter; sprinkle with Poppy-Seed Filling. Starting at long edge, roll up as for jelly roll. Carefully lift into greased and floured 3-quart fluted tube pan or 10-inch tube pan. Gently press ends together to join. Cover with towel and let rise in warm draft-free place until almost double in bulk, about 1 hour. Bake in 325° oven 1 hour 15 minutes (as soon as top is rich golden brown, cover loosely with foil). Cool in pan 5 minutes, then turn out onto wire rack. Sprinkle generously with confectioners' sugar. Cool. Store airtight at room temperature up to 3 days or freeze up to 3 months. To serve, cut in thin slices. Makes 1 coffee cake.

POPPY-SEED FILLING Whirl poppy seed about ¼ cup at a time in blender or all at once in food processor to very coarse powder; measure 1¼ cups into saucepan. Add ½ cup milk, ⅓ cup sugar and 10 tablespoons golden raisins. Cook over low heat, stirring, until blended and thickened, about 10 minutes. Stir in 1 teaspoon vanilla and cool.

Chapter

8

PARTIES, FEASTS AND BUSY-DAY MEALS

Opening your home, drawing people close, welcoming relatives, friends, neighbors, casual visitors—at Christmas our awareness of belonging to the human family broadens and deepens, and the mark of it is hospitality. We gather together to eat, drink and celebrate, to enjoy each other's company, and suddenly we realize that Christmas itself has come in the door. Hospitality at Christmas takes many forms, from entertaining unexpected callers to staging the big open house or sit-down dinner you plan weeks in advance. With a made-ahead stock of cookies, fruitcakes and snacks from the recipe collection in the previous chapter, you're ready any time for drop-in guests. With the menus, party ideas, recipes for festive foods and beverages and family meal guide given in the pages ahead, you can prepare peacefully for the special invitational events.

Versatile Just-Desserts Party

Like all the menus we suggest, this suits many holiday occasions. A dessert party is an ideal way to entertain in between or after meals—mid-afternoon, after dinner or following an evening event at the school, church or community center. You can make all the glamorous goodies at least a day ahead.

Menu

Cherry-Cream Crown*
Lemon-Curd Tarts*
Profiteroles with Bitter-Chocolate Sauce*
Christmas Cookies (see recipes, page 128)
Fruitcake (see recipes, page 133)
Coffee, Tea, Port, Sweet Sherry

*Recipe Follows

CHERRY-CREAM CROWN

Make a day ahead for thorough chilling.

2   packages (3 ounces each) ladyfingers, separated
1/4 cup brandy or rum
1   package (8 ounces) cream cheese, softened
1/2 cup sugar
1   pint heavy cream
1   teaspoon vanilla
1   can (21 ounces) cherry-pie filling

Brush ladyfingers with brandy. Line sides of 9-inch springform pan tightly with about half the ladyfingers, rounded sides against pan. Beat cheese with sugar until creamy; set aside. In large bowl of mixer whip cream and vanilla until stiff. Gently but thoroughly fold in cheese mixture until well blended. Spread a layer in pan; top with half the remaining ladyfingers. Repeat, then spread with final layer of cheese mixture. Cover and chill in refrigerator overnight (24 hours is even better). Carefully spoon pie filling over cheese layer. Chill several hours. Before serving, remove sides of springform pan and place dessert on serving plate. Serves 10 to 12.

PROFITEROLES WITH BITTER-CHOCOLATE SAUCE

The little cream puffs can be made and filled ahead. Store in airtight containers in freezer up to 2 months.

1   cup water
1/2 cup butter or margarine
1   teaspoon sugar
1/8 teaspoon salt
1   cup flour
4   large eggs
About 1/2 gallon vanilla ice cream
Bitter-Chocolate Sauce (recipe follows)

In medium-size heavy saucepan mix water, butter, sugar and salt. Cook over medium heat until butter melts, then over high heat bring to rolling boil. Remove from heat and add flour all at once. Beat vigorously with wooden spoon until well blended. Stir over medium heat 2 minutes or until mixture forms a ball, leaves sides of pan and begins to form a film on bottom of pan. Turn into large bowl of mixer or food processor and beat 1 minute to cool slightly. Add eggs all together and beat at medium speed until batter is very stiff and forms a ball. Drop dough by level tablespoonfuls about 2 inches apart on ungreased cookie sheets. Bake in preheated 425° oven 20 minutes. Reduce heat to 375° and bake 15 minutes longer. Turn off heat, remove cookie sheets with puffs and cut small slit in side of each puff. Return to oven, leaving door ajar, 10 minutes. Remove to racks to cool. When completely cool, split with sharp knife. Pack about 2 heaping tablespoonfuls ice cream into bottom half of each; replace top. On serving plate arrange profiteroles in pyramid. Store in freezer. Just before serving, drizzle with some Bitter-Chocolate Sauce; serve remainder in sauce boat if desired. Makes 36 profiteroles, or about 12 servings.

BITTER-CHOCOLATE SAUCE   In saucepan stir 8 squares (8 ounces) semisweet chocolate, 2/3 cup water and 3 tablespoons butter or margarine over low heat until chocolate and butter are melted. Stir in 1 teaspoon vanilla. Serve warm or at room temperature. Store any left over in refrigerator. To reheat, stir over low heat until warm. Makes 1 2/3 cups.

LEMON-CURD TARTS

Mix pastry day ahead. Use half for tarts; freeze other half for future use.

1   cup butter or margarine, softened
1   package (8 ounces) cream cheese, softened
2   cups flour
1/2 teaspoon salt
1   egg yolk mixed with 1 teaspoon milk
Lemon-Curd Filling (recipe follows)
Candied red-cherry slivers (optional)

In small bowl of mixer beat butter and cream cheese until blended. With wooden spoon or fingertips blend in flour and salt until pastry is smooth. Shape in flat mound on sheet of foil, wrap and chill overnight. Remove from refrigerator 15 to 30 minutes before rolling. Divide in half; refrigerate or freeze half. Divide remaining pastry in half. Roll out each half in rectangle about ⅛ inch thick. Fold in thirds over itself; roll out again; repeat. With cookie cutter or glass cut out 2½-inch rounds; fit (without stretching) in 1½-inch fluted tart pans, pressing pastry with fingers. Prick with fork. Dip finger in egg-yolk mixture and "brush" lightly on pastry. Chill about 30 minutes. Bake in preheated 375° oven 15 to 20 minutes or until lightly browned. Cool in pans on wire racks. Remove from pans and fill. (Or store unfilled shells in airtight container in cool, dry place; will keep up to 5 days.) Garnish each with cherry sliver. Entire pastry recipe makes 72 tart shells.

LEMON CURD In top of double boiler mix well 4 egg yolks, ½ cup sugar and the peel and juice of 2 lemons. Stir over simmering water until thickened and lemon-colored, about 10 minutes. Beat in ¼ cup butter or margarine. Cook, stirring occasionally. Cover loosely; chill. Makes about 1 cup, or enough to fill about thirty-six 1½-inch tart shells.

Hail the Hearty Supper Party

Here the focus is on informal entertaining after an activity outside the house—caroling, skating, skiing, an expedition of neighborhood families to a Christmas-tree farm. Decorate and set the buffet table before you leave home. Have the soup kettle ready to heat up and sandwich fixings arranged to put together assembly-line fashion.

Menu
Minestrone*
New York-Style Heroes*
or
Philadelphia Hoagies*
Vegetable Relishes
Christmas Cookies (see recipes, page 128)

*Recipe Follows

MINESTRONE
2 ribs celery, chopped
1 large onion, chopped
1 leek, chopped (optional)
1 clove garlic, crushed
¼ cup minced parsley

1½ teaspoons basil
3 tablespoons oil
2 carrots, sliced
2 potatoes, cubed
1 medium turnip, cubed (about 8 ounces)
2 to 3 medium zucchini, cubed
½ small head cabbage, shredded (about ¼ to ½ pound)
1 cup fresh shelled peas or 1 package (10 ounces) frozen peas
1 can (16 ounces) stewed tomatoes
1 quart beef or chicken bouillon
2 cups cooked great northern, navy or kidney beans (1 can, 15 to 16 ounces)
¼ pound elbow macaroni or spaghetti, broken up (1 cup)
Salt and pepper to taste
4 to 6 tablespoons grated Parmesan or Romano cheese

In large kettle sauté celery, onion, leek, garlic, parsley and basil in oil until tender, about 5 minutes. Add carrots, potatoes, turnip, zucchini, cabbage and peas; sauté 10 minutes, stirring occasionally. Stir in tomatoes and bouillon; bring to boil. Reduce heat, cover and simmer 45 minutes, stirring occasionally. Stir in beans and macaroni. Cover and cook 15 minutes or until macaroni and vegetables are tender. Season with salt and pepper. Serve in deep large soup bowls, sprinkle with cheese. Makes 8 to 12 servings.

NEW YORK-STYLE HEROES
6 Italian rolls (about 8 inches long), split
6 tablespoons olive oil
3 tablespoons red-wine vinegar
1 medium head lettuce, shredded fine
1 medium red onion, chopped coarse
36 thin slices Italian salami
Grated Romano cheese to taste
½ pound mushrooms, sliced thin and sautéed in 2 tablespoons butter or margarine, or 2 cans (4 ounces each) sliced mushrooms, drained
1 teaspoon oregano
18 thin slices provolone cheese
18 thin slices capocollo (smoked pork shoulder rubbed with paprika and red pepper)
1 cup black olives, preferably Italian cracked, pits removed
18 thin slices tomato (3 large tomatoes)
Salt to taste
Basil to taste
1 jar (12 ounces) *peperoncini* (mild Italian pickled peppers), drained (optional)
Potato chips (optional)

Remove a little bread from cut sides of each roll. In large bowl mix oil and vinegar thoroughly. Add lettuce and onion. Toss lightly to mix well. On bottom half of each roll arrange a layer of lettuce mixture, 6 salami slices, some grated Romano cheese, a few sliced mushrooms, a sprinkle of oregano, 3 slices each provolone and capocollo, some olives and 3 slices tomato. Season with salt and basil. Cover with roll top and cut in half. Good with *peperoncini* and potato chips. Makes 6 sandwiches.

PHILADELPHIA HOAGIES

6   hoagie or Italian rolls (about 8 inches long), split
Olive oil
24   thin slices capocollo
24   thin slices provolone cheese
24   thin slices cooked *cotechino* or Polish sausage
       (about 6 ounces)
36   thin slices Italian salami
1   medium head lettuce, shredded fine
6   tablespoons coarsely chopped sweet onion
18   thin slices tomato (3 large tomatoes)
Salt
Freshly ground pepper
1   teaspoon oregano
About 18 hot cherry peppers, halved and seeded

Remove a little bread from cut sides of each roll. Brush cut sides generously with oil. On bottom half of each roll place 4 slices each capocollo, provolone and *cotechino*, then 6 slices salami. Add a sixth of the lettuce, 1 tablespoon onion and 3 slices tomato. Drizzle with oil. Season lightly with salt, pepper and oregano. Add 4 to 6 pepper halves. Cover with roll top and cut in half. Makes 6 sandwiches.

Elegant But Easy Buffet Dinner

This beautifully balanced spread spares the hostess and the budget, yet serves up to ten people. The ham is pre-sliced; salad, casserole and fruit mold are all prepared ahead. Put plates, napkins and silverware at one end of the table and line up serving dishes in order given in the menu; hot trays or chafing dishes will keep meat and vegetables warm.

Menu

Ham with Honey-Mustard Glaze*
Brown-Rice Salad with Watercress*
Green-bean and Mushroom Casserole*
Cranberry-Apple Mold*
Assorted Rolls or Breads
Butter, Mustard
Mincemeat Pie
Rosé
Coffee or Tea

*Recipe Follows

HAM WITH HONEY-MUSTARD GLAZE

1   canned ham (5 pounds)
1/2   cup honey
1   tablespoon prepared mustard
1/2   teaspoon cinnamon
2   medium oranges, peeled and sliced crosswise
Watercress or parsley

Have meat cutter slice ham 1/8 inch thick and tie in original shape. Bake in 12x8x2-inch baking dish in preheated 325° oven about 1 hour or until almost hot. Blend honey, mustard and cinnamon; brush some over ham and bake about 30 minutes longer, brushing on more honey mixture and drippings occasionally. Place on platter. Carefully cut and remove string, fanning out ham slices slightly. Garnish with orange and watercress. Makes 10 servings with leftovers.

BROWN-RICE SALAD WITH WATERCRESS

4 1/4   to 5 cups chicken broth
1 1/2   teaspoons salt, divided
2   cups brown rice
1   cup minced watercress or parsley
1   cup diced radishes
1/3   cup minced green onions with some tops
1/4   cup oil
2   tablespoons red-wine vinegar
1   teaspoon prepared mustard
1/2   teaspoon freshly ground pepper
Lettuce leaves (optional)
Radish roses (optional)

In a large saucepan or a Dutch oven bring to boil the chicken broth (use smaller amount for long-grain rice, larger amount for short-grain) and 1 teaspoon salt. Stir in rice; return to boil. Reduce heat to low, cover tightly and simmer until rice is tender and liquid absorbed, 50 to 60 minutes. Cool completely (refrigerate if desired). Fluff rice with fork. Toss in watercress, radishes and onions. Mix well oil, vinegar, mustard, remaining 1/2 teaspoon salt and the pepper; pour over rice mixture. Toss just until blended. Chill to blend flavors. Serve in lettuce-lined bowl. Garnish with radish roses. Makes about 8 cups, or 8 to 10 servings.

GREEN-BEAN AND MUSHROOM CASSEROLE

4   packages (9 ounces each) frozen cut green beans,
       thawed, or 2 pounds fresh, trimmed and cut
       (about 8 cups)
Boiling salted water to cover
1/4   cup butter or margarine
1/2   pound mushrooms, sliced thin
1/2   cup minced onion or 1 tablespoon instant

minced onion soaked a few minutes
    in 1 tablespoon hot water
1/4   cup flour
1/2   teaspoon salt
1/8   teaspoon freshly ground pepper
2 1/2 cups milk
3   tablespoons grated Parmesan cheese
Minced parsley (optional)

In a large saucepan or a Dutch oven cook the beans in water: frozen, a few minutes; fresh, about 8 minutes or until crisp-tender. (Do not overcook; beans will cook further with sauce.) Drain and plunge into bowl of cold water. Drain well. In saucepan melt butter; sauté mushrooms and onion until mushrooms are tender, stirring often. Stir in flour, salt and pepper. Cook and stir until bubbly. Gradually stir in milk. Cook and stir until sauce thickens and just begins to boil. Pour over green beans and mix well. Turn into greased shallow 2-quart baking dish. Sprinkle with Parmesan. Cover and bake in preheated 325° oven 45 minutes. Uncover and bake 15 minutes longer or until bubbly. Sprinkle with parsley. Makes 8 to 10 servings. **Note** The casserole may be assembled ahead and then refrigerated.

CRANBERRY-APPLE MOLD

3   envelopes unflavored gelatin
1 1/2 cups cold water
3   cups cranberry-apple drink
1/4   teaspoon salt
2   cups diced unpeeled red apples (2 medium) mixed
       with 2 tablespoons lemon juice
1   can (20 ounces) pineapple chunks in own juice,
       well drained and halved
1   cup diced celery
Celery leaves
Mustard Mayonnaise, Creamy Yogurt Dressing (recipes
       follow; optional) or mayonnaise

In saucepan sprinkle gelatin over water. Place over low heat and stir until gelatin dissolves, about 3 minutes. Remove from heat. Stir in drink and salt. Chill until consistency of unbeaten egg whites. Stir in apples, pineapple and celery. Pour into 6-cup ring mold rinsed with cold water. Chill until set, 3 to 4 hours. Unmold on serving plate. Garnish with celery leaves. Serve with Mustard Mayonnaise or Creamy Yogurt Dressing. Makes 8 to 10 servings.

MUSTARD MAYONNAISE Mix well 1 cup of mayonnaise, 1/4 cup milk and 1 tablespoon prepared mustard, or to taste. Cover and chill until ready to serve. Makes about 1 1/3 cups.

CREAMY YOGURT DRESSING Combine just until blended 1 cup plain yogurt, 2 tablespoons honey,

or to taste, and 1 tablespoon grated orange peel (optional). Cover and chill until ready to serve. Makes about 1 1/4 cups.

Open House Holiday Buffet

The best way to serve either a large group at one time or a steady stream of callers passing through over a period of hours is with a special punch (see page 156) or cocktails accompanied by appetizers, snacks and easy-to-handle cakes and cookies. Everything can be made ahead; you need only replenish empty platters.

Menu
Mushroom-liver Pâté*
Turkey Pâté*
Cream-cheese and Crab Spread*
Savory Cheese Cup (recipe, page 122)
Sesame Cheese Wafers*
Salted Nuts   Olives
Fruitcake (see recipes, page 133)
Christmas Cookies (see recipes, page 128)

*Recipe Follows

MUSHROOM-LIVER PÂTÉ

1/4   pound mushrooms, chopped fine
1   tablespoon butter or margarine
1/2   pound braunschweiger, at room temperature
1/2   cup sour cream
2   tablespoons brandy
1   tablespoon chopped green onion
1/2   teaspoon sharp prepared mustard
Dash of cayenne
Parsley
Pimiento

In skillet sauté mushrooms in butter until very dark brown. Mix well with braunschweiger, sour cream, brandy, onion, mustard and cayenne. Pack in well-greased 2-cup mold; chill. To serve, unmold and garnish with parsley and pimiento. Makes 2 cups.

TURKEY PÂTÉ

2   cups ground cooked turkey meat and skin,
       lightly packed
1   onion, minced
2   hard-cooked eggs, minced
1/2   cup ground almonds
Salt and pepper
Generous dash of hot-pepper sauce
2   tablespoons Cognac
Mayonnaise

Mix all ingredients, except mayonnaise. Add just

enough mayonnaise to make a stiff paste. Put in bowl or container; chill. Makes about 2 cups. **Note** To serve, garnish with sliced olives or aspic, if desired.

CREAM-CHEESE AND CRAB SPREAD

1 package (8 ounces) cream cheese, softened
1 package (6 ounces) frozen crab meat, thawed, drained (reserve 2 tablespoons liquid) and chopped
2 tablespoons minced green onion (white part only)
1 teaspoon lemon juice
¼ teaspoon salt
⅛ teaspoon hot-pepper sauce
¼ to ⅓ cup sliced unblanched almonds
Bread rounds or crackers

In small bowl of mixer beat until creamy the cheese, reserved crab liquid, onion, lemon juice, salt and pepper sauce. Stir in crab meat. Turn into greased shallow 3-cup baking dish. Sprinkle with almonds. Bake uncovered in preheated 350° oven 20 to 30 minutes or until bubbly. Serve hot as a spread on bread rounds. Makes 30 to 40 appetizers.

SESAME-CHEESE WAFERS

½ pound sharp Cheddar cheese, shredded (2 cups)
1 cup butter or margarine, softened
1½ cups flour
½ teaspoon salt
¼ teaspoon hot-pepper sauce
⅓ cup Toasted Sesame Seed, cooled (recipe follows)

Mix well cheese and butter. Stir in flour, salt and pepper sauce; mix well. Cover and chill 1 to 2 hours or until firm enough to shape in rolls. Divide mixture in half. With lightly floured hands shape each half in 7-inch roll on sheet of waxed paper. Roll each in half the sesame seed. Roll up in waxed paper and seal ends. Chill several hours or overnight until firm. With serrated knife slice ¼ inch thick. Place ½ inch apart on ungreased baking sheets. Bake in preheated 350° oven 15 to 18 minutes or until edges are lightly browned. Cool on racks and store airtight. Makes 56.
TOASTED SESAME SEED Toast sesame seed in shallow pan in preheated 350° oven 10 to 15 minutes or until golden, stirring 2 or 3 times.

Traditional Turkey and Trimmings Feast

It's the old-fashioned favorite menu for the holidays and, elaborate though it may seem, you can still get a head start on this big, sit-down Christmas dinner. The rolls, stuffing and pie can be made and frozen up to a month in advance of the 25th and you can do the relish early Christmas week and the mold on the 23rd.

Menu
Celery, Green Onions and Black Olives
Grandma's Roast Turkey*
Mushroom-Celery Stuffing*   Giblet Gravy*
Sweet Potatoes or Whipped Potatoes (optional)
Acorn Squashes with Peas and Onions*
Double Apple-Cabbage Mold*
Cranberry-Orange Relish*
Brown-and-Serve Sally Lunn Rolls*
Butter or Margarine, Apple Butter or Jelly
Apple-Cherry Pie*

*Recipe Follows

GRANDMA'S ROAST TURKEY

1 turkey (10 to 12 pounds), thawed if frozen
¼ cup oil
2 teaspoons salt
6 bay leaves, crushed fine
1 teaspoon each pepper, poultry seasoning, paprika and thyme
Mushroom-Celery Stuffing (recipe follows)
About ⅓ to ½ cup butter or margarine, melted

As soon as turkey is thawed sufficiently, remove giblets and neck from body cavity; reserve for Giblet Broth, page 152. Wash and dry turkey. Mix well the oil, salt, bay leaves and seasonings. Rub or brush turkey with oil mixture to cover completely. Loosely wrap turkey to prevent drying. Refrigerate overnight or up to 2 days. Before roasting, rinse oil mixture completely off turkey; pat dry. Stuff; secure neck cavity, folding skin close to body and fastening with skewers. Tuck legs into skin flap or trussing hook. Place turkey breast side up on rack in shallow roasting pan. Brush generously with butter. Insert meat thermometer inside thigh. Roast in 325° oven 3½ to 4½ hours, basting occasionally with pan drippings or additional butter, until thermometer registers 180° to 185°, drumstick feels soft when pressed with fingers (protected by pot holder) or drumstick and thigh move easily. Halfway through roasting, release legs to allow heat to penetrate thigh joint. If turkey browns too quickly, crimp foil over browned areas. Remove to platter; let stand ½ hour before carving. Makes 8 to 10 servings. **Note** Reserve pan drippings for Giblet Gravy, page 152.

MUSHROOM-CELERY STUFFING

1   pound mushrooms, sliced thin
1½ cups chopped celery with leaves
    (4 to 5 medium-size ribs)
1   large onion, chopped fine
1   cup butter or margarine
7   cups soft bread cubes
2   teaspoons poultry seasoning
1   teaspoon salt
½   teaspoon pepper

In large skillet sauté mushrooms, celery and onion in butter until mushrooms are tender. Toss with bread cubes, poultry seasoning, salt and pepper. Makes about 9 cups stuffing, enough for 10- to 12-pound turkey. **Note** Stuffing can be baked in greased covered baking dish or casserole in 325° oven 45 to 60 minutes or until heated through. For drier, crispier stuffing, uncover last 15 minutes.

GIBLET BROTH In small saucepan place giblets and neck in water to cover; add dash of salt; cover and simmer until tender. (Liver will be tender in 10 to 15 minutes; neck, heart and gizzard in 1 to 1½ hours.) Remove giblets and neck; chop meat fine; reserve with broth for Giblet Gravy (below). Refrigerate until ready to use.

GIBLET GRAVY Pour pan drippings and browned bits from roasting pan into 4-cup measure or bowl. Skim off fat, reserving ½ cup. Set skimmed drippings aside. Place reserved fat in saucepan. Stir in ½ cup flour and cook until bubbly and lightly browned. Add enough Giblet Broth (above) to skimmed drippings to make 6 cups liquid. Gradually stir into flour mixture; add chopped giblets. Cook and stir until thickened. Adjust seasonings. Makes 6 cups.

ACORN SQUASHES WITH PEAS AND ONIONS

4   medium acorn squashes (about 1 pound each)
    Butter or margarine
1   pound small white onions
1   cup water
1   teaspoon salt
3   packages (10 ounces each) or 1½ bags
    (20 ounces each) frozen green peas (6 cups)

With large sharp knife or cleaver remove and discard ends, then quarter squashes crosswise, forming rings. Discard seeds. Melt 1 tablespoon butter in jelly-roll or shallow baking pan in 325° oven. Place squashes in pan; cover tightly with foil. Bake 1¼ to 1½ hours or until squashes are fork-tender. About 40 minutes before serving, bring to boil onions, water and salt. Reduce heat; cover and cook 15 minutes. Add peas;

cover and cook 5 minutes longer or until peas and onions are tender. Drain. If desired, add 2 tablespoons butter and toss to coat. To serve, place 4 to 5 squash rings around turkey and fill with peas and onions. Pass remaining vegetables in serving bowl. Makes 8 to 10 servings. **Note** If desired, 2 jars (16 ounces each) boiled onions, drained, may be used in place of fresh. Cook peas according to package directions. Add onions and heat through.

DOUBLE APPLE-CABBAGE MOLD

3½ cups apple juice or cider, divided
2   envelopes unflavored gelatin
⅓   cup sugar
3   tablespoons cider vinegar
½   teaspoon salt
2   cups shredded cabbage (about ½ pound)
¾   cup shredded carrot (1 large)
1   unpeeled red apple, chopped coarse

Heat 3 cups juice to boiling. In medium bowl mix well gelatin and remaining ½ cup cold juice. Stir in boiling juice, sugar, vinegar and salt until gelatin is completely dissolved. Chill until thick as unbeaten egg whites, 20 to 45 minutes. Fold in cabbage, carrot and apple. Pour into 6-cup mold. Chill until firm. To serve, unmold on serving platter. Garnish with parsley if desired. Makes 8 to 10 servings. **Note** If desired, dip thin slices of apple in lemon juice and arrange in bottom of mold before pouring in gelatin.

CRANBERRY-ORANGE RELISH

2   pounds fresh or frozen cranberries (8 cups)
2   cups water
1   cup packed brown sugar
1   cup golden raisins
2   oranges, peeled and diced

Combine cranberries and water in heavy saucepan. Bring to boil, then cook over medium heat until cranberries pop, about 5 minutes. Add sugar, raisins and oranges and cook over medium heat about 15 minutes or until thickened, stirring occasionally. Cool, then chill. Makes about 6 cups.

BROWN-AND-SERVE SALLY LUNN ROLLS

1   envelope active dry yeast
¾   cup warm water (105° to 115°)
¼   cup sugar
2   teaspoons salt
¾   cup warm milk
½   cup butter or margarine, softened and cut in pieces
3   eggs, beaten, at room temperature
5 to 6 cups flour

Make Ahead In large warm bowl sprinkle yeast into warm water and stir until dissolved. Stir in sugar, salt, milk, butter and eggs. Stir in 3 cups flour. With wooden spoon beat until well mixed, about 1 minute. Beat in enough additional flour (about 2¼ cups) to make a soft dough that leaves sides of bowl. Cover and let rise in warm, draft-free place until doubled, about 1 hour. Stir down and spoon into 24 greased muffin cups, filling each about ⅔ full. Cover; let rise until doubled, about 1 hour. Bake in preheated 250° oven 25 minutes or until rolls spring back when lightly pressed with finger. Cool in pan 25 minutes. Remove to wire racks and cool thoroughly. Wrap in plastic bags or pack in other containers; seal or cover tightly; refrigerate up to 1 week or freeze up to 1 month. (Thaw rolls before browning.)

Just Before Serving Place rolls on greased baking sheet. Bake in preheated 400° oven 10 to 15 minutes or until browned. Serve warm. Makes 24 rolls.

APPLE-CHERRY PIE

Flaky Pastry (recipe follows) or pastry for 2-crust pie
1　cup sugar
¼　cup flour
1　teaspoon cinnamon
½　teaspoon allspice
5　medium apples, cored, peeled if desired and sliced thin (about 3½ cups)
1　can (16 ounces) pitted tart red cherries, drained
2　tablespoons butter or margarine

Roll out ⅔ pastry; fit into 9-inch pie plate. Mix well sugar, flour, cinnamon and allspice; toss with apples. Layer ⅓ apple mixture, then ⅓ cherries in pastry-lined pan. Repeat twice. Dot with butter. Roll out remaining pastry; place on top of filling. Trim edges and flute rim; cut vents. Can be frozen at this point. Bake in 400° oven 50 to 60 minutes (if thawed) or 1¼ to 1½ hours (if frozen) or until filling is bubbly and apples tender. Crimp foil over browned edges to prevent crust from burning. Makes 8 to 10 servings. **Note** For easier oven cleanup, place cookie sheet or foil under pie to catch any drippings.

FLAKY PASTRY

Very easy to handle and roll out; needs no chilling.
2　cups flour
1　teaspoon salt
⅔　cup shortening
2　tablespoons butter or margarine, melted
5　tablespoons cold water
1　tablespoon vinegar

Mix well flour and salt. Cut in shortening and butter until coarse crumbs. Add water and vinegar, mixing with fork. Form in ball. Roll out. Carefully lift to pie plate (pastry is tender and may tear). Makes pastry for 2-crust 8- or 9-inch pie or 2 shells.

Colonial Roast Goose Dinner

The Christmas goose is a dinner tradition that goes back to the days when all cooking was done on the open hearth. Perhaps that's why many of us tend to think that it's just too challenging to undertake in the twentieth century. But after you've looked over our triumphant menu and easy-to-follow recipes, we think you'll hesitate no more. It's a modernized marvel.

Menu

**Consommé with Julienne Carrots
and Green Onions
Celery Sticks and Olives
Roast Goose with Apple-Prune Bread Stuffing***
Giblet Gravy*
Wine-Poached Apple Halves with Currant Jelly*
Skillet-Roasted Potatoes* **Red Cabbage***
Crescent Rolls **Butter (optional)**
Snow Pudding with Eggnog Sauce*
Red Wine
*Recipe Follows

ROAST GOOSE WITH APPLE-PRUNE BREAD STUFFING

1　goose (14 pounds), thawed if frozen (reserve giblets and neck for Giblet Broth, Page 154)
1　lemon, halved
1　tablespoon salt
½　teaspoon pepper
Apple-Prune Bread Stuffing (recipe follows)

Remove any loose fat from body cavity and render. Refrigerate for later use. Rub goose inside and out with lemon halves and mixture of salt and pepper. Spoon stuffing loosely into neck cavity. Fasten neck skin to back with skewer. Spoon remaining stuffing into body cavity. Twist wings and anchor behind back; tie legs together or tuck in band of skin or wire clamp at tail. Place goose breast side up on rack in large pan. Prick breast skin in several places to allow fat to drain away. Insert meat thermometer deep into inside thigh muscle. Roast in 325° oven until meat thermometer registers 185°, 4½ to 5 hours, or until the meaty part of legs feels very soft when pressed between fingers and juices run beige, not pink, when leg is pierced with fork. Spoon off fat from pan 3 to 4 times during roasting. Remove goose to carving board or platter and keep warm. Let stand 30 minutes before carving. Garnish with parsley if desired. Makes 10 to 12 servings.

APPLE-PRUNE BREAD STUFFING

1 medium onion, chopped fine
5 tablespoons melted goose fat, butter or margarine, divided
3 cups small toasted bread cubes
1 cup toasted slivered almonds (optional)
About 4 ribs celery with tops, chopped
About 2 medium-size tart apples, peeled and chopped (2 cups)
1 cup ready-to-eat pitted prunes, cut up
1 teaspoon each salt and poultry seasoning
¼ teaspoon pepper

In skillet sauté onion in 1 tablespoon goose fat until golden brown and tender. Remove to bowl; cool. Add remaining ingredients. Drizzle with remaining 4 tablespoons goose fat and toss to mix.

GIBLET BROTH As soon as giblets and neck are thawed and removed from goose, place all except liver in 3-quart saucepan with water to cover (about 5 cups), 1 small onion studded with 2 whole cloves, a few celery tops, 1 bay leaf and 2 teaspoons salt. Cover and simmer gently 1 hour. Add liver and continue to simmer 30 minutes. Strain broth and refrigerate. Chop meat fine and refrigerate. Makes about 3 cups broth.

GIBLET GRAVY In heavy saucepan melt 4 tablespoons goose fat, butter or margarine. Stir in ½ cup flour. Stir over medium heat until roux starts to turn light brown (do not burn). Gradually stir in Giblet Broth (recipe above) and cook and stir until gravy is thickened and smooth. Add ½ cup half-and-half (optional), chopped giblet and neck meat, 1 tablespoon (or to taste) each red-currant jelly and dry sherry. Heat through and season to taste with salt and pepper. Serve very hot in heated dish. Makes about 4 cups.

WINE-POACHED APPLE HALVES WITH CURRANT JELLY

1 cup sugar
½ cup each dry white wine and water or 1 cup water
2 strips lemon peel (about 2 x ½ inch)
Juice of 1 lemon
6 medium-size tart cooking apples, peeled, halved and core removed with measuring teaspoon
About ¼ cup red-currant jelly

In heavy saucepan bring sugar, wine, water, lemon peel and juice to boil. Add apple halves a few at a time. Simmer gently until tender when tested with pick but still firm enough to keep shape, about 10 minutes, turning once. Gently transfer to bowl. Cover loosely and refrigerate. Before serving, remove apples from syrup with slotted spoon. Arrange cut side up on platter around goose or serve separately. Fill each apple cavity with about 1 teaspoon jelly. Makes 10 to 12 servings. **Note** Use leftover syrup to poach other fruits.

SKILLET-ROASTED POTATOES

¼ cup goose fat, butter or margarine
6 large potatoes, peeled and quartered lengthwise
1½ teaspoons salt
½ to 1 teaspoon crushed cumin seed (optional)
¼ teaspoon pepper
2 tablespoons minced parsley

In large heavy skillet or Dutch oven heat fat until hot. Add potatoes, salt, cumin and pepper. Toss to coat with fat and brown over medium heat until potatoes turn golden, turning occasionally. Cover and simmer until tender, about 15 minutes. Sprinkle with parsley. Makes 10 to 12 servings. **Note** Goose fat does not brown potatoes as well as butter or margarine.

RED CABBAGE

¼ cup goose fat, butter, margarine or oil, heated
1 large onion, chopped (1 cup)
1 large head red cabbage (about 4 pounds), shredded (4 quarts)
2 large tart apples, cored, peeled and chopped coarse
⅓ cup red-wine vinegar, or to taste
2 teaspoons each salt and sugar, or to taste
¼ teaspoon each ground allspice and cloves, or to taste
¼ cup red-currant jelly (optional)
Minced parsley

In large kettle or Dutch oven combine all ingredients except jelly and parsley. Cover and simmer 1 hour or until cabbage is wilted and flavors are well blended, stirring occasionally. Stir in jelly and taste for seasoning. Sprinkle with parsley. Makes 10 to 12 servings.

SNOW PUDDING WITH EGGNOG SAUCE

Puréed thawed frozen strawberries or raspberries may be substituted for Eggnog Sauce if desired.

2   envelopes unflavored gelatin
1¼ cups water
6   egg whites
⅛   teaspoon salt
1   cup sugar
¼   cup cream sherry, brandy or bourbon
Eggnog Sauce (recipe follows)
3   tablespoons toasted sliced almonds
Preferred cut-up candied fruits (halved cherries, strips of angelica or crystallized ginger; optional)

In small saucepan sprinkle gelatin over water. Stir over medium heat until gelatin dissolves. Cool at room temperature. In large mixing bowl beat egg whites with salt until soft peaks form. Gradually beat in sugar until meringue is very stiff and shiny. Gradually beat in cooled gelatin mixture and the sherry until well blended. Pour into 6-cup mold that has been rinsed with cold water. Chill until set, at least 6 hours or overnight. Unmold onto chilled 2-inch-deep serving dish. Pour on Eggnog Sauce, sprinkle with almonds and decorate with candied fruits. Makes 10 to 12 servings.

EGGNOG SAUCE

6   egg yolks
⅛   teaspoon salt
¼   cup sugar
1½ cups milk, scalded
¼   cup cream sherry, brandy or bourbon, or to taste
½   cup heavy cream, whipped

In heavy saucepan or top part of double boiler combine egg yolks, salt and sugar. Beat in milk. Beat over low heat or simmering water until mixture coats metal spoon. Cover and chill. Just before serving, stir in ¼ cup sherry and the whipped cream. Makes about 3 cups.

Holiday Wines and Beverages

Wine adds to the festivity of any occasion, and it seems especially appropriate for holiday gatherings. What to serve and when? Individual dinner wines are described and suggested in the next few pages, followed by recipes for six wine punches and a creamy eggnog.

When you choose a wine to go with a meal, there are no ironclad rules. A selection is usually made according to food and wine affinities—red with beef, white with fish, various gradations between—that have been established through years of tasting.

For example, a crown roast of pork or ham for Christmas tastes great with a hearty white wine such as Gewürztraminer, Pinot Chardonnay or Moselle. A rosé is good too. A controversy exists on the proper wines to serve with turkey. Some authorities choose a full-bodied white such as Pinot Chardonnay or, with a highly spiced stuffing, Gewürztraminer, lightly spicy itself. Other experts insist on a light red wine such as Cabernet Sauvignon or a Bordeaux. Champagne is always appropriate and some authorities like sparkling Burgundy with turkey.

If roast beef is the Christmas entrée, a Bordeaux such as St. Emilion, a California Zinfandel or Pinot Noir or an all-purpose red table wine is good. This is the place for a rare bottle of old Burgundy if you have one. With duckling, goose, venison or other game serve a Châteauneuf-du-Pape, Hermitage (both wines of the Rhone valley), a California Zinfandel or Pinot Noir. The more complex wines complement these elegant meats, though a jug red wine can be served.

Dessert wines include sweet and medium-sweet sherries, port and Madeira, which takes its name from the island. These can be served with walnuts, plain buttery cakes such as pound cake, and cheeses. (Dry sherry traditionally is served with lightly salted almonds.)

When buying table wines, allow a bottle (4/5 quart or liter) for each four persons, a half-gallon jug for ten to twelve. Jug wines are easier to manage if decanted into carafes for the table, but showing the label expresses your pride in a bottle wine.

A few words about how to serve and store wines: A fine imported wine should rest several weeks or months after shipping or jostling in the bottle as you bring it home. But most wines are in good drinking condition a day or two after purchase. Very old wines should be handled gently in moving them from storage to table, since the sediment in fine old wines should be allowed to settle to the bottom of the bottle. If you do keep wines for long periods of time, keep the wine cellar (which may be a handy closet or cupboard) at about 55°F. If you buy wines a few days before serving them, store them at a cool room temperature—never in a cupboard over the kitchen range or near a radiator or wall heater. Bottles should be turned on their sides to keep the corks moistened, preventing the corks from shrinking and allowing air to seep into the bottles.

Red wines should be opened fifteen to thirty minutes before serving to allow them to breathe, which helps to develop the bouquet. White wines generally don't require much breathing time, perhaps only five minutes.

Much mumbo jumbo is circulated concerning the serving temperature of wines. In general, white wines are chilled and red wines are served at room temperature. However, excessive chilling kills the bouquet of white wines. About an hour in the refrigerator or fifteen to twenty minutes in a wine bucket with ice is ample to cool the wine to 50° to 55°F., considered ideal for Rhine, Chablis, Graves, Pinot Chardonnay and other dry white wines. Fine red wines should be served at about 60°F., somewhat cooler than normal American room temperature. A few minutes in the refrigerator brings red wine to this temperature. Rougher, fresh red wines such as Beaujolais often are served lightly chilled, almost as cold as white wines. Rosé wine is also served chilled, but not icy cold. Champagne is the only wine that is well chilled—three hours in the refrigerator or forty-five minutes to an hour in a champagne bucket with ice. The dessert wines—port, Madeira, Sauternes and Barsacs—may be lightly chilled but generally are served at cool room temperature. Some sherry fans chill dry sherry lightly when pouring it as an aperitif, but the sweet sherries usually are served at room temperature.

GLOGG (Christmas Wine)

1 cinnamon stick
12 whole cloves
12 whole cardamom pods
Peel of ½ orange or lemon in strips
2 cups sugar
2 bottles (1/5 gallon each) Burgundy
1 cup blanched almonds
1 cup raisins
½ cup brandy or Madeira (optional)

Tie in cheesecloth the cinnamon stick, cloves, cardamom pods and citrus peel. In heavy saucepan bring to boil the spice bag, sugar and 2 cups water. Reduce heat and simmer, stirring, 5 minutes, or until sugar is dissolved. Add wine, cover and remove from heat. Let steep 1 hour. Remove spices; add almonds and raisins and heat slowly until hot but not boiling. Add brandy, if desired. Put demitasse spoons in punch cups and ladle hot wine and a few almonds and raisins into each cup. Use spoon to eat almonds and raisins. Makes about 2½ quarts or twenty 4-ounce servings.

APPLE BISHOP

1 firm tart apple
Whole cloves
1 cinnamon stick
Peel of 1 orange, cut in spiral
1 bottle (4/5 quart) dry red wine (Burgundy, Zinfandel, Pinot Noir or Cabernet Sauvignon)
½ cup sugar
Apple slices

Wash apple but do not peel. Stud with 20 to 24 whole cloves. Combine apple, cinnamon, orange peel and wine in saucepan or chafing dish. Heat very slowly about 30 minutes, making sure wine does not boil but steams. Remove apple, orange peel and cinnamon stick. Stir in sugar. Cut apple slices in daisy or star shapes with small cookie cutters if desired. Stud slices with additional whole cloves and float on hot wine. Serve in punch cups or wineglasses. Makes 8 servings.

APRICOT WINE PUNCH

1 cup dried apricot halves
1 cup vodka
1¾ cups sugar
1 cup water
Peel of 1 lemon, cut in spiral
1 bottle (4/5 quart) Chablis, chilled
Club soda to taste

Soak apricots in vodka 2 to 4 weeks in covered glass jar. In saucepan over medium heat, cook and stir sugar, water and lemon peel until sugar dissolves. Add apricot-vodka mixture and cool. When ready to serve, place in small punch bowl and stir in wine and soda. Serve in sherry glasses or punch cups with some apricots. Makes about 12 servings.

PORT NEGUS

2 cups port
Lump sugar (large cubes)
½ lemon
½ cup boiling water
Nutmeg

In saucepan heat port slowly but do not boil. Pour into pitcher. Meanwhile rub 3 sugar cubes with lemon peel that has been grated lightly to break oil cells. Extract lemon juice. Add sugar cubes and lemon juice to port and stir until sugar is dissolved. Add boiling water, mix and taste. If desired, stir in more sugar. Serve in punch cups or wineglasses dusted with nutmeg. Makes 4 or 5 servings.

HOLIDAY CHAMPAGNE PUNCH

4   cups cranberry-juice cocktail
4   cups orange juice
½   cup lemon juice
1   cup sugar
1   bottle (4/5 quart) dry Sauterne or other white wine
2   bottles (4/5 quart each) champagne
Orange slices (optional)

Mix well cranberry, orange and lemon juices. Add sugar and stir until dissolved. Chill thoroughly. Add Sauterne and mix well. Pour over ice in punch bowl. Add champagne just before serving. Float orange slices on punch if desired. Makes 40 servings.

CALIFORNIA SHERRY SHRUB

1   can (6 ounces) frozen lemonade concentrate, thawed
1   bottle (4/5 quart) dry sherry
Maraschino cherries
Mint (optional)

In blender or with mixer, mix well lemonade concentrate and sherry. Cover and store in refrigerator 3 to 4 days. Serve over ice in short 6- or 8- ounce glasses. Garnish with cherries and mint. Any leftover shrub will keep several days in refrigerator. Makes 10 to 12 servings.

HOLIDAY EGGNOG

6   eggs, separated
¾   cup sugar
2   cups milk
2   cups heavy cream
1½   cups rye, bourbon or brandy
2   tablespoons dark rum
Nutmeg

In large bowl of mixer beat egg yolks until very thick and lemon colored. Add ½ cup sugar and continue beating until sugar is dissolved. Add milk and cream, then slowly stir in liquors. Refrigerate about 4 hours to allow liquors to "cook" the eggs. When ready to serve, pour into serving bowl. In large bowl of mixer, beat egg whites until stiff. Gradually beat in remaining sugar and fold into egg-liquor mixture. Sprinkle lightly with nutmeg. Makes 12 servings.

Simple Tricks For Beautifying Holiday Food

If the roast turkey, capon, goose, duck or chicken is to be carved at the table you'll make the carver happy by not surrounding the bird with elaborate garnishes. A sprig of some bright, hardy green and perhaps paper frills on the drumsticks are as far as you need go. Rub the green's leaves with salad oil (pour a little on a paper towel) to add luster. Store in a plastic bag or the refrigerator until needed for garnishing. Instead of crowding the platter holding the bird, place an arrangement of Cranberried Red Apples and Stuffing Balls in a separate dish beside it. The apples can be prepared ahead; they'll keep frozen for weeks or refrigerated for several days.

CRANBERRIED RED APPLES

3½   cups cranberry-juice cocktail
¾   cup sugar
8   red apples
Red food coloring (optional)

Bring juice and sugar to boil in kettle. Remove three fourths of core from apples, starting at stem end. Then, starting from top, cut ½″ peel from apple and cut skin into points halfway down. Put apples in boiling syrup, peeled side down, and simmer 5 minutes. Turn apples and cook until tender, basting often with syrup. If apples are not a pretty red, add some red food coloring to syrup. Serve hot or cold, garnished with mature Italian parsley or young spinach leaves and raw cranberries.

STUFFING BALLS

If your basic stuffing is dry, add butter or margarine and broth: enough moisture to hold mixture together. Shape in balls and arrange in greased baking dish. Brush with additional melted butter, margarine or pan drippings from the roasting poultry. Bake in moderate oven (350°F.) until a beautiful golden brown. If more convenient, bake ahead and reheat. Or if you prefer, bake stuffing in a casserole or baking dish. Cut in squares and arrange on a serving dish with the apples.

Almost everyone serves assorted cold cuts sometime during the holiday season, and the simplest way is to leave the meat in neat stacks all of a kind. This makes it easy for diners to serve themselves, the stacked-up slices do not dry out and change color, and no time is spent in rolling and twisting the slices into arrangements that generally end up having a handled look. Home-cooked, thinly sliced cold meat also fares better if stacked. In both cases, uneaten meat can be returned to the refrigerator for future use. Large slices can be cut in half. Put the stacks on leaves rubbed with salad oil; ivy or other nonwilting leaves work well. It's also good to use edible garnishes when possible. Our cheese pears are easy to make and equally appropriate for cold-cut platter, fruit salad, apple or mince pie.

CHEESE PEARS

When yellow Cheddar or process American cheese is at room temperature, shape into pears with hands. Paint a rosy cheek with a sprinkle of bright red paprika. Insert large whole cloves into stem and blossom ends, the clove bud showing at blossom end and clove stem serving as pear stem. Make many days ahead, if desired, and refrigerate in single layer in airtight container. Serve at room temperature. A pound of cheese makes about 8 pears.

If you're having a hot casserole, try crisscrossing the top with ½″-wide rows of chopped parsley. Put a pimiento star or square in each space. Do it after cooking to keep fresh. Chop quite a lot of parsley and keep in airtight container in refrigerator for ready use. Cut fancy shapes of pimiento or peppers a day or two ahead and refrigerate, *well covered.*

When you're serving a nongreen salad—chicken, seafood, turkey, potato, macaroni or mixed cooked-vegetable—serve it in a large round bowl decorated with an edible wreath of bite-size pieces of chicory or young spinach leaves. Parsley sprigs can also be used; Italian parsley is especially sturdy and attractive. Top with a big poinsettia, the petals cut from fresh or pickled sweet red peppers and the center little pieces of orange peel. Cover bowl with plastic wrap and refrigerate until serving time. Greens will hold up several hours.

Jewel-tone jellied salads and desserts are candidates for holiday tables. You can add even more sparkle to them by circling the turned-out mold with peeled seedless-orange slices. Soak half the slices overnight in grenadine or raspberry syrup and alternate these rosy slices with untreated ones. Put a bunch of white grapes on top and arrange greens, fake or real, around the base of the serving dish.

If jellied molds are to stand for a long time in a warm room it is wise to add an extra teaspoon of unflavored gelatin to each package of flavored gelatin or to each envelope of unflavored gelatin used. This is especially helpful if fruits or vegetables have been added. *Never* substitute the syrup from canned fruit for more than half the water called for or the mold won't set well enough to behave. Fresh or frozen pineapple cannot be used either.

To make breads and crackers more festive, line basket with alternating red and green cloth or paper napkins with the points hanging down over the side. Attach a jingly bell to each point with needle and thread. (Reinforce paper napkins with tape underneath.) Cookies can be served this way too.

Fruit juice, milk or other beverages become very gay and partylike if you tie a small real or artificial wreathlike garland onto the pitcher handle with a ribbon bow.

To slice fruitcake neatly, use a very sharp knife; dip it in warm water if cake proves sticky and fruit tends to pull out. A serrated knife is a help if a sawing action is used. Cut some big thin slices as well as cubes or sticks for those who want less. For the latter, cut slices 1″ thick, then cut 1″ cubes or long sticks. Store airtight.

Coffee cakes, fruitcakes, pound and other loaf or layer cakes look festive when glazed in white and decorated. To glaze, thin confectioners' sugar with lemon juice so that when spread on top it will run down the sides of any unfrosted cake. Top with homemade or bought marzipan fruit- or flower-shaped candies, or make red flowers and green leaves from bright gumdrops. Slice candy, then flatten by rolling between two sheets of waxed paper. Use shreds of lemon peel for centers.

Two-week Busy-day Meal Plan

Nobody wants to slight the family's everyday meals during the busy holiday season, and with a program like this one you don't have to. The menus are for quick, easy dinners that take advantage of convenience foods and fast cooking methods. Recipes are given for items with an asterisk*.

Sunday

Double-Shrimp Tarts*
Buttered Green Peas
Tomato-Cucumber Salad
Rolls   Butter
Minted Pineapple Chunks

DOUBLE-SHRIMP TARTS

1   can (10 ounces) condensed cream of shrimp soup, heated
¼   cup milk
¼   teaspoon salt
½   cup finely chopped celery (about 2 ribs)
2   tablespoons chopped green onions with tops (about 2)
1   can (3 ounces) sliced mushrooms, drained
2   cups cooked shrimps
2   teaspoons dry white wine
6   baked tart or patty shells (about 3-inch diameter)
Minced parsley
Lemon twists

Mix soup, milk and salt in saucepan. Add celery, onions and mushrooms; stir over medium heat until hot. *Do not boil.* Add shrimps; stir just until heated. Blend in wine. Just before serving, spoon into tart shells; garnish with parsley and lemon. Makes 6 servings.

Monday

Meatball Stew Dinner*
Celery Sticks
Pickles
Canned Peaches

MEATBALL STEW DINNER

2   cans (15 ounces each) meatballs with gravy
2   packages (10 ounces each) frozen mixed vegetables (4 cups)
1   tube (8 ounces) refrigerated buttermilk biscuits

In 2½-quart casserole mix well meatballs, gravy and vegetables. Bake uncovered in preheated 450° oven 10 minutes or until bubbly, stirring occasionally. Arrange biscuits around edge. Bake 8 to 10 minutes or until biscuits are lightly browned. Makes 4 servings.

Tuesday

Rice and Beans*
Broccoli Spears
Canned Apricots

RICE AND BEANS

3   to 4 cups cooked rice
1   can (16 ounces) black, pinto or kidney beans, undrained
1   cup shredded Cheddar cheese (4 ounces)

In large saucepan mix well rice, beans and cheese. Cook over low heat until cheese melts. Makes 4 servings.

Wednesday

Lemon Broiled Chicken*
Broiled Canned Sweet Potatoes
Italian Green Beans
Fruit Cocktail

LEMON BROILED CHICKEN

3   tablespoons each lemon juice and oil
1   medium clove garlic, crushed
1   teaspoon salt
½   teaspoon oregano
¼   teaspoon pepper
1   broiler-fryer (about 3 pounds), cut up

In large bowl mix lemon juice, oil, garlic, salt, oregano and pepper. Add chicken, turning to coat with marinade. Marinate chicken in refrigerator several hours or overnight. Broil skin side down 6 inches from heat source in preheated broiler 15 minutes, basting occasionally with marinade. Turn chicken, baste and broil 15 minutes or until chicken is tender and juices run clear when chicken is pierced with fork. Makes 4 servings.

Thursday

Jiffy Hash with Eggs*
Lettuce-Tomato Salad
Vanilla Pudding

JIFFY HASH WITH EGGS

¾ pound salami or 1 can (12 ounces) pork-ham luncheon meat, shredded or diced
1 package (16 ounces) frozen hashed brown potatoes (3 cups)
4 eggs

In large skillet brown salami, stirring. Stir in potatoes and cook until potatoes are lightly browned. With back of spoon form 4 shallow wells in salami-potato mixture; break egg in each. Cover and cook until eggs are of desired doneness. Makes 4 servings.

Friday

Tomato-Juice Cocktails
Sautéed Chicken Livers*
Mashed Potatoes
Braised Escarole
Applesauce

SAUTÉED CHICKEN LIVERS

1 pound chicken livers, halved
3 tablespoons flour
½ teaspoon salt
¼ teaspoon pepper
¼ cup butter or margarine
1 small onion, chopped (¼ cup)
1 medium rib celery, sliced thin
1 medium clove garlic, crushed
¾ cup beef broth
½ teaspoon Worcestershire
Mashed potatoes

Coat livers in mixture of flour, salt and pepper; set aside. In skillet melt the butter; sauté onion, celery and garlic until tender. Add livers; brown well on all sides. Add broth and Worcestershire; cover and simmer 3 minutes or until livers are still lightly pink inside when cut. Serve over potatoes. Makes 4 servings.

Saturday

Orange Ham Slice with Sweet Potatoes*
Green Beans
Gingerbread

ORANGE HAM SLICE WITH SWEET POTATOES

½ cup orange marmalade

1 slice (1 to 1½ pounds) fully cooked smoked ham
1 can (18 ounces) vacuum-packed sweet potatoes

In large skillet melt marmalade. Add ham and potatoes; turn to coat evenly. Cover and cook until heated through, 15 to 20 minutes, turning all once. Serve with pan juices. Makes 4 servings. **Note** To broil, place ham and potatoes on broiler pan, brush with melted marmalade and broil 3 to 4 inches from heat source until heated through, turning once and brushing with marmalade as necessary.

Sunday

Little Steak Supper*
Mashed Potatoes
Canned Plums

LITTLE STEAK SUPPER

4 cubed beefsteaks, thawed if frozen (about 1½ pounds)
2 medium onions, sliced thin
1 package (10 ounces) frozen peas or lima beans (2 cups)

In lightly greased large skillet over high heat quickly brown both sides of steaks. Remove; keep warm. Reduce heat to medium-low. Add onions to skillet and cook 2 minutes, stirring. Stir in peas. Return steaks to skillet, cover and cook 3 to 5 minutes or until peas are crisp-tender. Season to taste if necessary. Makes 4 servings.

Monday

Piperade*
Whole-wheat Toast
Carrot and Celery Sticks
Vanilla Ice Cream

PIPERADE (Basque Scrambled Eggs)

1 medium onion, sliced thin
1 clove garlic, crushed
1 each medium sweet red and green pepper or 2 green peppers, cut in ¼-inch strips (about 2 cups)
1 tablespoon oil (olive preferred)
1 can (16 ounces) tomatoes
1 teaspoon basil
⅛ teaspoon black pepper
4 eggs, slightly beaten with 1 teaspoon salt

In skillet sauté onion, garlic and sweet peppers in oil until tender; add tomatoes, basil and black pepper and simmer 15 to 25 minutes or until most of liquid evaporates. Pour in eggs; cook and stir lightly until set; serve at once. Makes 4 servings.

Tuesday

Hot Potato Salad with Knockwurst*
Pickled Beets
Pumpernickel Bread
Fruit Cocktail

HOT POTATO SALAD WITH KNOCKWURST

4   slices bacon
1   medium onion, chopped
4   teaspoons each flour and sugar
1   teaspoon each salt and MSG
¼   teaspoon pepper
½   cup cider vinegar
⅔   cup water
4   medium potatoes, cooked and cut in ¼-inch slices
3   knockwurst or 6 frankurters, cut in ½-inch slices
2   cups shredded romaine or other lettuce

In large skillet cook bacon until crisp; remove, crumble and set aside. Sauté onion in drippings until golden. Stir in flour and cook 1 to 2 minutes. Add sugar, salt, MSG, pepper, vinegar and water. Cook and stir until mixture comes to boil and thickens slightly. Add potatoes and knockwurst, mix gently but well; heat thoroughly. Stir in lettuce and bacon and serve at once. Makes 4 servings.

Wednesday

Broiled Open-faced Bean Sandwiches*
Corn Chips
Orange Salad on Romaine
Oil-Vinegar Dressing
Custard with Honey

BROILED OPEN-FACED BEAN SANDWICHES

1   can (16 ounces) tomatoes
1   large onion, chopped (1 cup)
1   large clove garlic, crushed
3   tablespoons oil, preferably olive
1   can (15½ ounces) mashed refried beans

1½ teaspoons chili powder
¼   teaspoon salt, or to taste
⅛   teaspoon hot-pepper sauce, or to taste
4   hamburger buns, split and toasted on both sides
1   small green pepper, sliced thin (optional)
1   cup shredded Cheddar cheese

Chop tomatoes; drain well and set aside. In large heavy skillet sauté onion and garlic in oil until tender, stirring occasionally. Stir in tomatoes, beans, chili powder, salt and pepper sauce. Simmer 5 to 10 minutes to blend flavors, stirring occasionally. Pile on cut sides of buns. Top each with a green-pepper ring and 2 tablespoons cheese. Broil about 6 inches from heat source 6 to 8 minutes or until hot and bubbly. Serve at once. Makes 4 servings. **Note** Sandwiches can be topped with bacon. Broil 12 slices bacon until crisp. Drain and halve each strip. Place 3 half strips on each sandwich before broiling. Top with pepper ring and sprinkle each with *only 1 tablespoon cheese*. Broil as above.

Thursday

English-Muffin Pizzas with
Cheese and Salami
Italian-style Slaw*
Tangerines

ITALIAN-STYLE SLAW

1   medium head cabbage, shredded very fine
1   medium onion, sliced
¾   cup plus 2 teaspoons sugar
1   cup cider vinegar
¾   cup oil
1   teaspoon each salt, celery seed and dry mustard

Put cabbage in large bowl or plastic container and add onion. Sprinkle with ¾ cup sugar. Bring to boil vinegar, oil, remaining 2 teaspoons sugar and seasonings; pour over cabbage. Cover and chill 4 to 5 hours. Mix well. Makes 8 servings.

Friday

Salad Plate*
Warm Onion Rolls or Garlic Bread
Canned Pears with Chocolate Sauce

SALAD PLATE

1   head iceberg lettuce

½ cup sour cream
¼ cup mayonnaise
1 tablespoon lemon juice
½ teaspoon each sugar and dry mustard
¼ teaspoon salt
⅛ teaspoon onion powder
2 cups raw or cooked vegetables marinated in oil-vinegar dressing
1 red onion, cut in rings
8 ounces (1 cup) cottage cheese
1 cup julienne-cut cooked turkey, ham, bologna or salami

Core, rinse and drain lettuce; chill. Just before serving, mix sour cream, mayonnaise, lemon juice, sugar and seasonings. Put in small bowl in center of platter. Cut lettuce in 4 wedges and arrange with marinated vegetables, onion, cheese and meat around bowl of dressing. Makes 4 servings.

Saturday

Curried Banana-Fish-Celery Skillet*
Steamed Rice
Steamed Spinach
Chocolate Ice Cream

CURRIED BANANA-FISH-CELERY SKILLET

¼ cup flour
2 teaspoons curry powder
¾ teaspoon salt
¼ teaspoon pepper
4 small firm bananas, peeled and halved lengthwise
1 pound fish fillets, thawed if frozen
1 tablespoon oil
3 ribs celery, sliced thin diagonally
4 tablespoons butter or margarine, divided
2 tablespoons lemon juice, divided

Mix flour, curry powder, salt and pepper, then coat bananas and fish; set aside. In large skillet, heat oil; stir-fry celery until crisp-tender, about 2 minutes. Remove celery and set aside. Add 2 tablespoons of butter to drippings; sauté bananas until golden and tender, about 1 minute on each side. Sprinkle with 1 tablespoon lemon juice; remove to warm platter. Add remaining 2 tablespoons of butter to drippings; sauté fish about 2 minutes on each side or until crisp and golden and fish flakes easily with fork. Sprinkle with remaining 1 tablespoon lemon juice; remove to platter with bananas. Reheat celery quickly in skillet; spoon over fish. If desired, serve with chutney. Makes 4 servings.

ENTERTAINING CHILDREN DURING THE HOLIDAYS

Christmas is celebrated because of a child. It is a festival of the family, a time when being and doing together is especially meaningful to both grown-ups and children. It's also a time of unusual busyness, during which a lot has to be accomplished by a few for the pleasure of many.

Particularly if you're having young overnight visitors or party guests—probably added to children of your own—you and your home need to be prepared for the extra holiday-accelerated excitement and commotion that youngsters generate. Here is our roundup of ways to facilitate all of the bedding-down, feeding, thirst-quenching and entertaining—with good thoughts for you even if you're merely living with resident kids during the holidays.

General Arrangements

Pick the most childproof area in your house and declare it *theirs*. Spray any upholstery in this area with fabric guard before your guests arrive. Spray fabrics in other rooms, too.

Ask families traveling by car to bring portable equipment, such as small folding cribs, sleeping bags, walkers, toilet-seat devices, if at all possible. Otherwise, borrow or rent necessities. Do this quite far ahead, for the demand is great. The Yellow Pages of the phone book list rental outfits.

Children find it a lark to sleep in sleeping bags (not a bad gift idea). Old-fashioned pallets on the floor can be just as much fun and solve the problem.

Have small inexpensive paper cups in full view for drinking water in places other than the kitchen. Try the powder room, utility room or bathrooms. Point out the nearby wastebasket, which is plastic-bag-lined—all cups aren't empty when they get thrown away.

If you live where it is snowy or slushy, plan ahead for dripping boots, snowsuits, coats. An extra boot tray and clothes rack in a utility room or entryway, with plastic spread for catching drips, can be most helpful. Racks can be rented, but a rolling one that can be taken apart and stored is often worth investing in. It can also be used for out-of-season clothing storage, drip-drying, or when sewing or ironing.

Put a roll of paper towels in plain sight and plenty of boxes of tissues for dripping noses, etcetera.

Give slipper socks as favors or gifts to children to put on as soon as they come in the house. This will help keep down noise and save wear-and-tear on your carpet and furniture.

Helpers   For part of the visit at least, hire a sitter to watch the children, even while the grown-ups are home. Since you're in the house anyway, a young, less experienced (and less expensive) one is perfect. He or she can read, tell stories, settle fights and play with the children.

Or, if there are several adults on hand, draw lots to see who gets which one- or two-hour shift as supervisor of the kids.

(*You* don't draw—you're general manager and ringmaster, full time.) It's hard on both kids and adults alike when all the adults are constantly bossing.

Children of just about any age can be put to work—and enjoy the responsibility. Depending on age and ability, a child can polish, chop, peel, grind, fold laundry, set the table, empty wastebaskets, answer the phone and door when you're "sticky," run errands, fetch and tote.

Activities/Games   If your own supply is nil or short, rent or borrow sleds, toboggans, ice or roller skates—whatever gear is appropriate. If you're a saver, get out any stored-away outdoor play equipment left from other times.

Check local events and shows for children and plan to take or send your charges. When necessary, make reservations and/or buy tickets well ahead.

Know when the most desirable holiday television specials for children are scheduled.

Send *everybody* out at dusk to drive around or walk to see the lighted houses and decorations or the store windows and outdoor crêches.

Plan on marching scrubbed shiny children to any suitable church services in your area or nearby. Include other children if possible. In fact, ask one or two neighbor children to join you on all your outings—and hope their mother will return the favor.

Have a box or drawer of doodads, puzzles, games, books, dress-up or other make-believe accessories ready for the "What'll I do nowww?" times. Also, see our list of specific ideas at the end of this chapter.

Eating and Feeding If you have fussy eaters (or sleepers), let them have their own way unless it interferes with others. You can't reform or even bend young twigs during such a season or in such a short time, and it can upset you.

Check the mother(s) of visitors on kinds and amounts of milk likely to be consumed. Stores are closed at times during the holiday season.

Have an extra big stock of soda on hand, as well as frozen, canned or dry lemonade and assorted fruit beverage mixes.

For your basic ice cream supply, choose vanilla. It's more easily removed when spilled and is popular.

Ice cream sticks can be thrust through paper plates to catch the inevitable drips.

For snacking, buy or unearth a huge glass jar and fill it with popcorn. Use margarine or oil when popping and it will keep two weeks, if closed between invasions. You might even consider giving an automatic popcorn popper as a family gift to guests and provide popcorn for trying it out at your house.

Mugs are more easily managed by little hands than glasses. Provide straws cut shorter than usual for the small.

For eating meals separately or for party refreshments, use a low table for the very small; put a card table with legs folded on top of cement blocks, boxes, stacks of magazines or the like, or use boards. In this way they can kneel to eat if they want to—or give them pillows (the inflatables are great and storing them later on is no problem). If they're eating in an area without a childproof floor, spread a plastic dropcloth under the low table before setting it up. Use a plastic tablecloth.

If very young children are to eat at the adult dining table, save work by laying a sheet of plastic or vinyl-coated fabric under their chairs. It may be the color of a plain rug. Clear plastic may be used, but it can be slippery. By-the-yard fabric is best, or use a vinyl tablecloth you have on hand. For tots opening gifts, a cardboard carton for the unwanted wrappings, ribbons and boxes can be disposed of quickly.

Have lots of paper napkins and cover-the-lap plastic aprons.

If a pet is visiting too, ask an adult of its family to be responsible for feeding it, letting it out or walking it at the right time.

Quick Cleanup Keep a bright-colored damp sponge in a dish here and there—behind draperies or books, for instance—for quick wipe-ups of spills. Let sitters and all adults in on the secret.

Buy the cheapest paper napkins and keep here and there for cleaning up after little ones and perhaps their pets.

Have a bottle of plain carbonated water handy for spills on carpeting; dash it on and wipe up at once.

"Drop-in" Children If neighborhood children are likely to drop in to see what Santa brought, invite them quite far ahead for a definite day and hour. Late Christmas afternoon after family gifts and dinner are all over could be a good time. Perhaps you want two groups, divided by ages, on different days; the older group can bear waiting longer. Plan festive but not elaborate refreshments and have gifts for them on or under the tree. Don't invite their parents. Sing carols, have a treasure hunt or some quiet games. A punch bowl and ice cream spell party to most children. Again, hold the activity in the nearest-to-childproof area.

Wrap extra gifts for children just in case unexpected ones turn up: puzzles, edibles, balls, a bag of balloons, jacks and such.

Protect/Prevent Never leave a Christmas tree lit without an adult present. A creeper, toddler or even an inquisitive older child can get burned by bulbs.

Don't leave candles lit where there are small children unless surely out of reach (a climber can reach almost any candle). When candles are to be lit or snuffed, children of school age can do it or help; they love the job. Have a few tapers rather than matches on hand for this purpose. Adult supervision is absolutely necessary and children should be cautioned against lighting candles on their own.

Keep matches, scissors, knives and other potential dangers out of reach.

If you have any really precious and nonreplaceable objects on low tables or shelves, put them away for the holiday season.

If you have a snappy or scratchy dog or cat, plan some protection for young visitors *and* it.

Ten Quick Answers to "What'll I Do?"

Idea: Instant cave. Needed: Card table or other crawl-under table and a blanket or sheet to toss over it.

Idea: String pretties. Needed: stiff cord or long shoelaces; beads, buttons, empty spools, macaroni or other stringables.

Idea: Scrapbooks. Needed: Safe scissors, glue or tape, blank paper, old magazines, Christmas cards, catalogs.

Idea: Wall or refrigerator murals. Needed: Large pieces of used wrapping paper, tape, crayons or colored markers.

Idea: Sorting games. Needed: Playing cards, poker chips, Mommy's button box—whatever can be sorted according to number, color or kind.

Idea: Rug pictures. Needed: Yarn scraps or string for making outline pictures on the carpet.

Idea: Art stones or shells. Needed: Pebbles, seashells or small stones and colored markers or paints to decorate them.

Idea: Water play. Needed: Plastic basin in the kitchen sink, plastic apron, sudsy water, plastic toys or doll laundry to do.

Idea: Station MOM. Needed: Tape recorder, tape that Mommy has prerecorded with new stories and old favorites.

Idea: Hydrophone. Needed: Different size glasses filled to different levels with water and a metal spoon to experiment in tapping out simple tunes.

CLASSIC CHRISTMAS SONGS AND READINGS

No sweeter literature exists than that of Christmas. It is devotional and whimsical, majestic and merry. Year after year we revive the old familiar songs and stories, knowing they are part of a precious continuity. Beginning with the words of Jesus' chroniclers in the New Testament of the Bible, these final pages offer a selection of Christmas prose and verse from writers famous and anonymous, words for you to read aloud and sing and best of all to share.

The Gospel According to St. Matthew

(1, 18-25; 2, 1-12; King James Version)

Chapter 1

18 Now the birth of Jesus Christ was on this wise: When as his mother Mary was espoused to Joseph, before they came together, she was found with child of the Holy Ghost.

19 Then Joseph her husband, being a just *man*, and not willing to make her a publick example, was minded to put her away privily.

20 But while he thought on these things, behold, the angel of the Lord appeared unto him in a dream, saying, Joseph, thou son of David, fear not to take unto thee Mary thy wife: for that which is conceived in her is of the Holy Ghost.

21 And she shall bring forth a son, and thou shalt call his name JESUS: for he shall save his people from their sins.

22 Now all this was done, that it might be fulfilled which was spoken of the Lord by the prophet, saying,

23 Behold, a virgin shall be with child, and shall bring forth a son, and they shall call his name Em-măn'-ū-ĕl, which being interpreted is, God with us.

24 Then Joseph being raised from sleep did as the angel of the Lord had bidden him, and took unto him his wife:

25 And knew her not till she had brought forth her firstborn son: and he called his name JESUS.

Chapter 2

Now when Jesus was born in Bethlehem of Judæa in the days of Herod the king, behold, there came wise men from the east to Jerusalem,

2 Saying, Where is he that is born King of the Jews? for we have seen his star in the east, and are come to worship him.

3 When Herod the king had heard *these things*, he was troubled, and all Jerusalem with him.

4 And when he had gathered all the chief priests and scribes of the people together, he demanded of them where Christ should be born.

5 And they said unto him, In Bethlehem of Judæa: for thus it is written by the prophet,

6 And thou Bethlehem, *in* the land of Juda, art not the least among the princes of Juda: for out of thee shall come a Governor, that shall rule my people Israel.

7 Then Herod, when he had privily called the wise men, inquired of them diligently what time the star appeared.

8 And he sent them to Bethlehem, and said, Go and search diligently for the young child; and when ye have found *him*, bring me word again, that I may come and worship him also.

9 When they had heard the king, they departed; and, lo, the star, which they saw in the east, went before them, till it came and stood over where the young child was.

10 When they saw the star, they rejoiced with exceeding great joy.

11 And when they were come into the house, they saw the young child with Mary his mother, and fell down, and worshipped him: and when they had opened their treasures, they presented unto him gifts; gold, and frankincense, and myrrh.

12 And being warned of God in a dream that they should not return to Herod, they departed into their own country another way.

The Gospel According to St. Luke

(1, 26-35; 2, 1-20; King James Version)

Chapter 1

26 And in the sixth month the angel Gabriel was sent from God unto a city of Galilee, named Nazareth,

27 To a virgin espoused to a man whose name was Joseph, of the house of David; and the virgin's name *was* Mary.

28 And the angel came in unto her, and said, Hail, *thou that art* highly favoured, the Lord *is* with thee: blessed *art* thou among women.

29 And when she saw *him*, she was troubled at his saying, and cast her mind what manner of salutation this should be.

30 And the angel said unto her, Fear not, Mary: for thou hast found favour with God.

31 And, behold, thou shalt conceive in thy womb, and bring forth a son, and shalt call his name JESUS.

32 He shall be great, and shall be called the Son of the Highest: and the Lord God shall give unto him the throne of his father David:

33 And he shall reign over the house of Jacob for

ever; and of his kingdom there shall be no end.

34 Then said Mary unto the angel, How shall this be, seeing I know not a man?

35 And the angel answered and said unto her, The Holy Ghost shall come upon thee, and the power of the Highest shall overshadow thee: therefore also that holy thing which shall be born of thee shall be called the Son of God.

Chapter 2

And it came to pass in those days, that there went out a degree from Cæsar Augustus, that all the world should be taxed.

2 (*And* this taxing was first made when Cȳ´-rē´-nǐ-ŭs was governor of Syria.)

3 And all went to be taxed, every one into his own city.

4 And Joseph also went up from Galilee, out of the city of Nazareth, into Judæa, unto the city of David, which is called Bethlehem; (because he was of the house and lineage of David:)

5 To be taxed with Mary his espoused wife, being great with child.

6 And so it was, that, while they were there, the days were accomplished that she should be delivered.

7 And she brought forth her first-born son and wrapped him in swaddling clothes, and laid him in a manger; because there was no room for them in the inn.

8 And there was in the same country shepherds abiding in the field, keeping watch over their flock by night.

9 And, lo, the angel of the Lord came upon them, and the glory of the Lord shone round about them: and they were sore afraid.

10 And the angel said unto them, Fear not: for, behold, I bring you good tidings of great joy, which shall be to all people.

11 For unto you is born this day in the city of David a Saviour, which is Christ the Lord.

12 And this *shall be* a sign unto you; Ye shall find the babe wrapped in swaddling clothes, lying in a manger.

13 And suddenly there was with the angel a multitude of the heavenly host praising God, and saying,

14 Glory to God in the highest, and on earth peace, good will toward men.

15 And it came to pass, as the angels were gone away from them into heaven, the shepherds said one to another, Let us now go even unto Bethlehem, and see this thing which is come to pass, which the Lord hath made known unto us.

16 And they came with haste, and found Mary, and Joseph, and the babe lying in a manger.

17 And when they had seen *it*, they made known abroad the saying which was told them concerning this child.

18 And all they that heard *it* wondered at those things which were told them by the shepherds.

19 But Mary kept all these things, and pondered *them* in her heart.

20 And the shepherds returned, glorifying and praising God for all the things that they had heard and seen, as it was told unto them.

A Right Jolly Old Elf

Much of what we know about Santa Claus we owe to the imagination of Clement Clarke Moore. In his famous narrative poem, written during the first quarter of the 19th century, Dr. Moore, a professor at General Theological Seminary in New York, described St. Nicholas' visit with such precision that the account become a kind of "authorized version." It has remained such a favorite that most of us can recite several lines from memory. Here it is in its entirety, an enchanting piece to read to your children, just as Dr. Moore first did in 1822.

A VISIT FROM ST. NICHOLAS

'Twas the night before Christmas, when all through the house
Not a creature was stirring, not even a mouse;
The stockings were hung by the chimney with care,
In hopes that ST. NICHOLAS soon would be there;
The children were nestled all snug in their beds,
While visions of sugar-plums danced in their heads;
And mamma in her 'kerchief, and I in my cap
Had just settled our brains for a long winter's nap,
When out on the lawn there arose such a clatter,
I sprang from the bed to see what was the matter.
Away to the window I flew like a flash,
Tore open the shutters and threw up the sash.
The moon on the breast of the new-fallen snow
Gave the lustre of mid-day to objects below,
When, what to my wondering eyes should appear,
But a miniature sleigh, and eight tiny reindeer,
With a little old driver, so lively and quick,
I knew in a moment it must be St. Nick.
More rapid than eagles his coursers they came,
And he whistled, and shouted, and called them by name;
"Now, *Dasher!* now, *Dancer!* now, *Prancer* and *Vixen!*

On, *Comet!* on *Cupid!* on, *Donder* and *Blitzen!*
To the top of the porch! to the top of the wall!
Now dash away! dash away! dash away all!"
As dry leaves that before the wild hurricane fly,
When they meet with an obstacle, mount to the sky,
So up to the house-top the coursers they flew,
With the sleigh full of toys, and St. Nicholas too.
And then, in a twinkling I heard on the roof
The prancing and pawing of each little hoof.
As I drew in my head, and was turning around,
Down the chimney St. Nicholas came with a bound.
He was dressed all in fur, from his head to his foot,
And his clothes were all tarnished with ashes and soot;
A bundle of toys he had flung on his back,
And he looked like a peddler just opening his pack.
His eyes—how they twinkled! his dimples how merry!
His cheeks were like roses, his nose like a cherry!
His droll little mouth was drawn up like a bow,
And the beard of his chin was as white as the snow;
The stump of a pipe he held tight in his teeth,
And the smoke it encircled his head like a wreath;
He had a broad face and a little round belly,
That shook, when he laughed, like a bowlful of jelly.
He was chubby and plump, a right jolly old elf,
And I laughed when I saw him, in spite of myself;
A wink of his eyes and a twist of his head,
Soon gave me to know I had nothing to dread;
He spoke not a word, but went straight to his work,
And filled all the stockings; then turned with a jerk,
And laying his finger aside of his nose,
And giving a nod, up the chimney he rose;
He sprang to his sleigh, to his team gave a whistle,
And away they all flew like the down of a thistle.
But I heard him exclaim, ere he drove out of sight,
"Happy Christmas to all, and to all a good-night."

Is There a Santa Claus?

A newspaperman named Frank Church was obviously someone who treasured "A Visit From St. Nicholas." Just 75 years after Moore wrote the poem, Mr. Church, a journalist on the staff of The New York Sun, *replied to a letter-to-the-editor from an eight-year-old girl who wanted "the truth" about the existence of Santa Claus. His answer, first printed in the paper in 1897, has become another Christmas favorite.*

Dear Editor: I am 8 years old. Some of my little friends say there is no Santa Claus.
Papa says, "If you see it in *The Sun*, it's so."
Please tell me the truth, is there a Santa Claus?
Virginia O'Hanlon
115 West Ninety-fifth Street, New York City

Virginia, your little friends are wrong. They have been affected by the skepticism of a skeptical age. They do not believe except they see. They think that nothing can be which is not comprehensible by their little minds. All minds, Virginia, whether they be men's or children's, are little.

Yes, Virginia, there is a Santa Claus. He exists as certainly as love and generosity and devotion exist, and you know that they abound and give to your life its highest beauty and joy. Alas! how dreary would be the world if there were no Santa Claus! There would be no childlike faith then, no poetry, no romance to make tolerable this existence. The eternal light with which childhood fills the world would be extinguished.

Not to believe in Santa Claus! You might as well not believe in fairies! You might get your papa to hire men to watch in all the chimneys on Christmas Eve to catch Santa Claus, but even if they did not see Santa Claus coming down, what would that prove? Nobody sees Santa Claus, but that is no sign that there is no Santa Claus. The most real things in the world are those that neither children nor men can see.

You tear apart the baby's rattle and see what makes the noise inside, but there is a veil covering the unseen world which not the strongest man, nor even the united strength of all the strongest men that ever lived, could tear apart. Only faith, fancy, poetry, love, romance, can push aside that curtain and view and picture the supernal beauty and glory beyond. Is it all real? Ah, Virginia, in all this world there is nothing else real and abiding.

No Santa Claus! Thank God! he lives, and he lives forever. A thousand years from now, Virginia, nay, ten times ten thousand years from now, he will continue to make glad the heart of childhood.

Favorite Christmas Songs

Verses for lullabyes, carols and hymns to sing or to enjoy as poetry:

Away in a Manger
Martin Luther

Away in a manger,
No crib for His bed,
The little Lord Jesus
Laid down His sweet head;
The stars in the heavens

Looked down where He lay;
The little Lord Jesus
Asleep in the hay.

The cattle are lowing,
The poor Baby wakes,
But little Lord Jesus
No crying He makes.
I love Thee, Lord Jesus,
Look down from the sky,
And stay by my cradle
Till morning is nigh.

Deck the Halls
Unknown; traditional Welsh

Deck the halls with boughs of holly,
Fa la la la la, la la la la!
'Tis the season to be jolly,
Fa la la la la, la la la la!
Don we now our gay apparel,
Fa la la la la la, la la la!
Troll the ancient yuletide carol,
Fa la la la la, la la la la!

See the blazing yule before us,
Fa la la la la, la la la la!
Strike the harp and join the chorus,
Fa la la la la, la la la la!
Follow me in merry measure,
Fa la la la la la, la la la!
While I tell of yuletide treasure,
Fa la la la la, la la la la!

Fast away the old year passes,
Fa la la la la, la la la la!
Hail the new, ye lads and lasses,
Fa la la la la, la la la la!
Sing we joyous all together,
Fa la la la la la, la la la!
Heedless of the wind and weather,
Fa la la la la, la la la la!

The First Nowell
Unknown; traditional English

The first Nowell the angel did say,
Was to certain poor shepherds in fields as they lay;
In fields where they lay keeping their sheep,
On a cold winter's night that was so deep.
(refrain)

Nowell, Nowell, Nowell, Nowell,

Born is the King of Israel.

They looked up and saw a star
Shining in the East beyond them far,
And to the earth it gave great light,
And so it continued both day and night.
(refrain)

This star drew nigh to the northwest,
O'er Bethlehem it took its rest.
And there it did both stop and stay
Right over the place where Jesus lay.
(refrain)

God Rest You Merry, Gentlemen
Unknown; traditonal English

God rest you merry, gentlemen
    Let nothing you dismay
Remember Christ our Saviour
    Was born on Christmas Day,
To save us all from Satan's power
    When we were gone astray.

(refrain)
O tidings of comfort and joy, comfort and joy,
O tidings of comfort and joy!

From God our heavenly Father,
    A blessed angel came;
And unto certain shepherds
    Brought tidings of the same:
How that in Bethlehem was born
    The Son of God by name.
(refrain)

Now to the Lord sing praises,
    All you within this place,
And with true love and brotherhood
    Each other now embrace;
This holy tide of Christmas
    All others doth deface.
(refrain)

Hark! the Herald Angels Sing
Charles Wesley

Hark! the herald angels sing,
"Glory to the newborn King;
Peace on earth and mercy mild,
God and sinners reconciled!"
Joyful all ye nations rise,

Join the triumph of the skies,
With the angelic host proclaim,
"Christ is born in Bethlehem."
(refrain)

Hark! the herald angels sing,
"Glory to the newborn King!"

Christ, by highest heaven adored,
Christ, the everlasting Lord,
Late in time behold Him come,
Offspring of a virgin's womb.
Veiled in flesh the Godhead see;
Hail, the Incarnate Deity,
Pleased as Man with man to dwell,
Jesus, our Immanuel!
(refrain)

Hail, the heaven-born Prince of Peace!
Hail, the Sun of Righteousness!
Light and life to all he brings,
Risen with healing in His wings.
Mild He lays His glory by,
Born that man no more may die,
Born to raise the sons of earth,
Born to give them second birth.
(refrain)

Here We Come A-Wassailing
Unknown; traditional English

Here we come a-wassailing,
Among the leaves so green.
Here we come a-wandering
So fair to be seen.
(refrain)
Love and joy come to you,
And to your wassail too,
And God bless you and send you
A Happy New Year,
And God send you a Happy New Year.

God bless the master of this house,
Likewise the mistress too,
And all the little children
That round the table go.
(refrain)

I Saw Three Ships
Unknown; traditional English

I saw three ships come sailing in,

On Christmas Day, on Christmas Day,
I saw three ships come sailing in,
On Christmas Day in the morning.

Pray, whither sailed those ships all three?
On Christmas Day, on Christmas Day,
Prayer, whither sailed those ships all three?
On Christmas Day, in the morning.

O, they sailed into Bethlehem,
On Christmas Day, on Christmas Day,
O, they sailed into Bethlehem,
On Christmas Day, in the morning.

It Came upon the Midnight Clear
Edmund Hamilton Sears

It came upon the midnight clear,
    That glorious song of old,
From angels bending near the earth
    To touch their harps of gold:
"Peace on the earth, good will to men
    From heaven's all-gracious King"—
The world in solemn stillness lay
    To hear the angels sing.

Still through the cloven skies they come
    With peaceful wings unfurled,
And still their heavenly music floats
    O'er all the weary world;
Above its sad and lowly plains
    They bend on hovering wing,
And ever o'er its Babel sounds
    The blessed angels sing.

For lo! the days are hastening on
    By prophet bards foretold,
When with the ever circling years
    Comes round the age of gold;
When Peace shall over all the earth
    Its ancient splendors fling,
And the whole world give back the song
    Which now the angels sing.

Joy to the World
Isaac Watts

Joy to the world! the Lord is come;
Let earth receive her King;
Let every heart prepare Him room,
And heaven and nature sing,
And heaven and nature sing,

And heaven, and heaven and nature sing.

Joy to the earth! the Saviour reigns;
Let men their songs employ;
While fields and floods, rocks, hills and plains
Repeat the sounding joy,
Repeat the sounding joy,
Repeat, repeat the sounding joy.

He rules the world with truth and grace,
And makes the nations prove
The glories of His righteousness,
And wonders of His love,
And wonders of His love,
And wonders, and wonders of His love.

O Christmas Tree
(O Tannenbaum)
Unknown; traditional German

O Tannenbaum, O Tannenbaum,
How lovely are your branches!
In beauty green will always grow
Through summer sun and winter snow.
O Tannenbaum, O Tannenbaum,
How lovely are your branches!

O Tannenbaum, O Tannenbaum,
You are the tree most loved!
How often you give us delight
In brightly shining Christmas light!
O Tannenbaum, O Tannenbaum,
You are the tree most loved!

O Tannenbaum, O Tannenbaum,
Your beauty green will teach me
That hope and love will ever be
The way to joy and peace for me.
O Tannenbaum, O Tannenbaum,
Your beauty green will teach me.

O Come, All Ye Faithful
(Adeste Fideles)
Unknown; old Latin hymn

O come, all ye faithful, joyful and triumphant;
O come ye, O come ye to Bethlehem.
Come and behold Him, born the King of angels;
(refrain)

O come, let us adore Him, O come, let us adore Him,
O come, let us adore Him, Christ the Lord.

Sing, choirs of angels, sing in exultation,
Sing, all ye citizens of heaven above:
Glory to God, in the highest:
(refrain)

Yea, Lord, we greet Thee, born this happy morning,
Jesus, to Thee be glory given;
Word of the Father, now in flesh appearing:
(refrain)

In Latin
Adeste fideles, laeti triumphantes;
Venite, venite in Bethlehem;
Natum videte, Regem angelorum;
Venite adoremus, Venite adoremus,
Venite adoremus, Dominum.

O Little Town of Bethlehem
Phillips Brooks

O little town of Bethlehem,
How still we see thee lie!
Above thy deep and dreamless sleep
The silent stars go by;
Yet in thy dark streets shineth
The everlasting Light;
The hopes and fears of all the years
Are met in thee tonight.

For Christ is born of Mary,
And, gathered all above,
While mortals sleep, the angels keep
The watch of wondering love.
O morning stars, together
Proclaim the holy birth!
And praises sing to God the King,
And peace to men on earth.

How silently, how silently,
Their wondrous gift is given!
So God imparts to human hearts
The blessings of His heaven.
No ear may hear His coming,
But in this world of sin,
Where meek souls will receive Him still,
The dear Christ enters in.

Silent Night
Joseph Mohr

Silent night! Holy night!
All is calm, all is bright,

Round yon Virgin Mother and Child.
Holy Infant so tender and mild,
Sleep in heavenly peace!
Sleep in heavenly peace!

Silent night! Holy night!
Shepherds quake at the sight;
Glories stream from heaven afar,
Heavenly hosts sing alleluia;
Christ, the Saviour, is born!
Christ, the Saviour, is born!

Silent night! Holy night!
Son of God, love's pure light
Radiant beams from Thy holy face,
With the dawn of redeeming grace,
Jesus, Lord, at Thy birth,
Jesus, Lord, at Thy birth.

We Three Kings
John Henry Hopkins, Jr.

We three kings of Orient are,
Bearing gifts we traverse afar,
Field and fountain, moor and mountain,
Following yonder star.
(refrain)

O, star of wonder, star of night,

Star with royal beauty bright,
Westward leading, still proceeding,
Guide us to Thy perfect light.

(Melchior)
Born a King on Bethlehem's plain,
Gold I bring to crown Him again,
King forever, ceasing never,
Over us all to reign.
(refrain)

(Caspar)
Frankincense to offer have I,
Incense owns a Deity nigh;
Prayer and praising, all men raising,
Worship Him, God on high.
(refrain)

(Balthazar)
Myrrh is mine, its bitter perfume
Breathes a life of gathering gloom;
Sorrowing, sighing, bleeding, dying,
Sealed in the stone-cold tomb.
(refrain)

Glorious now behold Him arise,
King and God and sacrifice;
Alleluia, alleluia:
Earth to the heavens replies.
(refrain)

RECIPE INDEX